Praise for *Almost a Foreign Country*:

" …It's with his tales of foreign experiences and observances that Wolf shines. From discussing the quiet success of Muslim women in Western Europe, to the fact that drug dealers are allowed to deduct firearms and pit bulls as business expenses in the Netherlands, the author engages readers with interesting points. He also offers the interesting perspective of an immigrant who has absorbed a large part of American culture but questions the rest…"

— Kirkus Discoveries, October 8, 2009.

"…Wolf's columns are written in the tradition of the Feuilleton, a form of personal literary essay popular with European journalists but never really adopted by English-language writers. Digressing from seemingly random observations made on Taraval Street or in Helsinki, Wolf meditates on everything from San Francisco teenage semiotics to the dating game of AARP members…"

— Charles Pfister, *Westside Observer*, July/August 2009.

"…His point of view is always unflinching, original, and unapologetic. It is as if he's culled and condensed some of the most flavorful and charming cultural observations from a large collection of personal commentaries down into chapter-sized pearls of wisdom… This is the sort of book literary Mensans … would find a thought-provoking read."

— Paul Payton, *San Francisco Regional Mensa*
"Intelligencer," September 2009.

"…Here is another fable of America, as seen by another wise foreign-born writer (Nabokov comes to mind) whose love for his adopted country is coupled with keen-witted irony and a total absence of sentimental cant…"

— Maurice Bassan, Amazon.com review, January 25, 2009.

Survival in Paradise

Sketches From a Refugee Life in Curaçao

Manfred Wolf

SURVIVAL IN PARADISE
SKETCHES FROM A REFUGEE LIFE IN CURAÇAO

iUniverse books may be ordered through booksellers or by contacting:

iUniverse LLC
1663 Liberty Drive
Bloomington, IN 47403
www.iuniverse.com
1-800-Authors (1-800-288-4677)

ISBN: 978-1-4917-2264-0 (sc)
ISBN: 978-1-4917-2263-3 (e)

Printed in the United States of America.

iUniverse rev. date: 6/04/2014

To the memory of my brother
Siegfried Robert Wolf (1932 - 2012)

Contents

Acknowledgments

I am ever grateful to Yael Abel, my unfailingly helpful editorial assistant, advisor and friend.

I owe a special thanks to Anne Dinning for rescuing the hard copy of the manuscript, which was languishing in a state of near dormancy until she scanned it into the computer. That gave me the push to revise and finish the book.

My genuine thanks too to those trusted friends who made excellent suggestions for revision and improvement: Betsy Davis, Edward Fortner, Ralda Lee, George Leonard, Merete Mazzarella, Connie Stroud and Marjorie Young.

I am also thankful to those friends and acquaintances, almost too numerous to list, who have expressed a genuine liking for my writing, whether in this form or in the short essays that make up my recent book, *Almost a Foreign Country*: Steve Arkin, Saumya Bajada, Maurice Bassan, William Bonnell, Jane Cutler, Susan Ellis, Anke Ente, Helen Fauss, Herbert Feinstein, Marijke Huisman, Lyn Isbell, Kay James, Edie Jarolim, Ken Johnson, John Kaye, Vernon Kerr, Marjorie Kewley, Michael Krasny, Leo Litwak, Tina Martin, the late Henk Romijn Meijer, Joan Minninger, Debby Nosowsky, Paul Palmbaum, Charlotte Prozan, Harriet Rafter, Ina Rilke, Scott Rollins, Helen Steyer, Paige Stockley, Paul Vincent and Dan Wick.

And I am especially pleased by the encouragement of my sons, Dana, Michael and Paul.

MW

Prefatory Note

Except for the first and last chapter, these sketches cover my years in Suriname and Curaçao as a very young World War Two refugee from 1942 to 1951. Chapter One details my family's flight from Holland in 1942 to France, Spain and Portugal, while the last chapter traces my journey from Curaçao to America.

Though I have sometimes streamlined certain episodes or merged two characters into one, on the whole the events set forth in this book are exactly as I remember them.

Some of these chapters have appeared in somewhat different form in the following publications. Wherever appropriate, permission to reprint is gratefully acknowledged.

"A Special Case," in *San Francisco State University — College of Humanities Magazine*, Fall 1998.

"So much Bleating, So Little Wool — School Days," as "Schooldays in Curaçao," in *College of Humanities Magazine*, Spring 1989.

"Singing for the Queen," in *Midstream*, April 1996.

"A Small Emotion," in *College of Humanities Magazine*, Fall 1997.

"Ever More Tropicalized," in *College of Humanities Magazine*, Fall 1995.

"Mundi and the Coming Autonomy," in *College of Humanities Magazine*, Fall 1999.

"A Jewish Word," as "Dutch and Jewish in the West Indies," in *Judaism*, Spring 2002.

"The Dance School," in *The Literary Review*, Summer 1998. Also included in *Beacon Press Best of 1999*.

"Emile and Yahnchi," in *College of Humanities Magazine*, Fall 1994.

"The Two Witch Doctors," in *The Literary Review*, Spring 2001.

"The Gentiles Have Patience," as "Icke-judar har talamod," Swedish translation by Bertel Stenius, in *Nya Argus*, Summer 1992; and as "The goyim hebben zo'n geduld," Dutch translation by Henk Romijn Meijer, in *Maatstaf* #6, 1993.

Brief passages from "The Tree of Memory" have appeared in "At Brandeis in the Fifties," *Brandeis Review*, Spring 1995.

Part I: Flight

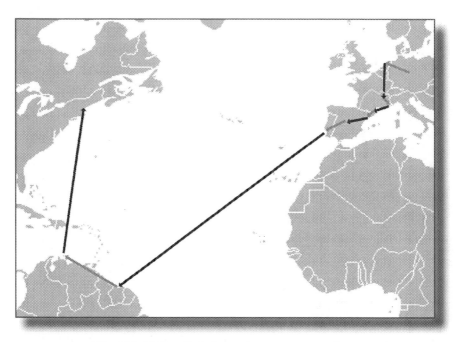

The Wolf family's long journey to safety

Chapter 1. 1942

Standing on the deck of the ship *Nyassa*, on its way from Lisbon in Portugal to Suriname, my mother started crying and could not stop. Why does she cry now, I wondered, now that it's all over and we're safe?

The other refugees were all out on deck. We knew some of them from the waiting rooms of Dutch consular offices in Lisbon. One family we met in our hotel in Nice. Others had found their way to this refuge from the far corners of Europe. They surrounded us, some of them waving to people they knew on the wharf.

The ship inched away from shore. My father stared unseeing at the waving crowd. My brother stood next to him and looked up to see how tall the ship was. My mother blew her nose and sobbed. I didn't want to look at her. I ran to the other side of the ship and soon saw a limitless ocean. I was glad to be away from the crying and happy to scan the future.

We had been on the run for almost a year. And everywhere we went, the Nazis threatened. We fled Holland in February 1942, a year and a half after the occupation of the Netherlands by the Germans. I was seven years old when we escaped from our pretty villa town of Bilthoven in the center of Holland, not old enough to understand fully what danger we were in. After this year, it became ever more real to me, though I continued to hope for a while that I could resume the happy life so abruptly interrupted.

The scene leaving Lisbon is as sharp and clear in my mind today as it was when I was almost eight — on that December day in 1942 when we sailed away from Portugal on the *Nyassa*, headed for a distant place called Suriname. Other memories of our flight from Nazi occupation are like scenes from a rushing train — blurred and hazy. And then there are those indelible, slow-motion memories — half recollection, half reconstruction, powerfully with me during the years of childhood and adolescence in Suriname and Curaçao, and continuing into my American life.

Still other memories — such as my family's years before Holland in Nazi Germany — are vivid. But I was really too young to remember. They seem compelling now because I heard them retold so many times within my family. All these memories live within me, in a kind of perpetual present tense; they cast their shadow over our new life in Curaçao, much as I tried to evade them, and are still powerfully present in my life today, where I know them to be inescapable.

My father emigrated from Poland to Germany in 1922, when he was seventeen. He settled in the Saxon town of Chemnitz; he liked the small, busy city, gray but clean. Like many other Jews in that town, he prospered. A few years later he met and married my mother. Her parents also came from Poland but lived in Holland for a long time before settling in Chemnitz. My parents loved Germany, the country of their new prosperity, but neither of them gained German citizenship.

My brother and I were born in Germany, Siegfried in 1932 and I in 1935. Our names reflect my parents' warm feeling toward Germany, feelings later shattered by the Nazis. Neither my father nor my mother ever wanted to leave Chemnitz. In 1937, when I was two years old, my father had a large textile factory and a devoted German staff. "Fräulein Weiner," he later said, "cried when we left for Holland. She was actually one of the few who knew that we planned to go." Both my parents referred to her for many years, the ever-attentive, kind secretary in the business.

My mother was warned to leave Germany by the Nazi parents of her German high school friend. In our flat in Chemnitz, I remember brown suitcases stacked up against white furniture. My mother and a driver took us in the middle of the night on the autobahn from Chemnitz to Leipzig. I dimly knew that my father would join us in Holland later. On a damp, star-stunned night, the car came to an abrupt halt, and my mother got out and ran to the side of the road and heaved violently.

A few months later I was sitting with both my parents on a large chair in my maternal grandparents' flat in Scheveningen, happily learning Dutch. Scheveningen had a boardwalk and a splendid beach, where my mother, my brother, and my little Belgian cousin Paulette, a mere infant, played in the sand. Here I tasted my first ice-cream. My most profound memory from those days is a happy, thrilled anticipation. I couldn't wait for the next ice-cream cone, which I somehow knew would come soon.

My first years in Holland are a blur. A large flat in The Hague. Walks in a park carpeted with flowers. A holiday near a windy Dutch lake. My father in a raincoat on a sailboat. Our move — for safety's sake — inland to the central province of Utrecht.

"Why do we move?" I asked, a question I was always asking, until years later we arrived in Curaçao and stayed. By then it was clear to me why we had always moved.

The war started in 1940 with the German invasion. We were living in a small house in the town of Bilthoven. At around that time, I was overcome with longing for a bicycle, and I got it almost immediately. At six, I rode it in the park across the street, the Rembrandtplein. A more chronic longing was to go to school. My brother had started the year before, and my mother and I walked him there every morning to the large school building on a leafy street. That longing for school soon turned into a passion.

One early morning we awoke to an aerial bombardment of a nearby military airport. Our windows were taped up with broad strips of brown tape. Every few minutes the house shuddered and shook. I was frightened, but no bombs fell on our street or even in our town.

That day, my father received a letter. All morning he sat next to the heavy coal stove that stood in the middle of the living room while the distant explosions boomed. His thick black hair fell over his face, and he did not cover his eyes when he cried. For hours he sat and wailed, sometimes howling like a helpless animal. Once in a while, he stroked my hair forward and murmured, "Little sheep, little sheep." The letter told of his father's heart attack and death in the Urals, to which he had fled from Nazi-occupied Poland.

The German invasion made it impossible for us to use the visas we held for Bolivia and Peru. Now all borders were sealed. The year before, my father wondered if we should go there. But maybe Holland would remain neutral — after all, it had in World War One. On the other hand, the Germans were threatening. We had to go. Perhaps we could stay closer by, go to England? How could we live in Bolivia? La Paz is at such a high altitude; people had been known to develop heart trouble there. And in Peru it had rained only once in six months!

After the invasion, he, and even I, knew that those possibilities were gone. The persecution of the Jews in Germany made him get those visas, but since we were by then in Holland the danger still seemed remote. But now the Germans were here. My father started talking to himself, aloud. "How will we get out? No, I don't want to go to Spain. There's Franco, Hitler's friend." He looked at the maps, and I looked with him. "South America is where we should have gone. Maybe we still can." We looked at the atlas for hours. "Anywhere but Europe. But how do we get out now? You know, I wish we had a tank."

At the same time, my parents started searching for a little house tucked away in the Dutch countryside. "In the woods," said my father, "in the woods we'll be invisible." But every house we looked at was close to a road; Holland was just too small to hide that way. We saw a beautiful red-brick house in what looked to me like a forest, but it could be seen from a fine, paved road.

My father took me every other day to a cafe in Bilthoven where slow-moving men played billiards, good-natured men who fussed over a little boy. My brother had lessons across the street while we waited for him here. Hours passed before he came out; I felt a little bored but deeply content, while my father slowly and musingly drank tea. When my brother emerged from his lesson across the street, we all bicycled home, I in the back of my father's bicycle, my legs searching quickly for the footrests, and enjoying the support they gave. I thought of my playmates, and of how happy I'd be to finally go to school.

A few months after the war started, I played a portable phonograph out in the backyard, delighted by the sounds of a Dutch popular song that issued forth. "The fixing man... has got himself a real sedan... and he drives it like a king... through the streets of Amsterdam..."

In the first year of the Occupation, there was a lull in our anxiety. Life was harder but we adjusted. I was six years old in the late spring of 1941. On a long bicycle trip to Arnhem in the east of the Netherlands, we stayed in a paradise of green, a large hotel in the woods, with flocks of geese in a park in the back. My nineteen-year-old uncle Paul put me on his shoulders and ran through the fields chasing the geese. Row upon row of misty trees and hedges promised an endless future. But rumors of new measures against Jews soon turned us back from the resort to our home in Bilthoven.

Now in the care of Nina, a servant girl, my brother and I drifted with her through the summertime-hot streets. A heart-stopping memory I have is of one day hearing a choked, suffocating sob from an abandoned-looking caravan. Nina, looking frightened, shouted wildly and listened to the muffled voice inside, then bent toward a hatch on the side of the wooden trailer, somehow unlatched it, and a young gypsy boy my age crawled out of a kind of storage space and ran off faster than I had ever seen anyone run. Had he been locked up by his parents? Were there people bad enough to do that to a child? Ever after, I have felt a choking sensation when I remember that. I could not imagine something like that happening to anyone I knew.

In late 1941, prohibitions against Jews followed each other in quick succession. The Nazis forbade Jews the use of a radio. We turned ours in, and arranged with a Gentile neighbor to play his loudly. Every late afternoon we stood in the garden listening. The news was broadcast in Dutch from London. England was being bombarded; the German occupation of France — and so much of Europe — remained unchallenged. The bulletins spoke of resistance in the occupied countries and occasionally promised that the war would be over soon.

In that same year, Jewish children were no longer allowed to go to school. My disappointment was intense, and I disliked the improvised lessons I got from a distracted rabbi. This was not school at all. I continued to hear many conversations about escape routes between my parents and their friends. Certain words stood out because they were spoken with such fright and horror, always in German, which was what my parents often spoke to each other. *"Nach Polen geschickt."* Sent to Poland. *"Abgeführt."* Deported. These words were surrounded with such gloom that when I heard them I felt a sense of dread and a weight of melancholy — a vague, brooding disappointment, a sadness, for they foretold that happy plans for tomorrow would be dashed and wonderful projects spoiled.

In the first year and a half of the German occupation, our little town of Bilthoven still seemed safe, the hated green uniforms and hoarse singing rarely in evidence. My thoughts were on my new bicycle and on hoping, after all, to go to a real school some day. But further restrictions came one by one: no cars, no radios, no recreational activity.

Summers in Holland are gusty and green. In that little Dutch town, on the square outside the little house with its slanting roof, tall trees encircled meandering bicycle paths. When it rained, as it often did, I dreamt and drew pictures of the life I expected to lead. I drew a picture of the woods near our house and the little cottage where my friends Jan and Els Romeel lived, where we often visited.

Their parents — Mr. and Mrs. Romeel — had the same problems we did. On one visit in 1941, they scrutinized their passport lying before them on the dining room table, staring fascinated at the luridly large visa to Morocco, which the year before would have enabled them still to flee. But Mr. Romeel insisted the Dutch woods were safer than Morocco.

"Useless," he said to my father now, without taking his eyes off the passport. "Useless," and he grasped his forehead with both hands. "Have I been a fool? Should we have gone? At least I should have gone. Women and children will be safe in any case, just as they were in World War I."

"Oh," said Mrs. Romeel, "don't reproach yourself about it. The war will be over soon. Maybe in a few months. You'll see." She put her hand on his shoulder.

"Who can guarantee that?" Again he grasped his forehead.

"The war won't come here," his wife said. "Hardly any Germans in this little town."

It got dark in the house. The heavy curtains were drawn. The Germans would shoot you if you disobeyed the blackout. No light that could guide Allied bombers was allowed to be visible from the outside.

"This passport," resumed Mr. Romeel, carefully putting a hand under his chin and staring at the little dark-blue book lying flat on the table before him, "this passport could have taken us to Morocco. But, Max, I was afraid. What would I do there?"

My father did not answer. He had a way of looking, seeing, not seeing, hearing some things but not others, an absent-mindedness and yet a deep thoughtfulness too. He ran his hands through his thick black hair. His own passport was nonexistent. His preliminary Dutch naturalization papers were nowhere close to a passport, though he always carried them with him and once in a while unfolded them on the dining room table, where they shone white under the electric lights. My mother's "papers" were in better shape, closer to real naturalization.

We fled Holland when the young Dutch cop tipped us off that the Nazis were planning to deport us the next day. "You must leave at once; there is no time to spare," he said. I had seen the young, pink, smiling man in our house a few times, having a drink with my father, who befriended him. "We really liked him," my father said later, "but also… you never know what this kind of person can do for you some day." It was a connection that saved our lives.

I had just turned seven. February 15, 1942, the day of our flight from Holland, was a blur of train rides and yet more train rides. In our compartment, four young German soldiers, unaware of our being Jewish, gave candy to my brother and me and spoke German to our pretty, young mother. She was able to talk to anybody and did not "look Jewish." But my father did. Suddenly frightened, my father took me on his back and, before the train had fully stopped, jumped onto the onrushing platform of the next station. A few meters further, my mother calmly got off with my brother. Evidently nobody noticed. We changed to another train and continued our first day of flight.

Afterwards my mother always said that those soldiers were too young to care about Jews who escaped. "Or maybe I just did not know yet what was at stake."

And nobody noticed when, just before the Germans checked passengers' papers at the Belgian border, we got out of the train car. We acted as if we belonged in the town where the train stopped and hastened over the ice-cold platform to a nearby farm.

Uncle Paul and Uncle Itscho had found a farmer living near the Belgian border and visited him several times. They talked to him and his wife about the terrain and how easy or difficult it would be to cross; they left gifts and made arrangements for the day we would come through.

The farmer was not at the station, but we knew how to get to his farmhouse. With few words exchanged, he walked us over his fields into Belgium, where the first of a whole series of trams took us to Antwerp.

Dog-tired, we somehow got to Brussels, and my father's brother — later to perish in Auschwitz — danced my brother and me around and showed off his wife and new baby. I do not know to this day how his wife and child escaped.

A whole succession of tiny rooms in shabby hotels later found us in Besançon in northeastern France. Now a new word — *passeur* — ominously intruded on my reveries of toys I wanted and toys I had left behind. A small boy in the hotel's grubby back yard rode a miniature car, and I passionately wanted to do so too. But I wasn't allowed to: it might call attention to us.

By asking other Jews in town, my father finally found a *passeur*, a smuggler, who would take us across the Demarcation Line, the border between occupied and unoccupied France. For some reason, the Germans did not take southern France in their invasion in 1940. Most *passeurs* were French farmers, risking their lives for money and sometimes for the anti-fascist cause. Our *passeur*, whose name was Klein, was Jewish.

On a windy spring night, we crossed the border. Mr. Klein told our little group that German patrols were nearby but would not come closer unless their guard dogs picked up our scent. He knew we could avoid them. Every few hundred yards in those deep-black fields punctuated with clumps of shrubs and the occasional bright fence, the dogs started barking. Immediately, our little band of about fifteen dropped to the ground, motionless.

When we did not move the dogs fell silent. Each time they started barking, we crouched. Some people flung themselves down, other sank slowly. I tried it both ways. Either way, my bare knees got cold, and soon my feet did too. My high-top shoes were muddy, and I saw my mother's heels caked with thick brown dirt. She had her felt beret pulled over her curly brown hair, which made her look as if she had no forehead. I listened intently. The barking sounded closer sometimes, but then farther again.

After a few hours it started to pour. A musty, dank smell enveloped me. The *passeur* was small, dark, nervous; his beret looked glued to his head. Inexplicably, he spoke German. "Sir, it is raining," I said to Mr. Klein, trying to be helpful, and he sternly brought his fingers to his lips, shushing me. I was scared now and stayed quiet. Soon I was too tired to walk and my father carried me the rest of the night on his back through the rain-sodden fields till morning came. In the little town of Lisle, we found a hotel that seemed prepared for people who arrived in the early hours of the day.

That ordeal over, a brief illusory euphoria overtook us. Though run by collaborators, unoccupied Vichy France was not German-infested. We found a hotel room in Lyon and started making plans. The city had narrow little streets with pink and blue fronts, shops which sometimes sold toys. Uncle Paul was in Lyon, as were other members of the family. In that dark hotel room, my father declared to Cousin Jacob that we would spend the war years in the French Alps making cheese.

My father was seriously wondering if we could sit out the war in unoccupied France, though my mother argued against that and he himself thought better of it. Once in a while, a totally unexpected streak of grim playfulness emerged in him. He and my uncles discussed changing their names and frenchifying them. My father became obsessed with turning into Monsieur Loup, Monsieur Wollfus, Monsieur de Volphe, trying out any number of combinations on my mother, who already then struck me as improbably patient.

But soon, life in Lyon dragged us down. As transients, my parents had to register every day with the police. My mother and her brother Paul drafted a letter to the police requesting residence in Lyon, and they affixed a number of official-looking stamps on the forged references they enclosed. We spent much time in our room, which seemed to be made of cardboard. A push against a closet door would leave a huge dent. The floors billowed strangely and creaked with every step.

One morning before we went out for our daily walk to the banks of the Saone river, Uncle Paul rushed into our hotel room. He and his wife Melitta were staying in another hotel across town. At twenty-one, Paul was the most active of the family, talking to people, gathering information about escape routes. He was handsome, funny, quick, his lithe, athletic body rarely at rest. Today his long, usually impeccably combed hair flew to one side of his head. "Lucky we were not in the hotel last night. There's been a raid against Jews, a sweep, a *razzia*; they took everybody away."

I remember distinctly the hoarseness of my father's voice. "Who took them away?" he asked, still in his pajamas. "There are no Germans here."

"No, not yet. It was the Vichy French police. These Jews had no papers."

"No papers?" asked my father. "Where were you?"

"Melitta and I were out." Paul smiled mischievously.

"Out?"

"Yes, we were at a place called the 'Lido.' Dancing."

My father looked at his hands. "How is it possible?" he said.

As if to divert him, Uncle Paul now looked at the documents my father had spread out on the deep sill of our dormer window. "These papers won't get you far," he said. "They look false and shabby. We need to bribe consuls, get them to give us something. But it has to be legal, look legal, or the French won't let us out."

Lyon was dangerous and felt so even to me. A ragged urchin threw a rock at me, for no reason. People jostled us. The Vichy police, the local Lyon police, and different kinds of gendarmes whose uniforms my brother and I recognized, looked for stateless Jews, or refugees without documents, or Resistance activity. When not feeling frightened, I was fascinated by the numerous shabby men, their heads bent, their eyes glued to the pavement, picking up cigarette butts. When they gathered a fistful, they slit them open with a dirty razor blade, pushed the tobacco together, and rolled them into nasty-looking gray cigarettes.

For once, I did not mind leaving. "Nice is quieter," my father announced. "No one will bother us there."

We arrived in Nice in April 1942. A glorious family photograph on the Promenade des Anglais shows an amazingly youthful extended family — dapper uncles, short-skirted aunts, prosperous blooming children. My brother and I were sent to the Ecole de Notre Dame, where I, as a foreign child, was put in a slow class and the teacher, her uncombed hair and faded housedress still vivid in my memory, recited endlessly, "cho-se... po-se... ro-se..." pronouncing the second syllable of each word as distinctly as the first. The boys wore shorts and sandals and had long hair. Meanwhile a ragged kid next to me clipped his toenails with oversized scissors. I couldn't imagine why he would do this in the classroom.

A young girl was hired to walk my brother and me along the sea, and my pre-pubescent reverie of her merged with the walks we took into the hills overlooking the gold and brown old city. I was happy.

Though food was scarce, my mother cooked potatoes in the room night after night. They were filling, and we rarely complained. But when some refugees got wind of a restaurant where "chicken is served," we immediately went. So did many other Jews. No other restaurant had meat. At long tables, the language of conversation was Yiddish, German or Dutch. The chicken was delicious but looked darker than chicken usually does. We went there many times.

My mother took a particular liking to a Dutch family from Utrecht with a seven-year old girl, who always wore a little bow in her hair. She had grown-up, ladylike manners.

From them we heard that the Romeels, just as they were getting ready to go into a friendly Gentile's basement, were summoned to Westerbork, the infamous Dutch transit camp to Auschwitz. The four of them were last seen by a surviving family friend, who reported years later that Mr. Romeel tried to show his passport and Moroccan visa to a barking German soldier before vanishing forever.

We kept seeing this family with the impeccable little girl until the restaurant experience came to an abrupt halt. Another rumor now went around: that we had been eating rats. But Nice felt safe, a vacation place — beautiful, sunny, warm — not like Holland. I was astonished by its intense colors and rounding shoreline. The beach had white, round pebbles instead of sand. Several times the whole family went swimming, all of us wearing tennis shoes to protect against the stones. My father hired two Dutch university students, Jewish refugees, to teach my brother and me something of what we were missing in school. A young man with wireless glasses, blond hair and light down on his chin taught my brother algebra, while he furthered my own passion for geography.

His colleague, a Talmudic-looking fellow with curly hair, became excited when he noticed the sink and grimy little hot plate in a dark, closet-like space in our hotel room. I watched him bending over it, then leaping to some documents he spread out over the table. Quickly he lifted a gray egg out of a boiling pot, dried it on a towel, then rushed to the table and rolled the steaming shell over a signature in an open passport, only to roll it again over an empty page of another passport he was creating. Once he copied a whole page this way. Official-looking papers now covered the whole table. We started calling him The Consul, because he forged numerous documents.

My father often wrung his hands, impatient, wondering aloud whether these documents would work, inquiring whether the boys could also make a *Sauf Conduit*, the required Safe-Conduct out of France, a sort of exit visa. He inspected a white card they crafted for him, a French identity-card attesting to the legality of our being in France, with a profiled passport picture at the top next to freshly printed "Recepisse" and a brand-new date and several stamps. Without it, any French official could immediately arrest us. My father looked at it, frowned, and stared as if he did not quite see it. "These papers," he reiterated to my mother, "these papers will help, but we need a real passport, a real visa, and a real *sauf-conduit*."

The words almost became a refrain, and I knew its importance — that we needed better papers. But I found Nice so irresistible, its golden hills inspiring my desire to walk along their paths, the dark-haired girl taking care of my brother and me so enchanting, that I forgot those words from time to time. Lisette had lovely black bangs and a mild, gentle manner. Where would she take us today? Would we be able to climb up the undulating hills in back of the Old City and look out over the whole town? Her voice was soft, and I understood most of the French she spoke. And when I didn't, I hypnotized myself with the sound of her voice. Returning to our room instantly set off a whole wave of anticipation for the next day.

My maternal grandparents were in Nice, as well as their children, my mother's brothers Itscho and Paul, with their wives Rita and Melitta. My mother's sister Anna was there, with her husband Isaac and four-year old daughter Paulette, my cousin. She had been in a convent school in Villard de Lans, a town in the French Alps, and occasionally still said, to everyone's merriment, "*Je suis Ca-co-lique*." Then my father's cousin Jacob joined us. Except for my father and Jacob, everyone spoke good French, my mother best of all.

"You know," smiled Uncle Paul, "with all these dark Frenchmen around, it's easier here to pass for Gentile. But we cannot stay in Nice. We must go. What happened in Lyon will happen here."

Half running to the closet, my father picked up a pair of my shoes. He then, laboriously, cut one of the soles away from the shoe and extracted three dark-green U.S. hundred-dollar bills from between the soles. They looked black around the edges. "Try Liberia, Paul," he said urgently. "Tell the Liberian Consul I lost my Dutch passport, but he can put the visa on this document." And he unfolded our gray-white naturalization forms. Uncle Paul had visited the Liberian Consulate several times, since Liberia was rumored to be giving out visas. No other country was so inclined.

My father resumed his pacing, his face gray, his eyes expressionless. He looked so old, I thought, but then he is thirty-seven! He got carried away with an idea or plan and repeated it endlessly. Already then I knew that he did not really know where Liberia was. "There are ships in Marseille; they can take us there. Liberia," he half-chanted in a monotone. "Liberia, we must have Liberia … Why can't we live in Liberia? Of course, we can. "

"Monrovia," I said, showing off. I had learned the capitals of most countries.

"Monrovia?" asked my father. "Yes, of course, it's far, far from here, so it's good."

But Uncle Paul was back that same morning without a visa to Liberia. That conversation has been told and retold in our family.

"The Consul will take the money," he reported, "but he wants something else."

"Other than money?"

"He wants me to get his novel published."

"How does he think you can get his novel published?" asked my father.

Uncle Paul smiled slyly. "Well, I played the role of a journalist."

"Why, for God's sake?"

"Max, you're not following me. At first he didn't even want to talk to me, but I could tell he was an intellectual, so I pretended to be a Dutch journalist, like Cousin Herman."

"Okay, but can you get his book published?"

"Of course not," answered Paul, irritated at my father's slowness. "Of course not, Max. But now he'll talk to me."

"And what will you talk about? We need a visa, right away."

"I know that. So I told him I could get his book published. But he said if he gave me a visa, I would just leave, and he'd never hear from me again."

"So what did you say?"

"I said since his book was in English anyway, it couldn't be published in France or Holland. I would send it from Liberia to my English uncle, a famous publisher in London. He answered that he would consider it. Then I gave him a hundred dollars. More when I get the visas."

Liberia remained out of reach. Before he could return to the literary consul, Uncle Paul was arrested on the street by French police, who, holding one of his documents to the light, seized him. They beat him on the head and called him a forger, interrogated him all night and occasionally hit him with a chair. Then suddenly they offered him cigarettes.

Paul remained polite and even jovial throughout. He swore in his best French that his identity papers were genuine, and suddenly the officers let him go. In parting, Paul gave them five packs of Gauloises he bought on the black market and promised to come back with more.

I watched my father as he tore our own forged papers into tiny little pieces and flushed the toilet repeatedly. He was mumbling to himself, "These are not good enough." That same morning the crew in the hotel set to work on improved identity cards. When we finally left Nice for "safer" Monte Carlo, we displayed some of these forgeries. They were not detected.

*   *   *

From his American exile, the Prince of Monaco announced that no Jews would be harmed in his tiny principality, and great numbers of them traveled there from southern France. We took a toy-like train to Monte Carlo and found an idyllic little hotel outside of town, grapevines around the trellises, distant music along the hillsides. The owner was friendly and patted me on the head. I wondered how far it was to walk into town and swim in the sea. I wanted to stay here forever.

One night I woke up to loud, insistent voices coming from my parents' room. At first I thought I was having a bad dream, but the voices did not stop and grew louder; several men were talking commandingly to my mother, and I could hear her replying patiently, but she sounded different, a frightened edge in her voice. My brother and I got out of bed and looked out the window: policemen and men with guns stood in the garden. Military-looking vehicles were parked on the street. In the distance, the lights of Monte Carlo flickered less reassuringly than earlier in the evening.

We walked into my parents' room, and one policeman said, almost softly, "*Voici les enfants,*" 'Here are the children.' My mother turned to him and told him I had been ill and needed further treatment, but her protestations did not help: the two policemen insisted we come along with them. My father looked hurriedly through a briefcase, found a document. He put a hand on the sleeve of one officer. He tried to show the document. But without looking, the officer brushed his hand away.

Unbeknownst to us, the Vichy French had overrun Monaco and were now doing the Nazis' work. "*Vite, vite,*" — 'Quick, quick' — said one of the policemen. We were driven back to Nice in a closed truck which we entered from the back, my father lifting me up the two steps. My mother tried to talk to the plain-clothes driver but he did not respond. The winding road of the Grand Corniche looked windswept and forlorn in the dark. We stopped before a large building. Along with groups of people from other trucks, we were hurried into a huge assembly hall where we sat on long, straight benches. In that room of the doomed, I asked one of the policemen for a glass of water. He handed it to me wordlessly.

Policemen and other officials bustled around. My mother called out to a young officer with important-looking braids on his shoulders that we were Dutch and that his orders were to round up Eastern European Jews only. She showed him our tattered papers, including one homemade document, and spoke gently but vivaciously to him. He bent over the forged identity cards and the naturalization papers, which my mother called "a Dutch passport." He looked at her and told her to come with him into one of the rooms off the hall; I could see them disappearing behind a huge door. My father sat motionless and silent.

The three of us now waited on that bench; a low, agitated hum of hundreds of whispers fills the air. As in a dream, the sound undulated from silence to ear-shattering to murmuring quiet. Families, old people, young people, children, all were either mute or very noisy. Every once in a while a stifled sob came from somewhere, but I did not want to look. Next to me, my brother sat straight and said something to my father. The door from which my mother could emerge opened constantly but always with policemen walking importantly in and out. My brother asked my father if we should inquire, but he whispered, "Better not."

Suddenly there was my mother, looking drawn but somehow relieved, accompanied by a smiling policeman. He spoke to her in French that sounded almost Italian, and I could make out something like, "Correct. This is technically correct." She smiled at him and said to my father in Dutch but making sure the man would understand, "We can go. Thanks to this gentleman." We all got up to leave, but my mother now spotted the family with the little girl whom we had met in the restaurant. She said rapidly to the parents, "We'll take her with us." I looked at the little bow in her hair. Her parents wordlessly talked to each other and the man replied, "Thank you. We don't want to be separated from each other." This exchange took less than a minute.

I cannot forget that they and all the others in that room, shipped back to the Nazis, are now dead. That thought was with me in Curaçao, and is with me still. It is not survivor's guilt I feel — merely an unspeakable horror at the slenderness of that thread which has unaccountably held for me and not for others, like that little girl with the impeccable manners and the bow in her hair.

Free once again, we boarded the next train to Perpignan, near the Spanish border. My parents spoke wildly, incoherently, to each other. For the first time I heard that the nice ruddy-cheeked man I used to see on the stairs in the hotel in Nice hanged himself after he gambled his escape money away in the casinos. I heard about the money that saved us, and would save us again, sewn into shoulder pads or rolled tightly into vaginal plugs. I saw one of those plugs, when in Nice my mother held it up for my aunt, who laughed hard. A long flat, yellow sausage — I wondered, "Where did that go?"

Through it all my parents even made jokes: the refugee Jews called the narrow dollar bills *"lokschen,"* Yiddish for noodles, and the squarer sterling, *"farfel,"* farina. And in the midst of it all, a new anxiety-filled word was spoken, urgent, insistent, frightening: *Visa de Sortie*, Exit Visa.

We did not have this all-important paper. It would be hard to get with our inadequate Dutch passport. Somehow the *Visa de Sortie* had to be extracted, bought, forged. My father traveled from Perpignan to Pau and tried to obtain a Spanish visa without it. He bought the visa with money and a gift, but the Consul told him it will be worthless without a *sauf-conduit* and a *Visa de Sortie*. But on the other hand, the visa was indispensable.

Two Jewish refugees in the hotel in Perpignan attempted to enter Spain without visa or *sauf-conduit*. The morning of their departure they sat motionless next to their luggage in the small hotel lobby; the man had a pale bald head and his tall wife extraordinarily gray skin. They barely spoke. After they were refused entry into Spain, they tried a later train, and on their second return from the Spanish frontier town, husband and wife hurled themselves under an approaching train in the French border town of Cerbères.

Somehow, somewhere, my father found a mysterious angel: a young Dutch man named Sally Noach who worked for the honorary Dutch consul in Lyon, the Frenchman Maurice Jacquet. Animated, bright-eyed, Jewish, Noach was a self-appointed wheeler-dealer, a man who liked playing the diplomat. But in the process he did an immense amount of good. He befriended Jacquet, a brave anti-fascist French businessman, and together they ran a semiofficial Dutch consulate in Lyon, the "*Office Néerlandais.*"

If a refugee could show the slightest connection to Holland, Noach would give him Dutch identity cards or whatever other documents he could. Sometimes he provided the names of *passeurs* who could lead the way to Switzerland or Spain. When word of his activities got out in the fall of 1942, Noach fled Lyon, first making his way to Spain, then to England. While helping my father in Perpignan, Noach was himself in flight.

"I had heard about Noach in Lyon, and heard that some of the 'good' Dutch diplomats helped him," my father told us later, "but that he now was in Perpignan was a stroke of luck. We had so many strokes of luck."

Incredulous, I asked, "Did he have his blank papers and documents with him when he was in flight?"

"Noach was odd, kind and greedy at the same time. I didn't even get in to see him without presenting him with a fine leather briefcase."

"How did you know to do this?"

"Oh, everything I knew I knew from other refugees. Just talking."

The document Noach gave us in Perpignan was designed to make our improvised passport look more genuine. He certified that the naturalization papers were an "interim passport," as valid as a regular passport. We now had what it took to get the French authorities to give us a *sauf-conduit*, which made possible a *Visa de Sortie*, which activated the visa to Spain, which made the French let us go and the Spanish let us in — which allowed us to live rather than die. Passports, visas, government stamps and official seals on documents were from then on always discussed in our household in hushed, reverential tones.

While my parents had some legal documents, which allowed us to enter Spain, my grandparents had none. Everybody else had a different document story. Uncle Paul held a visa, made out unaccountably to Miss K. Paula. He might have crossed into Spain legally, but he chose to accompany his parents who could not get a visa, not even a good forgery. After he hired *passeurs* recommended by a cafe owner, he also rented an ambulance and a Basque driver with a Red Cross armband, and the whole family crossed the border at a rarely used checkpoint where the driver "had a cousin."

One hour's drive into Spain, the driver let them out. The *passeurs* now took over, two young men in suit jackets and dirty slacks, and the whole group started climbing up a footpath "where the *guardia civil* is too lazy to go." The *passeurs* who had earlier spoken pleasant French now snarled at them in Spanish to walk faster, climb more rapidly. The higher they went, the nastier the *passeurs* became. In a freezing cold valley where my grandfather slumped down on the ground, exhausted, holding his chest, one *passeur* demanded another "*cientos.*" My uncle Itscho gave him pesetas, then tried francs, but the man yelled, "*Dólares, carajo, dólares.*" Itscho gave him a yellowed hundred-dollar bill.

The *passeur* growled and told them to "*subir mas alto.*" They climbed again and walked toward a farmhouse. As they got closer, the farmhouse turned out to be a Spanish police station. The *passeurs* vanished. The police arrested the stragglers.

The women were sent to Figueras prison, the men to Miranda de Ebro. They were lucky compared to those refugees who crossed into Spain a few weeks after them: those were sent back to the Nazis, who by then had swallowed up unoccupied France as well. We had left Perpignan three days before the Nazis took over southern France. My jailed grandparents, aunts and uncles survived the war.

On the platform in the Spanish town of Port Bou, the *Guardia Civil* admitted us but sent back the man with the broad-rimmed hat who had been in our compartment. He had written in his passport. Even his Spanish visa and his *sauf-conduit* could not save him.

"He wrote in it," exclaimed my father with a mixture of despair and scorn. "How could he write in his passport?"

"Max, he must have had a reason. Was he trying to add to it, make it more official? Probably he was fudging something."

"But he had a perfectly good passport," lamented my father. "How could he be so careless?"

"Maybe his visa wasn't complete."

My father remained despairing on the man's behalf. He looked somber as he repeated several times, "Everything must always be done carefully, carefully. You have to check this over, again and again."

"Yes," affirmed my mother with a sigh, "everything must be carefully checked. But we are in Spain now."

"Yes, Bertha, as long as Franco doesn't send us back. We must go farther, far away; we are still not safe. Across the oceans, across as many seas as possible."

"Oh boy," said my brother. "A ship."

"You children should know," said my father, now becoming more expansive, his face almost relaxing into a smile, "in normal life it's not necessary, but we Jews will probably never lead a normal life again. Papers, documents, we'll always be looking for papers, always scurrying around to be safe."

"I know," answered my brother, "but won't it ever be normal? Like after the war? Won't things get back to normal?"

* * *

Lisbon, December, 1942. My father looked strangely relaxed. "This'll be a formality, Bertha. All we need is a permit to land in Suriname. The Dutch won't deny us that."

But he came back looking dejected. "I saw the Vice-Consul, who turned out to be a real dog. Said he couldn't give me any documents authorizing us to go to a Dutch colony because our papers were not legal. I told him we were almost naturalized, but he said that did not matter; the naturalization papers were not final. *'Bijna is nog niet half*... 'Almost isn't even half,' he said a few times. What does that even mean?"

"Oh," explained my brother, "it's an expression we learned in school. It means if you come very close, you still haven't achieved anything."

"Then I asked him," my father continued, "what should we do?

"And he said, 'That is up to you, of course, Mr. Wolf, but why not stay in Portugal and sit out the war here? You'll be safe. Portugal is neutral. No Germans here.'"

My father continued. "At that moment he received a phone call — and spoke German to whoever it was. *'Einverstanden*,' he kept saying. 'Agreed.' I asked him, 'How do you suppose I can get the papers to stay in Portugal and last out the war here?'"

My father now drew himself up, imitating the vice consul. "'That is not the concern of the Kingdom of the Netherlands.' Those were his exact words. 'That is not the concern of the Kingdom of the Netherlands.'"

Much as I hated to miss out on the ship and crossing the ocean, I thought it would be good to stay in Lisbon, which reminded me of Nice. The warm sun on the pink and white houses, the little hills rolling up toward the sky, the yellow tram at the bottom of the steps right outside our hotel — and in the evening, strange, sad music throbbed in white-washed houses.

My mother suddenly looked up and remembered that someone we met, a refugee, had said that the official in charge of documents was bad, but another official, a kind of assistant to the consul, was good. "We can just see this other man. We have no time to waste. I'll find out when the first one isn't in the office. Or better, I'll call him away from his office."

"How will you do that?" pondered my father, looking at his hands.

"I'll call him away myself. And when I do, you go to the Consulate, with the same request for a permit as before."

Next morning she put on her coat and said I could come along. My father would go to the Consulate with my brother. She found a public telephone and asked in Dutch to speak to the official, then switched to German and said sternly, "You are urgently requested to meet an important visitor. Can you meet Herr Schutzen in the main lobby of the Hotel Majestic in one hour's time? He is wearing a flower in his lapel." And she hung up without waiting for an answer.

That afternoon, my father returned from the embassy with a big grin. "This assistant consul is '*tov*,'" he said, using the Hebrew word for 'good.' "He said our passport wasn't real, but it was real enough to leave this sad continent. 'Close enough, close enough,' he kept saying. 'We can do our part here.' He said he himself would like to go to England to join the fight against the Germans."

At last, on the Portuguese ship *Nyassa*, I stood alone, watching the ocean. Soon my parents and my brother came looking for me. But my mother started crying again. Fortunately, a fellow refugee joined us and said in German:

"It's Europe you're leaving behind, Frau Wolf, not your youthfulness."

I did not know what he meant; my mother was thirty-one .

Now very composed, my mother answered, "I feel a decade older than a year ago when we left Holland."

That conversation and the German refugee's odd formality were reiterated often by my parents. But in subsequent years they never spoke of the crying again.

[L. to r.] Manny's mother's sister Anna and her husband Isaac; Rita and her husband, mother's brother Itscho; mother, Bertha, and father, Max; Melitta and her husband Paul, mother's youngest brother. In front, Manny and his brother Sieg. Nice, France, autumn, 1942

Engagement photo of Manny's parents,
Chemnitz, Germany, 1930

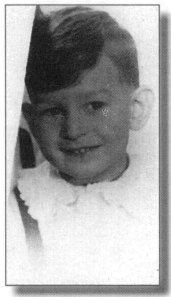

Manny, 2, Chemnitz, Germany,
1936 or 1937

Sieg, 5, and Manny, 2, at a German or Czech
resort, ca. 1937

Sieg, 5, Manny, 2, and their mother; in Chemnitz,
Germany, ca. 1937

Manny, 4, and Sieg, 7, The Netherlands, ca. 1939

Sieg, 7, Manny, 4; on the beach in Scheveningen,
The Netherlands, ca. 1939

Mother, Paramaribo, Suriname, 1943

Father, Manny, 10, and his grandfather, David
Kornmehl, Curaçao, ca. 1945

Manny, 13, in Curaçao, 1948

Father and mother in Curaçao, ca. 1949

Part II: Refuge

Chapter 2. A Special Case

We had sailed from Lisbon in mid-December and observed the arrival of 1943 — and my eighth birthday — on board the Portuguese steamship *Nyassa*, and still the sea was everywhere around us, blue, green, white, misty, clear. On stormy days, it seemed to hover above the ship, and then the passengers huddled on deck; even Mr. IJsland would give up his pacing. My brother and I called him Mr. IJsbeer, Polar Bear, which is also the Dutch term for endlessly pacing back and forth. Tall, white-haired Mr. Ginsberg, whom the passengers called with a mixture of sarcasm and respect Mr. van Ginsbergen, stood ramrod straight at the railing, in wind and rain. He talked mainly to his wife, a worried-looking lady with thin, sharp features, whose Dutch was so formal that some of the other refugees doubted she was Jewish.

One night, without prior announcement, we were called on deck. The ship was too large to enter Paramaribo, Suriname's capital, so we would be unloaded at sea. A wave of anxiety swept over the passengers. "Unloaded, how?" Were we going to be refused entry? "You'll see, they'll dump us out yet," said Mrs. IJsland and started crying softly as she stood next to her husband. A few weeks ago, they had been abandoned by their Basque smuggler, who was to take them across the Pyrenees to Spain. They groped their way back and attempted to take the train across the border but were sent back to unoccupied France because they lacked a proper Spanish visa, and there was no way they could legally get it, visas no longer being issued. Mr. IJsland had to forcibly keep his wife from throwing herself under the train at the border town of Port Bou. Only a last-minute forged document, bought from a fellow refugee with a printing press, had admitted them into Spain and finally into neutral Portugal. I caught her anxiety and felt instantly certain that we would never see the new land I so longed for. How would they unload us?

Nearby, a tall, bony woman, Mrs. Hotz, stood very still, clutching her ragged little suitcase. Her glasses were wet, but she did not wipe them off. She had had to divorce her Gentile Viennese husband, which somehow enabled her to escape. The story was vague, but she so lovingly reiterated at every turn *"Mein Mann aus Wien,"* "my husband from Vienna," that my parents kept having the same conversation about her:

"How could she leave that man?" wondered my father and looked contemplatively at his hands, as he always did when he was perplexed.

"How could he let her go?" answered my mother, a worried, sympathetic furrow on her youthful features.

"What?" said my father, still looking at his hands, and not seeming to listen. "Maybe she didn't even really have to go."

"Yes, after all, he wasn't Jewish. She might have been OK," said my mother.

"Did she make the right choice?"

I felt sad for Mrs. Hotz and wondered why her husband hadn't come with her but never asked my parents.

She had established herself on board as a pedicurist. "Someone who knows how to do something," pronounced my father frequently, almost dreamily, "is never out of work." She came to our cabin twice a week, more for the company than because my parents needed her. Only when she spoke of her former husband did she smile. "My husband in Vienna, you know, he always looked after me. We had a fine house." My mother asked many kind questions.

We stood on deck. It was now the middle of the night. The sea was choppy, the night as black as in one of the pictures of a book I loved. We stood for what seemed like hours. Then our Portuguese captain said in French, "You will be picked up here. *Ici, ici.* "

"Here, here, how can we be picked up here?" wailed Mrs. IJsland, her curly brown hair limp on her forehead. Mr. van Ginsbergen looked sternly at her. In the damp night, he wore a double-breasted blue blazer with an insignia, which I could just barely make out: Batavia Yachting Society. He had been an attorney for the Dutch colonial government in the East Indies until a few years ago. After looking at her for a few long seconds, he said, "Quiet, please." And then he turned to an unlikely person, a small, bent man who was forever looking in back of him, to the side of him, around him. He had a shuffling gait and, though he spoke excellent German, was thought of as an "Eastern Jew," "a real Polish Jew," by the rest of us, a little shifty, too unassimilated; but everyone knew his sad story: he had left a wife and son in Holland. "Don't you think it is time we showed some dignity?" asked Mr. van Ginsbergen. "Aren't we Europeans, shouldn't we try to set an example?" "Yes, yes," said the little man, looking to all sides, barely understanding the Dutch. "*Sicher,*" he said in German.

Suddenly below us, out of the darkness, emerged a small steamer, its hull gray-white, its decks tiny. It heaved on the waves and sought to come closer, making several approaches. But then it retreated, which caused our little band of refugees to lurch forward. "Are they leaving?" called a desperate voice in the back. "Leaving without us, stranding us? God help us." Finally, the captain shouted a few hoarse orders, and we surged to an opening in the railing of the deck that seemed to lead nowhere. Their torches lit, the Portuguese sailors gestured to a long, bouncing stairway along the ship's side.

"No," I heard myself screaming, suddenly convinced that there was no little boat in the deeps below. "No."

For a moment my panic knew no limit. I yelled again, "No, no, no."

My father tried to carry me, but the gangplank heaved and shook. My panic now receded and made way for a gray sense of dread. It was as if I had already fallen into that foaming sea, the showers of which we could feel where we stood.

"Forward," commanded Mr. van Ginsbergen.

I took a few steps toward the gangplank, drenched and slippery, my father tugging at my hand. I knew I had to do this if I wanted to get to the new country.

Two abreast, we clambered down the groaning stairs into the noisy spray, and finally into a small launch, which we stepped or fell into, four or so at a time. The rest waited at the bottom of the stairway over the roiling waters. In our little boat, we drifted and maneuvered to the side of the small vessel, where another, even wetter stairway hung next to its hull. From this distance, the *Nyassa* looked like a floating skyscraper.

On board of the little steamer, miraculously, Dutch words were spoken in a strange sing-song by genial black men in white shirts. In the warm night air, they smiled and moved quietly, purposefully. One of them handed me a drink, and to this day I remember its foreign, bitter-sweet taste, the acute thrill of my first Coca Cola. The black men settled us on deck chairs, and a few hours later, as the sun rose, we steamed slowly into the harbor of Paramaribo, its long, flat river banks making way for a sudden protrusion of streets and wooden frame houses. Palm trees rose out of the brown earth, creating spots of shade in a wide field of glare. Sleepy, warm, I glanced around me; the Dutch flags were comforting, as were the black voices speaking Dutch. Could we live here as we had in Holland? I looked at my mother, who had tears in her eyes, while my father stared straight ahead, thinking his own thoughts.

For two months we were not allowed to leave our internment camp in Paramaribo. We slept in barrack-like dormitories, and almost instantly the children were organized into an open-air school taught by a woman who had been a teacher in the Netherlands. Our curriculum was meticulously Dutch, except for a song about "Suriname's proud streams, Suriname's stately trees, Suriname's sacred land." Under the circumstances the words rang true to us. We were happy in school.

The adults appeared more abstracted, a little dazed; in their tropical outfits they looked clumsy and displaced, though eager enough to do what was asked. Some of them wanted ardently to do something but did not quite know what. Every morning on the sandy lots surrounding the barracks stood little clumps of men hatching plans and having serious discussions. One man declaimed earnestly, his skinny arms pointing out of his sport shirt, his face beaming under his large Panama hat: "This country has water and Surinamese. And it's our job to sell the water to the Surinamese."

An intense desire for normalcy prevailed. We had somehow escaped the chaos of Europe and here in 1943 we embraced order and regularity. Not only was there school and homework for the children, but for the adults different activities, from sewing classes for women to political discussions for men. Mr. van Ginsbergen gave a lecture on "The Genius of European Civilization," which reminded me that our teacher had called one of the boys a genius. The Dutch Jews socialized mainly with each other, as did the German Jews, while the handful of Eastern European Jews somehow looked most out of place. Several men were drafted into the Dutch Army in Exile and started appearing in uniform. A certain Captain Feder, as Aryan in manner as any Aryan, was always in uniform; not a popular figure in our boys' barrack when he had the watch, he was envied for his captain's stars, which he had earned by being an engineer.

At the end of the second month, a large variety show called "An Evening in Europe" culminated in a beauty contest. First a juggler performed magic tricks, and a slender man recited in nasal tones the medieval ballad of Sir Halewine. Then a woman sang *"La Donna e Mobile"* to the accompaniment of a large piano, and as a planned encore a coy rendition of a popular French song that required much rhythmic clapping. Finally, two young women in bathing suits shared first prize for the most beautiful legs. I did not realize adults could be so enthusiastic; there was much applause and many mutters of appreciation. "Just like back home, in Europe," said Mr. Handelsman, his round face glowing. "Omi," he yelled to his mother-in-law, "they want you on the stage too." She waved at him appreciatively. "It shows we still belong to Europe," said Mrs. Klein contentedly. They were all so rapt, though I noticed that Mr. Remak disapproved and kept saying, "Kitsch, kitsch." My parents too did not join in on the fun: my father looked dazed, unseeing, and my mother uncharacteristically detached.

Less than three years before, in 1940, just before the war came to Holland, we lived in the Dutch town of Bilthoven, my father still youthful, my mother cheerful, though both of them anxious. One day my father announced that he would take us all to see a "real German cabaret — just the way it used to be in Germany." His best years were spent in Germany, where as a young man he had married my mother and prospered. Leaving Germany for Holland in 1938 was one of the many losses he sustained in his life.

I was five years old but remember the train ride from Bilthoven to Utrecht along the woods and green fields that seemed from the train to point to an eternally beautiful future. On the platform at Utrecht stood a cat so perfect, so rounded and symmetrical, that for a moment I disbelieved its existence. Despite the noise of the loudspeakers and the bustle of passengers, it did not move until a gold-braided conductor scooted it out of the way.

The lights in the theatre were orange and blue, and I had never seen so many people in one place. On the stage, a slender young woman wearing only her bra, girdle and stockings stretched her arms and patted her bottom and sang coquettishly, "A corset is... oh... so practical." She kept stroking herself while she sang languorously, her stockings giving off a purple glow. The applause from the audience, probably mainly German refugees, was tumultuous.

Soon the master of ceremonies, a slight figure in devilish black, burst on the stage and sang: "Let no alien shadows fall... on your loveliness..." Now his mood changed. He approached the woman with a shoe in one hand and shrieked to the audience: "How can we get excited about a shoe and a man... eh?" He put his hand on the woman's bottom, and then he looked at the audience, and at her.

The woman turned to all us and smiled. He pointed the shoe at her. "Yes, why is that? ...Eh, Frau Schuuuuu... mannnnn?" he screamed. The audience roared at this play on shoe and man.

The evening stayed with me. The magical lights blended with the look of relaxation on my parents' faces. I saw them as they were then, as I wanted them to be now, as I myself wished to be in the future. In subsequent years I asked them about that evening, but they never seemed to remember.

We fled Holland almost two years later in early 1942 when the first waves of deportations started. It was during that period, as we now understood it, that small, shuffling Mr. Remak went boldly to the Gestapo, requesting permission to be exempted. He told them he was a "Special Case" because he had volunteered as a Polish seventeen-year-old to fight for Germany in the desperate last battles of the First World War. "I brought along my Iron Cross to show them what I had done for Germany. They laughed at me and locked me in a cell for two days and nights." Then they let him go and told him he would soon be "repatriated," though perhaps "a little more easterly" than he expected. When Mr. Remak came home that day, he learned that his wife and son had been arrested by the Gestapo. No one he dared to speak to could tell him anything about their fate. He went into hiding and later found his way into southern France and then crossed the Pyrenees into Spain. Now he was here.

We were sitting in one of the tiny rooms sometimes used by families in the camp to be together. Even inside there was a glare, and my father kept adjusting the wooden shutters.

"Do you think they arrested his wife and child because Remak called attention to himself?" asked my father, still looking at the window.

"Hard to say," sighed my mother. "What must he think? What goes through his mind? God forbid that he should blame himself."

"Not his fault. But how could he not feel responsible?"

"I don't know. What is going to happen to all those people they transported to Poland?"

"We aren't even sure that's where they went, Bertha."

"It isn't going to be easy for Mr. Remak to find another wife," said my mother, her dark-blond hair glinting in the light.

"Why not?" asked my brother, then eleven years old.

"He's so strange. So sad. Nebbish. Poor man."

"Nebbish," affirmed my father.

"He lost everything."

Was Mr. Remak always looking around because he had lost something, I wondered.

"But he still may find a wife," insisted my brother.

"Yes, of course."

"Besides, why should you think his wife will die?"

"Well," answered my mother. "Perhaps she and the child will return after the war." Her frown undermined her soothing words.

"It's much harder for a woman to remarry," said my father.

"True, Max, much harder."

"Why?" asked my brother, closing his book, which displayed a zany-looking man in an old-fashioned suit.

"Because when a woman isn't married at a certain age, she becomes odd and difficult."

"Even if she is a widow?" my brother wanted to know.

"Yes."

"There will be more women than men after the war," said my father. In World War I they didn't kill women. At least not deliberately."

"Maybe they won't this time either."

"Maybe."

"You children should play now," said my mother.

"I'm getting too old to play," said my brother, who was eleven. "Besides, I'm reading," he said, "about someone who goes around the world in eighty days."

"That's not very fast," I piped in.

"No, not now, silly, but then it was."

"I'm reading about a boy who goes camping in the Dutch woods, and on the heather. I wonder if we can go camping here in Suriname."

"No," said my brother. "You'd be eaten up by tigers."

"If we went camping, we'd be just like Dutch kids."

"Forget about camping. We will never be Dutch kids again," answered my brother. "I'm not going to read about Holland anymore."

"Remak," said my mother. "Remak… so close to Remarque, the great writer. What a wonderful man that is. He knows everything about what we went through, and about love…"

"Love?" asked my father.

"Yes, love. His name is Remarque. Erich Maria."

"All Quiet on the Western Front," said my father proudly, who had not read the book. I knew that because he was always reading newspapers, never books.

"Remarque. It's a pseudonym," explained my mother. "Kramer spelled backward. I think he is one of us. Hitler burned his books a few years ago. But the Germans liked him still."

"Yes, like Einstein," said my father.

"Yes."

"When the Germans thought Einstein was wrong, they announced that the Jew Einstein was wrong. When he got the Nobel Prize, they said the German Einstein won. And now ..." My father paused as if he had forgotten what else he was going to say. He could go from expansiveness to melancholy in a moment.

"Who knows what goes on there now."

"There are going to be plenty of mixed marriages after the war," brooded my mother. "Meanwhile, you children be nice to Mr. Remak."

We did not seek him out but always stumbled across him. Just now, Mr. Remak was walking on the damp sand paths between the barracks. In the afternoon heat, he wore a limp straw hat, which from time to time he took off to wipe the sweat from his forehead. He suddenly paused, his hands Germanically behind his back, and looked to one side as if he were speaking with someone next to him who had made a startling point.

"What?" he asked and seemed to hear a reply.

"*Aber wass.* That is not possible." He walked further.

We had never seen him so strange; maybe that was how he behaved when he was by himself. He looked like a figure in a story book, trudging slowly across an endless plain.

Suddenly he stood completely still, calmer now. "How can anyone ..."

Then he turned around and asked me in German, "How old are you, little boy?" His forehead was mottled with little glistening spots.

"Eight."

"Good, but that is very good. Yes, good. Eight years old. *Ach.*"

"You do not rest in the afternoon, Mr. Remak, with the other adults?"

"No, kind of you, such a small boy, so thoughtful."

"My father says the afternoon heat is the worst."

"Everything is the worst sometimes. I have a boy, older than you are ..."

Suddenly Mr. Remak turned his head, and I heard a shout that sounded like a sob, and he was gone. I was proud to have had so grown-up a conversation, but I wanted to get away from Mr. Remak. I wanted to be with the other children, and I became eager to storm a hill that some of the boys used as a fort in a protracted series of war games. My brother was usually more patient than I: he was a good, polite listener. He encouraged people to speak their minds, though he found little to say to Mr. Remak.

Soon the refugees left the camp and found housing in different parts of town. The camp stayed on as a social center, a kind of club, but few people came to visit. On an unpaved street lined with palms, one family called their little house "Summer's Cottage." We moved to an apartment with a wooden verandah over a shoe store in Paramaribo, and my brother and I played in a ragged back yard with brownish, sticky palm trees. After each heavy rain, fast-flowing rivulets appeared, and we planned to build a boat and float it into the jungle, which seemed to begin next door where an empty lot faded into a pale-green wilderness. Actually, the real jungle was miles away, but you could always see a tropical thicket wherever you happened to be. On our way to the refugee school at the camp, we saw a panther carcass with three perfectly round holes in its hide hanging alongside a truck. The panther resembled a long, stretched-out cat, with that same perfect roundness I admired in cats, but it was a stiff, punctured cat now. A tall black man stood nearby, as if he were waiting. His long hair and loin cloth marked him as one of the Surinamese Bush People, proud descendants of runaway slaves, who live in the jungle and to this day do not like to come into town.

"What if a panther gets into our back yard?" I asked my brother.

"They rarely come into town," he answered, not quite reassuringly.

My brother liked to be measured in his speech, even when tormented by a heat rash all over his body. He always was more controlled than I, more purposeful, more practical and methodical. He embraced his studies with a passion. He would have done so anywhere. It was not easy to do it here, but he did it anyway. Both of us sweltered under our mosquito nets, a nearby fan providing little breeze. The legs of our beds stood in little pots of oil that protected against centipedes. For me, our new South American home could not compete with memories of cool, crisp Holland. I did not question our luck in being here but became nostalgic for all things Dutch, even potatoes, since our main staple now was rice. In our Surinamese kitchen hung little wooden cabinets with bits of food surrounded by buzzing flies.

Most of the refugees left Suriname within a year. The first to go was Mr. Remak. He had appealed to the Dutch authorities to release him first because of his special circumstances. "I told them about my case," he said to my father, "and I told them about my uncle in Mexico."

"I thought your uncle was in Cuba."

"Did you?" A sly expression crossed his face. "No, Mexico; Veracruz. Besides, I'd rather go there anyway."

"Why is that?"

"Well, in Mexico they don't bother people like me."

"People like you?"

"Yes, people like me, who are not in one piece. Besides," Mr. Remak now looked almost cheerful. "That country has a border, a dry border with the U.S, if you know what I mean."

"You mean..."

"Exactly," gurgled Mr. Remak. "From there, I can smuggle myself into the United States."

He explained to my father that he would stay "in the New World" till the war was over and then return to Europe. For some reason, we went to see him off. Clutching a copy of a Spanish primer, he pulled down his straw hat over his eyes and buttoned and unbuttoned his white suit jacket. Still looking around him, looking everywhere but straight ahead, seeming to peer under the propeller, he climbed with two other passengers into a small float plane and within minutes it took off, leaving two powerful, horizontal funnels of white spray.

Shortly thereafter, it was our turn. We had been told that the other Dutch colony in the region, Curaçao, would admit refugees and that it offered a "far more normal Dutch environment" than Suriname. Curaçao was drier, less jungly; it had a large Dutch community and more Jewish inhabitants. My parents would find work there. The small DC-3 lifted off, and before the curtains were drawn over the tiny portholes to keep any potential spies among the passengers from reporting the lay of the land to the enemy I caught a last glimpse of Suriname's wide brown rivers, the "proud streams" of our song. The land looked flat and pale-green in the shimmering sky. I would have my ninth birthday after my first plane ride. I looked forward to 1944 in that new land, which our teacher called "almost like home."

But not quite yet. Our plane made a stop-over in Trinidad, and we were instantly separated from the other passengers and led into a secluded office. Two British police officers sat behind paper-laden desks; they wrote down everything my mother said. In their white short-sleeved shirts with dark-blue tie, they looked friendly but serious. Occasionally, they smiled politely. Since my parents did not speak English, the conversation took place in French, which my mother spoke well. The older, red-faced officer was unhurried and thorough. He explained that to further the "war effort" he needed to know as much as possible. "Spare no detail," he urged. Though they had been in Trinidad since the war started, he said almost apologetically, there was a great deal the authorities knew, but they could always learn more.

I was impatient to be back on the plane. Would we be left behind with no new home to go to? The young police officer slowly began his questioning. The little town on the border between unoccupied and occupied France where the Nazi guard dogs were barking that night in the summer of 1942 when we fled over the Demarcation Line from occupied to unoccupied France — what was it called? My mother hesitated and looked hopefully at me. "Lisle," I said. "We arrived there the morning after our crossing." Without looking at me, the man paused and wrote it down. Why did the Vichy French police let us go after having arrested us in Monte Carlo? "Because," said my mother patiently, "I persuaded them that we were Dutch, not Eastern European Jews." My mother seemed extraordinarily calm; conversation always quieted her.

"I don't understand exactly. Why did that make a difference?"

"Well, you see, that week it did. That's what it said in the French newspapers."

The policeman looked puzzled but he wrote it down. He seemed genuinely to want to know. And he seemed genuinely not to understand. Sometimes he appeared to be writing things down because he had been told to. Now he started asking about our fellow refugees in the camp. Occasionally he peered at a long typed list. The scheduled hour's stop in Trinidad turned to three. Each deafening sound of a plane taking off scared me. Was it our flight? Surely our plane would leave without us. My father was silent, just as he had been over a year ago when we were arrested by the Vichy police in Monte Carlo. But these were English, it was different, they were our allies; still, why did they detain us while all the other planes were taking off? Could they blunder into sending us back, somewhere, somehow?

My parents looked upset but not surprised. Not once did my mother ask why we were being interrogated. My father looked gray, his face rigid and mournful. He did not understand French but seemed to know what was being said. Only once did he look up, when the questioner repeated, "Remak, Remak," as if he were pronouncing the name of a fine old French wine. The younger police officer also tried out the name and looked at the list. "That's the Tangiers list, not the Suriname list," he said in English. My mother explained what happened to Mr. Remak, in Europe, before he ever came to these parts; but the two officers seemed not fully to comprehend and asked such questions as, "Why did he think he was a Special Case?" At last the older one asked, "Is this Mr. Remak?" and he showed each of us a blurry picture of a young man with big muscles in a bathing suit.

My heart starting thumping excitedly. What if Mr. Remak was not who he said he was? What if he had made things up, made everything up? Maybe he had been in disguise all along and really was the man in the picture. And later, in Curaçao, on the rare occasion I thought about him, I felt light-headed and almost giddy at the thought that all those horrid things had not happened to him.

But long after our interrogation in Trinidad, when we were established in Curaçao, a story appeared in the Curaçaoan papers that a certain Karl Radek had been captured in Colombia. He had passed himself off as a refugee and spent time in a refugee camp, but he was actually a Czech spying for the Germans and sending them radio messages about possible submarine landing sites on the north coast of South America. The picture in the paper showed a handsome man, dwarfing two Colombian women on each side of him. Because of his great height, the locals nicknamed him *El Gigante*.

So Radek was not Remak. Unfortunately, Mr. Remak's sad story of the loss of his family had been true. I had hoped that he was an impostor, an adventurer, a spy. For my sake, I hoped that one more tragedy would turn out not to be. It would have made it easier to forget him.

But after the war, it was easier to forget him anyway. There were many like him; he had not been such a special case after all.

Chapter 3. So much Bleating, So Little Wool—School Days

Shortly after our arrival in Curaçao in January 1944, at the age of nine, I went to my first real school, the Hendrikschool in Willemstad. I had passed the large concrete building a few times and was terrified by the noise from the playground at recess, the children running and yelling and fighting. Once enrolled, I turned to my brother for protection during recess. In class I thought I would get it from my teachers. Much as I had longed for a real school, this was not at all what I expected; the Dutch schools I had read about so fondly in my children's books did not resemble the Hendrikschool.

Thirty of us seated at tiny desks, all boys, mostly black, some brown, some white. We all wore short pants with neat, short-sleeved shirts. Most of the boys looked large and muscular. I felt scrawny, vulnerable, unused to so many alien creatures. They paid little attention to me, and when I tried to talk to them they ignored me. The teacher, a small, brown-skinned Curaçaoan man, with a gold pince-nez, was the younger brother of the island's most famous politician, who sought to lead Curaçao, a Dutch colony, toward autonomy and independence. I felt scared of something unpredictable in Mr. da Costa Gomez's manner, his eyes glassy but flickering like those of an excited, wild boy. In his shiny white suit, he stood behind his desk slowly stroking his curly black hair. He looked almost lazy as he asked a series of questions about the Dutch history textbook:

"Hipolito, when did the Romans come to our country?"

"The Romans came to our country in 50 A.D."

"Where did they have a large settlement, Benjamin?"

"They had a large settlement in the town we now call Nijmegen, sir."

I tried very hard to memorize the children's names. The teacher kept on asking questions. "Why was it easy for the Romans to settle in our country?"

"Because there was little resistance from the local tribes overwhelmed by superior armaments — and only the rivers served as a barrier in that flat, wet land."

"Very good."

This part looked easy; I would do my homework and answer questions. Memorizing textbooks and excelling on tests — these were what I expected. Dealing with the other children would be harder; they seemed not to take school seriously even when answering the teacher's questions. I looked around the room with its brownish desks and graying walls. All the windows were open, but the room was airless. A sweaty smell hung in the air. The boys' bobbing faces looked feverish, dreamy. As the long day wore on, everything began to feel like a game, an overheated ritual.

The teacher spoke Dutch and the kids answered in Dutch, but to each other they talked in Papiamentu. "A Creole language," the principal explained to my mother. "Derived from Spanish, Portuguese and Dutch. Some of the grammar goes back to West Africa and the slave past," he elaborated. My mother had nodded respectfully.

"And what tribes were living in our country then, Frank?"

Frank shifted in his seat. He was a light-skinned boy whose shirtsleeves were rolled up to his shoulders. "They were the... eh... eh. I don't know, sir."

"Have you done your homework?"

"No, sir."

"Why not, Frank?"

"Well, my sister got married, and I had to be ring-bearer."

I was afraid for Frank, but he looked unworried.

"What has that to do with homework?" Mr. da Costa Gomez took a short step forward but Frank sat up boldly.

"Sir, I didn't have time because we had to rehearse."

"The explanation doesn't correspond, correspond, correspond to the original problem. Do you hear me, Frank? Correspond, correspond, correspond."

"Yes, sir."

"Do you understand what I mean by correspond, Frank? Correspond is an important word not enough people pay attention to," said Mr. da Costa Gomez loudly without looking at Frank.

"Yes, sir."

"Sometimes people search for the word, but it doesn't spring to their lips. Do you know which word I refer to, Ivan?"

"Correspond, sir."

"That's right, Ivan, correspond — a supremely important word, a word for which there are many uses and a variety of occasions. I warn people who haven't done their homework. I have a new stick. And you know what I call this stick?" He now stared expectantly at the class.

Several voices, cheerful enough. "No, sir."

"I call it the Pir-lala."

"The Pir-lala, the Pir-lala," several boys repeated, almost in unison.

"Yes, that's what I said, the Pir-lala. Now let me show it to you, especially to people who do not find the time, or have the energy, or possess the intellectual wherewithal to study. There should be a correspondence, a clear correspondence, a transparent correspondence, a pellucid correspondence, between homework and the Pir-lala. Do you follow me, Frank?"

"Yes, I do, sir." Frank smirked at the boy next to him. I would be frightened if a teacher talked to me like that, and it surprised me that other kids did not seem to care.

"Now, let's unveil the Pir-lala." Mr. da Costa Gomez ceremoniously opened a large closet in a corner of the classroom. His eyes glittered, and his voice was soft, almost soothing. "Yes, I see my collection of other sticks: the Sparkling Fire-Giver standing there quite contentedly, alongside the Teacher's Ultimate Aid, looking none the worse for frequent use; and the Adult's Final Support, with its many ferocious knots; and finally the cleverly named Last Curaçaoan Waltz. But where, where now is the Pir-lala, which a good friend cut for me on the wild northern shore of this beautiful but harsh island? Where is that gorgeous stick? I do not see it." He wheeled around quickly, "Do you, Frank?"

"No, sir."

"It was here yesterday."

"Sir," called out Wilmoo, a tall, light-skinned lad in an unusual pale-blue sport shirt. "I saw the Pir-lala yesterday." He grinned excitedly.

"Yesterday, Wilmoo, you saw the Pir-lala yesterday. Where did you see the Pir-lala yesterday?"

"Sir, I saw it on a car."

"And so did I," interjected Benjamin, a small, very dark boy, with an elegant round head and fine, mobile features, who impressed me with his quiet manner and evident good sense. "I saw it on a car too, tied with twigs to the front bumper."

I was planning to make friends with Benjamin, but I couldn't understand why he was saying these strange things. How could you see a stick on a passing car? And was it even true?

A chorus of voices now: "Yes, I saw it also; no, no, sir, I was the one who saw it, I saw it: it was near Westpunt, the car was going very fast."

"All those sightings of the Pir-lala, boys. It makes my head spin." Mr. da Costa Gomez raised his hands dramatically.

The shouting now grew louder, which he did not seem to mind. His eyes, feverish behind his little glasses, flickered. He stood with his arms still upraised like an orchestra conductor, the voices cascading towards him: "I saw it, I saw it. The Pir-lala, of course, man, how can you say you saw it when I was the one who did? I saw the Pir-lala. I saw the Pir-lala, of course I saw it. It was speeding by without a car; it flashed by my house like magic."

"I saw it pass my house in the middle of the night; it was beautiful and shiny; I had never seen anything go so fast; it whipped by me."

Several boys were standing now, turned to the others, grinning, their hands half raised or on each other's forearms as if to interrupt each other, though they kept looking at the teacher. I wondered why he allowed this to go on so long and wanted him to stop it.

"Yes, I heard it singing, I heard that," said Hendrik, and he started swaying in his seat, singing the words, his long body throbbing and shaking.

"Well, boys, a good thing the bell just rang because these stories aren't going anywhere; they do not bear on anything, if you grasp my meaning. They do not correspond, correspond, correspond. But the subject is important enough for us to dwell on some more, in another time, though not in another place."

"Is he crazy?" I asked my brother on the way home from my first day.

"Of course not. How can a teacher be crazy?"

"He seems so strange."

"Well, Manny, that's the way they are here. If you do your homework, you'll like school."

I had not gone to school in Holland, because when I reached school age in 1941 the occupying Germans forbade Jews to attend school. I used to look longingly at a picture of my brother, taken in first grade, standing proudly next to a pretty, smiling teacher.

So in 1941, instead of going to that kind of school, I had "rabbi lessons," as I called them; I was the only pupil and did not really want to hear about things Jewish, while the distracted, heavy-browed rabbi showed no interest in my drawings of cars or birds. He stroked his beard with a preoccupied manner and looked right past me. How I wished I could have been in the school to which my brother had gone.

In Nice, in 1942, I was again briefly enrolled in school, the Ecole de Notre Dame. The teacher was a middle-aged Frenchwoman with a dowdy bun. The children wore shorts and sandals and had long hair. They seemed intimidatingly large.

And the year before this one, in 1943, I was in our little makeshift school in Suriname, taught by one of the refugees. She was a blonde, warm-hearted Dutch lady, copious in her praise. We sat on long benches under a thatched roof supported by four slender poles. I liked it, but it wasn't a real school.

"How is school in Curaçao?" asked my mother, looking concerned but right past me at two small cartons of pots and pans she was unpacking. We had just moved into a tiny house off a dusty square.

"It's strange."

"Well, a new school is always strange. But you like it, don't you?" She sounded almost cheerful and was trying to smile.

"Yes, I like it. Do you think we'll move back to Holland after the war?"

"Sure," she replied wearily. "That may well be."

"When?" I demanded.

"We've moved around so much."

"But this would be different. We would be moving back," I said.

"True, we wouldn't be fleeing, but if you consider all the countries we've already lived in, Germany, Holland, France, Suriname …"

"But once we return to Holland we won't ever have to move again."

"How can anyone be sure of that?" She looked away.

All during this time, in the fall of 1944, my parents found it hard to listen to my school stories. My father stared absent-mindedly at me, his eyes remote, a pained, blank look on his oval face, and I soon stopped talking about school. Once in a while he said, "Hard to believe we're here."

"We saved our lives," said my mother quietly.

"How is it possible?" answered my father. "And what about the others?"

"Only fifteen years ago," said my mother, "I graduated from high school. My best friend Tzilly — did she reach Australia? And Becka?"

"Becka is OK — she married a Gentile," said my father distractedly.

Now my mother was staring the way my father usually did. "But what if the Nazis shipped her to Poland?"

Mr. da Costa Gomez asked what the typical diet in Greece contained. He wanted someone to say "goat cheese." His pince-nez seemed to be slipping off his shiny face. Now a small quarrel broke out between two pupils.

"Sir," shouted a tall boy from the side of the classroom pointing dramatically at Benjamin, "that boy said 'correspond.'" And he swiveled around, looking straight at Benjamin. "Wait till teacher finds out that you never even saw the Pir-lala. You are going to be in big trouble; you're going to catch water." And he made that funny up and down gesture with his hands the boys made when they said "catch water."

"What," said Mr. da Costa Gomez to Benjamin, "you didn't see the Pir-lala a few weeks ago? Are you now going *linea recta* against your earlier testimony?"

"No, sir," smiled Benjamin. "That boy is lying. Or at best guilty of a *contradictio in terminis*."

"Explain," said the teacher, who now put down his pince-nez on his desk and rubbed his eyes like a sleepy child, "what the contradiction consists of and why it is *in terminis*. I see it as an accusation, either true or untrue. Certainly *per definitionem* it is not a contradiction."

"Well, sir," replied Benjamin, cocking his round head, "*mutatis mutandis*, it is a false accusation."

"A serious matter, a very serious matter. Especially *coram publicum*." Mr. da Costa Gomez was now rubbing his cheeks.

"Indeed, sir," answered Benjamin gravely, "but consider the unreliability of *vox populi*."

"You are," said Mr. da Costa Gomez, "a bright lad, an exceedingly bright lad, an inordinately bright lad. You may come up here and light my Zippo."

"Oh, boy!" Benjamin ran kiddishly to the teacher's desk. They both took turns lighting the lighter, the teacher occasionally admiring the swiftness of the flame and the leanness of the wick. Benjamin's elegant, oval head was tilted to one side, while Mr. da Costa Gomez gazed intently down at a succession of slender reddish and blue flames. "The rest of you," he called without looking up, "remember, we stopped at The Domain of Plants, bottom of page 43."

From the back row a sudden murmur: "Your mother's domain of plants." It was starting again, this strange buzzing. And, as usual, it was done in the local language Papiamentu, which I was beginning to understand.

A Dutch boy, Peter, smiled at me. He whispered, "Look back, Manny. This is so weird."

I looked around at a brown-skinned, curly haired lummox, his face close to that of a heavy-set black boy. "No, your sister's domain of plants."

"Man, your sister asked me to look at her bushy plant. Your sister's plant was so dried out she begged me to water it."

"Yeah, she told me about it. She said your nozzle was so limp only a few drops came out."

"I'm telling you, I couldn't see the earth for the bush."

"Listen, brother-in-law. I take my sister's bush over your mother's nether lips. Those are so large a ship from the oil company could sail in."

The curly-haired kid looked indignant, while the other fellow scowled, but this was not a quarrel. It was just something the boys did, couldn't help doing, another life beneath the life of the class. The only thing that surprised me was the suddenness of these eruptions.

Perhaps some day I would take part in this strange ritual, but I didn't even know what everyone was saying. "Bush" I could understand, but what were "nether lips"?

"Hey, look, Manny got a haircut." Frederik came over to me and carefully gave me a measured slap on the back of my head, at the place where bare skin met the hair-line. He intoned, *"Mi ta batisabu,"* "I baptize you."

About ten boys now lumbered toward me. I shrank back, frightened, but one by one, they gave me careful pats on the back of the head, saying "I baptize you." They looked congratulatory. I felt a joyous relief.

Wilmoo clasped my head from side to side and looked closely at the hair-line on the back of my head: "It's a *corta bajo*, a good Caribbean straight low cut, not one of those stupid-ass tapered Dutch hair-cuts. Hey, Wolf, you're one of us."

Mr. da Costa Gomez and Benjamin were now lighting a whole set of lighters from a large carton to see if the Zippo was actually the fastest. Every time the flame would appear, Mr. da Costa Gomez studied it with a fascinated stare, while Benjamin stood quietly. A few boys tried to approach the desk, but Mr. da Costa Gomez hissed, "Let me concentrate." Some flames were blue, some orange, but the Zippo was the fastest. Both praised the Zippo till our attention was suddenly diverted by a powerful fart. *"Lie-bo,"* intoned the farter. *"Lie-bo,"* everyone responded in a kind of chant. This was funny: it had the same prayerful gravity as the responses at Friday night services in the synagogue. "*Lie-bo,*" I said also, but so softly that no one could hear.

It was easier to join in at the movies where it was dark. If the film broke or the projector failed, the audience cried out, "Shon Popo, Shon Popo." I did too, at first just calling it out but gradually yelling louder, "Shon Popo, Shon Popo." My friends looked approvingly at me, and I felt happy to be included in the group, though I knew it was not the sort of thing that would be done in Holland. It took me years to find out that a man named Shon Popo had been the first to run a movie house in Curaçao, and that his primitive equipment in those old days failed regularly. "Shon Popo" was a mock chant to recall this legendary figure to his duties.

Mr. da Costa Gomez was one of several Curaçaoan teachers, but most of our teachers were Dutch. Often from small towns in the Netherlands, they taught as the Curaçaoan teachers did, looking for specific answers and sticking earnestly to the text, but, unlike the Curaçaoan teachers, they used language defensively, the driest expressions serving as a bulwark against the lushness of their surroundings. I see now that they wanted to extend a European rationality, a rigid Dutch normalcy, to the colonies, and so they praised common sense or deflated the extravagance of the children they taught.

Many had arrived on the island before World War Two. "It was either the East Indies or the West," one teacher explained in class, "and I chose you, though sometimes I wonder why." Most of those teachers seemed unready for what they found: a rocky, hot, starkly beautiful place, with cactus silhouetting a barren landscape, inhabited predominantly by black Curaçaoans and white Dutch people, and by Hindustanis, Surinamese, British West Indians, Polish and Levantine Jews, Portuguese and Venezuelans. I myself was among the most recent arrivals:

a refugee from Europe, a small survivor from that distant war. One or two teachers were enchanted by this mix; the rest reacted with aversion or indifference.

And yet I liked them. They came from the place where I wanted to live, and they worked hard on this strange island. My parents knew some of these teachers. They too admired them and now occasionally listened to my brother and me discuss them, evidently interested, sometimes even wanting to hear more. But the war was coming to an end, and in the spring of 1945, right after I turned ten, a series of harrowing stories from the continent we fled only two and a half years before drifted over like cinders from a distant fire. With the liberation of Auschwitz, Bergen-Belsen, Buchenwald, Dachau, one concentration camp after another, the true meaning of the fate we had managed to evade became clear. A photograph in *Life* magazine showed grim-faced GIs looking at hundreds of naked bodies stacked on top of each other outside a wooden shed. Making an effort to keep my voice from shaking, I asked my brother: "When were these people killed?" and he answered, "Must have been just a few days before the picture was taken. Long after the Germans knew they had lost."

My father paced from one end of our small living room to the other. "Bertha, I am in despair." He squeezed his hands together and stared at them, as if they contained some solace.

My mother looked somber. "Can we find out more? Maybe your brothers survived. Maybe the Red Cross or the JOINT…"

"The JOINT?"

"Yes, you know, the Jewish JOINT Distribution Committee. They may know how many of your brothers survived."

My father looked blank. "Survived?" he asked as if he did not understand the word. "Survived?"

"There may be hope, though it's unlikely that your mother…"

"Yes," he said, "hope." He looked at his hands and slowly wrung them.

"Thank God the Germans are losing the war, Max."

"Against us they won."

"We must keep working, Max. It is good for us."

"Yes," said my father, suddenly almost cheerful, "work. We are lucky to be here. And thank God the children like school. That is important."

Such talk always made me feel bad, and I often tried to change the subject, conscious of having to push something away, a heavy lump, a weight that loaded me down and made me gloomy and strangely tired. Only when I thought of the future was the heaviness completely gone.

May 5, 1945, the German capitulation: I was ten years old. It was, as usual, sweltering. Suddenly, in the classroom, a stir. A few cars, sounding their horn as if at a wedding procession, drove by into the Bredestraat, Willemstad's main artery and the pride of Curaçao, already then one of the Caribbean's best known shopping streets. Classes canceled, the whole school now gathered in the gymnasium. All of us attempted to cheer, very difficult to keep up for more than a few minutes when there is somehow no clear direction, no immediate center. But we knew we had to cheer, and I made a sort of dry-throated effort myself. I was happy. Maybe now we would go back. I would ask my parents tonight when that would be. Some of the more inventive Curaçaoan boys, for whom the war was remote anyway, since the island had not been affected by it, made Tarzan sounds. But the principal, Mr. van Leeuwen, a stocky, red-faced Dutchman, would have none of this. He began his speech to the assembled boys by saying: "Just because the war is over doesn't mean you can scream."

Right after liberation, several more teachers arrived from the Netherlands. They too wanted us to repeat the formulas of our textbooks. And they wanted them said calmly, matter-of-factly. Mr. van de Water, our new French teacher, a tall, blond, blushing man, was plaintive:

"Why is everyone bouncing around so? You may look older than your years, but you behave as if you have St. Vitus' dance. You aren't spastic, are you? Don't be so animated. Just give the answer, calmly, quietly, directly. No need for emotion, you hear?"

"We're southern people," said Benjamin.

"Yes, southern, OK, but remember: 'If a donkey is too happy he'll dance on the ice.' Oh well, let's return to the lesson. Where were we? Page 33." And he wrote on the board, *'Jean patine sur l'étang.'*

As soon as Mr. van de Water's tall back was turned, Frederik, a lanky boy with the beginnings of a mustache, stood up, thrust his crotch forward, and grabbed it. *Patine* meant prick in Papiamentu. Other boys guffawed.

I felt annoyed. Those big boys always gave everything a dirty twist.

"Could you explain *'patine'* a little more?" asked Wancho, not to be outdone.

"Of course, Whan-choo," sneezed Mr. van de Water happily. "You see, the verb is *patiner*...."

"No, I mean *patine*. What are they doing on the *étang*?"

"Oh, you mean skating."

"Yes," said Wancho innocently, "skating — what is that?"

"Oh, yes, yes, I guess you don't do much of that around here."

"Well," said Wancho, "we use our *patine* but not for skating."

Mr. van de Water looked puzzled at the laughter, but since he did not know what *patine* meant in Papiamentu, or what anything meant in Papiamentu, and since Wancho himself kept a straight face, he did not catch on.

I felt bad for him, but I thought he was almost too naive. He should have seen through the boys. Still, I liked his seriousness, the way he told us about first going to Paris as a young man and the waiter chiding him for calling him *"garçon"* (*"Garçon, c'est vous"* — "you are the boy.") I pictured myself as a young man in France, like Mr. van de Water. I too would go to a cafe and watch the people drift by. Mr. van de Water brought Europe to our classroom, and even if the other students did not want it, I did. Would it be as beautiful as I remembered it?

My favorite teacher taught Dutch. Mr. Gos was a gaunt, balding man in his late thirties, but unlike the others, passionately interested in the island, its history and language. I liked his cheerful manner and admired his enjoyment of everything he did. An amateur painter, he came in the classroom and quickly drew a caricature of one of us on the board. He enlivened the textbooks with stories of his own. But he was as bound to those books as were the other teachers.

"Let's do Style now. Complete the following. Wilfredo, let me call on you. What beautiful names you have here in Curaçao, Wilfredo, Benjamin, Hipolito, Wancho. In the Netherlands everybody is Jan and Piet. And you obviously like your names; you find them beautiful. Curaçaoans know how to live. You're not only precocious but artistic. Anyway, Wilfredo, complete the following: "Grab the bull by the …?""

"Horns," shouted Wilfredo.

"Hungry lice bite…?"

"Sharply."

"If you want to marry the daughter, woo her…? "

"Mother."

"Manny, what is an unlaid egg?"

"An unlaid egg is an uncertain egg." I liked these proverbs. They were concise and clear.

"Why are we doing these?" inquired Benjamin.

"To impose order," beamed Mr. Gos, "to shape, to form, to guide, to control. A mature culture has such expressions, and Holland is especially rich in them."

"How do they create order?"

"By teaching prudence, carefulness. I love Curaçao, but some Dutch normalcy would not be amiss here."

A stream of children's books, printed long before the war, started flowing in from the Netherlands. In my favorite, a young boy went into the woods with his friends, and on one colorful illustration a neatly starched child with a straw hat and a large bow-tie joined a welcoming group of boys for an adventure on the heather, their tents nearby. A curly-haired boy held an open book. The heather was colored purple, just as I remembered it when our family had stayed at a country hotel before the war and my uncle Paul swung me on his back and played football with my brother and me. I remembered the happiness of those walks, the bicycle trips in the open air, myself on the back of my father's bicycle or trying out my own.

In these books there was no war, nor the chaos of the makeshift schools I had attended, nor the wildness of the Caribbean whirl around me. Children were eager to learn but had fun, adventures and intrigues. They were never in danger. I became a reader and a diligent student. On the wall of my study still hang two prizes given to the best student of Dutch, in 1946 and 1949. In one, old Queen Wilhelmina gazes down sternly; in the other, a young and glamorous Queen Juliana, swathed in ermine, casts an approving look.

I asked Mr. Gos if he owned a book of sayings, and he brought one in, *Proverbs from the Whole Wide World.* "Just got this from Amsterdam," he said. "Look, it may be printed on cheap paper, but it's beautifully typeset. No one can beat the Dutch at printing. And here it is one year after Liberation, and everything is all the way back to normal."

"Except for the dead, of course. They'll never be back," I said without thinking.

"Don't be morbid, Wolf."

It was the first book I had seen printed in Holland after the war, and at the age of eleven it excited me to think how many more there would be. Maybe Mr. Gos was right and everything would be normal again. I wanted things to be just as they had been before the war: the small Dutch town, the cheerful sounds of Dutch, my looking forward to being a big boy. At least these sayings had not changed. I read the book from cover to cover, but when I came to "Jewish Expressions" I was startled to see some of my father's odd proverbs: I never thought those would be collected in a book. Jewish things always felt private, unwholesome, an uneasy secret — certainly not something you would expect to find in a Dutch book.

Along with Dutch proverbs, the teachers enjoyed a caustic summing up. If no proverb came to mind, they made one up, the more biting the better. "God gave you a great physique and balanced it out with your mind." "With a face like yours, further punishment is unnecessary." "Putting on airs? You'll end up paying income taxes on that, even on this island." They wanted things to be plain and orderly, and that made sense to me, but unlike them, I did not hate extravagance. Much as I disliked people who "put on airs," who pretended, who professed feelings loudly, I did not think you should be punished for calling attention to yourself, as Dutch people did. "Little birds that sing too early in the morning get eaten up by the cat," went a proverb, or "If you burn your ass, you'll sit on blisters," or "Just be yourself — that's weird enough." I liked those sayings but sometimes joined in with the Curaçaoans who laughed at them.

Curaçao was always hot, but in June of 1947 we had a heat wave: in the blue sky, an American Piper Cub circled over the sea right by the large picture-window of our classroom; it climbed steeply, then fell, then seemed at the last moment to rescue itself within yards of the dark blue water. I was now twelve and feeling restless. How free that plane looked, and how hungry for movement it made me. All eyes strained at the toylike plane, bodies contorting to follow its acrobatics. The teacher, Mr. Wilder, white mane over his forehead, paused. He had been explaining that Cabinet ministers as well as foreign ambassadors to The Hague always had to be addressed as "Your Excellency," but that, under certain clearly definable circumstances, it was permissible, even good form to address the Queen simply as "Madam," instead of "Your Majesty." Now he walked slowly to the large pane of glass, absurdly large for such a hot climate, peered through it and pronounced, still looking at the ambling sports plane: "That joker, doesn't he know he is interfering with the class?"

But Mr. Wilder made up for lost time. He ran through the work at top speed, roaring out questions and answers.

"Geography and Topography of the East Indies. The capital is Batavia, we know that. But what is that cool city in the mountains?" Mr. Wilder grinned at the thought of a cool city.

"It's Bandung, sir."

"What is Bali known for?"

While Frederik started pantomiming large breasts, Wancho shouted out, "Volcanoes!"

"Good. Now Religion of the Indies. I hope to God we never lose our beautiful Indies. . . . Temples on the island of Java?"

"Borobudur, sir."

"Good. Next: Economy of the Indies. What did the Dutch establish for the natives?"

"Banks, for saving their money."

"You should identify them — Dessa Banks."

"I meant Dessa Banks."

"Meant? Meant? No one can tether his horse to meant. But go on: why is there little industry on Sumatra, Frederik?"

"The natives are lazy."

"No, Frederik. The answer is 'The natives lack the necessary industriousness.' That is what your book says, and that is what you should say."

Mr. Wilder also taught biology. "What do apes and people have in common?"

"A Common Ancestor."

"Yes, a Common Ancestor, but what is the Missing Link?"

He said a few words about the mystery of the Missing Link, but a little song erupted, about a loose-limbed, dreamy giant of a boy, Eduardo, with long apelike arms. "Eduardo is the Missing Link."

"Trap shut," bellowed Mr. Wilder, at which point the little song went underground as a sort of hum, about Eduardo the Missing Link.

Distracted by the hum, Mr. Wilder mumbled, "So much bleating, so little wool."

Just then, the principal and Mr. Gos, carrying huge clipboards, entered. I dreaded these yearly visits to ask each of us where we were born. Finally it was my turn, "Chemnitz, sir," I said, "but we moved to The Hague when I was two."

"That doesn't count," snapped the principal. "Just say where you were born."

"Germany," I whispered. I hated being linked to Germany in any way.

"Manny is a German," yelled the kid next to me, and it almost became a little song, but the principal scowled at him. I felt enraged.

Mr. Gos said kindly: "Our great Dutch poet Vondel, the Prince of all our poets, was born in Germany."

"Was he Dutch?" Peter asked.

"Of course he was Dutch — our greatest poet."

"Is Manny really Dutch?" asked Peter with real surprise.

"Certainly he is," beamed Mr. Gos. Did he mean it? And was it true? If I belonged with anyone, it was with the Dutch. I was not wild enough to be Curaçaoan. It pained me to have to always explain that I was Dutch. My hope for the future lay in the Netherlands. But maybe I did not belong anywhere.

It had been arranged for weeks that I would meet the parents of this same Peter, a tall, flaxen-haired Dutch boy, who was almost Curaçaoan in his interest in dirty jokes and bawdy stories.

Peter's father sat up straight in a large overstuffed chair islanded in a sea of dark-brown parquet. Dr. Voscus was a dentist. He looked extremely old to me, his wispy gray hair lifeless on his head, his small brown eyes darting left and right. He spoke to his wife as if he had not known we were coming, "Now, look here, mother, isn't that nice? Peter has brought a friend home."

Peter stood up straight, one hand toying nervously with his flaxen hair: "Father, Mother, this is my friend Manny, from school."

Mrs. Voscus smiled broadly and got up from a small, straight-backed chair in a little alcove off the living room. She was younger than her husband, tall and blonde. I had seen her out shopping a few times and admired her lithe, energetic walk. She addressed her husband with a show of enthusiasm, "Jan, what a fine occasion."

"Yes," said Dr. Voscus, "an occasion for rejoicing."

"We like to see Peter bring friends home," said Mrs. Voscus.

Dr. Voscus slowly removed his glasses and blew on them. "This warrants taking down the cookie tin, doesn't it? It's important once in a while to be festive, to put the little flowers outside." Mr. Gos had only recently explained this quaint Dutch saying: if you were going to celebrate, with dancing and carrying-on, then you would prudently put the flower vases and pots outside, to prevent breakage.

Mrs. Voscus stood on tiptoe and took down a large tin box from the top shelf of the stately bookcase. She opened it slowly, arm extended, and leaned over Dr. Voscus as if he were an invalid.

Though all the cookies appeared identical, Dr. Voscus studied them a long time. "Many piglets," he said jocosely, "thin out the swill-trough."

"But Jan," protested his wife, "what are you saying? Surely there are a great many here, so this swill-trough hasn't thinned out yet."

"These are tasty," said Dr. Voscus slowly. "We must get more of them when we're on leave in the Netherlands."

"Oh, our leave, what a wonderful thought; to be cold again for a change." Mrs. Voscus gave a happy, anticipatory shiver.

Peter looked embarrassed but I did not know why. I too wished I could be cold for a while. And I wished my parents would talk like that — and be like that.

After we had each taken a cookie, Mrs. Voscus stretched out her arms and carefully put the box back in its place on the top shelf. Her pulled-up skirt revealed the back of her knees and calves more muscular than I would have thought.

Dr. Voscus turned to me and with a friendly furrow in his brow said: "I hear that you are a litterateur."

"Yes," I replied, "I have written poems and stories."

"Oh, and do you mean to publish those?"

"Yes, certainly. After all," I said, now trying a proverb myself, "paper is patient."

"How wisely observed. I am glad you're Peter's friend in school."

"Art is long, life is short," noted Mrs. Voscus.

Dr. Voscus now sat forward and spoke in a brooding monotone: "I have a brother, a good man, but his creative efforts led to journalism."

"Well, that would suit me," I said. "I think I would like that." I felt expansive in this company. Odd that I was so different here than at home — or even at school.

"You see, Jan, you regard brother Jacques as a failure, but Manny here wouldn't object to such a career."

"Yes, I suppose so, Nellie, but we have all been men of science in our family. That's why I went into dentistry. But journalism... What do you think, Peter?"

Peter didn't think, so he said nothing and munched on his cookie, and occasionally glanced up at the top shelf of the book case. At school, he and I had once devoured the better part of a cake my grandmother had sent along for the whole class. I felt unaccountably happy during this visit.

✳   ✳   ✳

That evening, my brother and I were trying to evaporate huge flat trays of water in the living room. We had learned in school that Dutch people in Java cooled down their houses that way.

"Was it nice at the home of your friend?" asked my mother with a frown of interest.

"What friend?" asked my father.

"You know Max, Manny is friends with the son of the dentist Dr. Voscus."

"You children are lucky to have so many Dutch friends. You're accepted as Dutch even by Gentiles." My father looked both pleased and distant, a look peculiar to him.

"We are," I reassured him, wishing it were true.

"It's good to lead a normal life, in a normal, wholesome school."

"Yes," I said, "but I want to be in school in Holland."

"Oh," said my father, "maybe some day."

"You're just saying that."

"What?" asked my father distantly.

"You always just say things. It doesn't mean anything."

"Don't be upset, Manny."

"Why can't we ever be like other people?"

"Other people didn't go through what we did."

"We'll never move back, will we? We're never, never moving back."

"Move back, move back. What do you mean?" My father's attention was now clearly flagging.

"I mean, move back, move back to Holland."

"What's wrong with Curaçao? Yesterday, I saw your old teacher, Mr. da Costa Gomez. He's very nice."

"He's weird."

"Sure Curaçao is odd, but it's a good place. You like it here, don't you?"

"Yes."

"When I was a child in Germany," my mother said, "friends and school were the most important thing in the world."

"In Germany, in Germany," brooded my father and trailed off as if he had lost his thought. "In Germany we were really at home, even more than in Holland. In Germany... yes, but then the Nazis came. Who knows where anyone is at home?"

Chapter 4. Singing
for the Queen

It was August 31, 1944, the birthday of Queen Wilhelmina of the Netherlands, and once again time for the yearly musical tribute, the "Aubade," on the Caribbean island of Curaçao. My brother and I stood in separate rows in the merciless heat, as we would for all aubades through the forties. From schools in the country as well as the capital Willemstad, boys and girls in crisp white clothes streamed in procession to the large square in back of the Governor's palace, a broad, two-storied building whose front faced Curaçao's handsome harbor. There we stood for hours until the other processions arrived and until the Governor and the Inspector of Schools came to the balcony to receive our songs in homage to the Queen.

I felt hot and sweaty. In the hottest time of the year on the ever-sweltering, ever-humid island, this event took place during the hottest part of the day, the late afternoon. Thousands of black, white and brown faces peered out of white-starched costumes; we sang for God and Christendom, for Queen and Land (Holland), for the welfare of those (especially the Governor) who protected us. The land we paid homage to hadn't been able to protect itself from the Germans in the war — but the words had their own life and held their own truth. I didn't think of what I was singing, and probably no one else did either.

When at last the Governor came to the balcony, a tremendous cheer went up from all over the huge square. He was a small, dignified-looking man in an elegant white suit. Whereas the other Dutch notables wore a stiff, chalky white, his suit had a touch of cream in it. He was said to have literary ambitions and had a somewhat bohemian air about him. As always he was introduced as "His Excellency, the Governor of our islands, Dr. Piet Kasteel." Because *kasteel* means castle in Dutch, the Curaçaoan nickname for the governor was Jan Paleis, John Palace, which a few kids mumbled.

After the cheering, all the various groups from all the schools sang the Dutch national anthem. This stately old seventeenth century hymn to the Father of the Netherlands, Prince William of Orange, had lately been altered: where it described the Prince as saying that he was of *Duitsen* blood, of German blood, we were now made to say *Dietsen*, which removed the offensive German connotation but sounded archaic, and made little sense, as if we were now suddenly pronouncing German as Gooman. The Curaçaoan kids sang lustily about the Prince's loyalty to the fatherland without any sense of incongruity that a far-off country and not their own Curaçao was intended.

During the high-school years, some of the larger boys at the aubade were beginning to whistle at the girls standing in other rows, but there was little rowdiness. My friend Sigmund, whom we called Mundi, a tall lanky black kid, said once, "We Curaçaoans like this kind of stuff better than you people." I could tell from my first days on the island that Curaçaoans loved ritual, drama and song. They admired choreography: the way all the groups would slowly fill the whole enormous square, the manner in which the red, white and blue Dutch flags alternated with the orange of the House of Orange, the way the Governor would step onto his balcony at just the right moment. It did not seem to interest them that as the years went on some black faces started appearing with the Governor on the balcony.

If the Curaçaoans loved the singing, and the Dutch kids felt patriotism, the aubades reminded me of being a refugee — Dutch, but not really accepted as such, too unchristian, too unblond. On such occasions I felt more an outsider than ever. I envied those who could be so wholehearted in their celebration, and I wished I were fully Dutch or Curaçaoan, either very fair or black. But much as I longed for Holland, I did not revere the Queen. On the occasional newsreels we saw at the movies, she was a remote, small figure, who spoke from her exile in London in strange, formal tones. Some Dutch people in the movie theatre applauded.

After one such aubade when we were back at our school, I told Mundi this, and he answered, suddenly attentive:

"How come you feel that way? Isn't she your Queen?"

"Well, yes, but you know we're refugees."

"I know that," he said impatiently, "but don't you have refugee things you celebrate?"

"No, I guess we don't... Hey, want to come back with me and play chess?"

"Not me," said Mundi. "I have to help my parents get ready for Queen's Birthday fiesta; it's at our house and we'll be dancing till tomorrow morning," and he started doing a slow motion rumba, his hips swiveling languorously from side to side, his arms holding an imaginary sensuous partner. "There'll be masks, Wolf, like the masks people make in Brazil." A nearby teacher shot him a puzzled look. "*Mijnheer,*" said Mundi suddenly. "What do you do tonight to celebrate?" and he switched over stiffly to a fox-trot, his right arm distantly and formally around an imagined Dutch lady's waist, his left arm stiffly extended.

The teacher was in a hearty mood: "Well, well, Sigmund, maybe we will have a little dance and raise a small glass too."

Another year, this same teacher was less good-natured. During the long recessional back to our respective schools, some of the noisier boys were still singing but giving a kind of mock Curaçaoan accent to the Dutch songs, and a stern word or two from him silenced that. Mundi was again exuberant, talking about another Queen's Birthday dance, this one at the house of his uncle. He started gyrating and lowering his long body as if doing the Limbo when this teacher said irritably: "Don't you know what kind of day this is, you dumb kaffir?" 'Kaffir' had been an insult in the Netherlands ever since the Bantu people had risen up against the South African settlers of Dutch descent.

"Why does this man always say kaffir?" mumbled Mundi. "Hey, Wolf, what actually is kaffir?"

"A kaffir is a South African," I answered.

"What does that have to do with me?" wondered Mundi.

We lived in a hermetically sealed world where one teacher, himself a Curaçaoan, though very light-skinned, would always say, "Whole tribes who never understand a thing," and we all knew that Europe no longer had tribes but Africa did — and yet no racial slur seemed intended or heard.

In the younger grades in Curaçao we celebrated another Dutch ritual, which held much more interest for me. On Sinterklaas, Santa Claus, held on December 6, the festivities taking place all over the Netherlands were copied. St. Nicholas, the fourth- century bishop of Myra, whose fame spread all over the Mediterranean world after he entered the home of three destitute girls and left dowries for them, was said to arrive by steamer from Spain. "There comes the steamship from Spain again. It brings us St. Nicholas; I see him standing there," we all sang, and indeed the white-haired old man in his scarlet bishop's robes with the golden miter in his hand sat in the back of a convertible which was driven onto the school grounds, where a group of children and teachers was waiting, and then was escorted into the gymnasium in which the rest of us had congregated.

Santa traditionally had a helper, Zwarte Piet, Black Peter, a fearsome figure dyed black, presumably a Moor. The major way in which our Curaçaoan ritual diverged from the one in the Netherlands was that here St. Nicholas had two black Peters, and they did not require blackface because they were in fact black. Nor did they inspire fear, because we all were either surrounded by black faces or had them. Every once in a while, you could see them trying to make the hideous broad grins they were supposed to have in the colder countries where blacks were a rare and frightening sight.

The principal welcomed Santa and thanked him for taking time out from his busy schedule to visit this school in this distant land. Santa smiled serenely and stroked his white beard. Soon the attention turned to the good children who deserved presents and candy, especially those who had good grades. Santa's helpers scattered candy and small gifts, grinning broadly. The children jostled each other jumping for the candy. We all exaggerated the excitement of this.

Then came the high point of the ceremony.

"Are there any children who have been bad?" croaked Santa ominously.

It grew very still. The principal announced regretfully that there were.

"And where are these children?" asked Santa.

"Your Grace," said the principal in his gasping, sweaty way, "I will read the names of the children who have not behaved and who were very bad."

Now Santa gestured to his black helpers, who slowly unfolded large burlap sacks.

The names were read and the children stepped forward, some brazen, some frightened. One small boy bounced up jauntily when called and made the sign of the stiff prick behind his back, his middle finger extended between rounded index and ring fingers.

Santa reprimanded the offenders sternly and shook his miter and then ordered the 'worst' children to be put into the sack. "There you go," he said, sounding suspiciously like one of the teachers not present at the assembly. The helpers grabbed two children and put them unceremoniously into their sacks, one of them head first, and then they went outside, "back to Spain," the principal bellowed, "where they know what to do with such children." It was not uncommon to see the feet of a seven- or eight-year-old child violently thrashing around inside the closed brown sack.

How bad were those children, I pondered? Were there ever children bad enough to deserve being taken away? I thought of that gypsy boy, trapped beneath his wagon. Did we save him, that day in 1941, when we opened the latch of his little prison? What about all the ones who were carried away but definitely had not been bad? Why had they been selected for that fate? No one had come to save them, that I knew.

In subsequent Sinterklaas festivities, two black Peters turned into three and four. Sometimes they did a little dance before they dispensed gifts or opened their sacks. They started to shake rattling gourds and soon seemed to be playing for each other. Gone were some of the Dutch songs. One year the Peters brought large drums, and the drumbeat throbbed through our auditorium to the pleasure of most of the children. The Dutch teachers looked surprised.

"*Wiri, wiri,*" yelled the kids, asking for an old Indian instrument, a kind of pipe that musicians scraped with a key. The kids were swaying to a sort of rhythmic clapping and chanting. Some of them became loud, while others made low humming sounds, like the ones I always heard in class, subterranean voice-overs to whatever was going on. It all made me long for the way the celebration was done in Holland, without exaggeration and display.

Four years earlier, in 1940, when I was five, we lived in Bilthoven, in the Netherlands. On Sinterklaas, all family members were invited to attend the celebration at my brother's school. I remember walking there with my mother through the wintry lanes of our woody town. In back of all the houses — we invariably called them villas — stood tall trees, which even in their present leafless state beckoned to be climbed. I knew that there would be endless summer evenings of play waiting for me, and my one worry was that I had more plans than there would be time for: the tree house, playing soldier with my brother, the bicycle, and all the inevitable school activities.

This was certainly the town in which I would live the rest of my life, marry and have children, though my parents would still be there to take care of my brother and me. The length of the walk to school, the way the road stretched never-endingly made all time fall away. The anticipation I felt for the day's festivities was the strongest feeling I had ever had. Near the school on that cool Dutch day was a small police station in front of which stood a bored-looking German soldier in his green uniform. Other signs of the Nazi occupation were few. I felt a fierce desire to be at that school, just like my brother, and to have a satchel like his.

In the Gymnasium we were all gathered together when Santa was escorted in. All of us, including the visitors, sang loudly: "Santa Claus, Santa Claus, put something in my shoe and something in my boot. Thank you, little Santa Claus."

Santa had left any number of things in the shoes I had put out the day before, but my far greater joy was to be here, in this school auditorium, and to think that some day I would take part in it.

To my brother, Santa said, "Your name may be Wolf but you don't eat like a wolf." My brother's pretty teacher smiled warmly at him. My brother promised to eat more in the future.

And one child was carried away in a sack. But such a fate seemed easy to avoid. I would simply see to it that it did not happen to me. You could avoid such things if you were careful. Nothing could really spoil my happiness and my anticipation of that day, especially in view of my future attendance in that school.

Soon thereafter the Germans forbade Jewish children from going to school. Instead of walking to the large building with its noisy playground I was taken, satchel in hand, to a Rabbi's house, where I seemed to be the only pupil. He talked a lot about Jewish holidays, and he did not want to talk about Santa Claus.

My next Sinterklaas was at the house of our friends, the Jagers, where my brother and I played in the afternoons. The Jager boys had created a whole world in their attic. Large ships stood ready to sail the seas. A model airplane was miraculously spacious enough to take us in. The attic's windows faced a mysterious wood, which I planned to explore in the future. Someday I would walk through those woods on warm afternoons and gather mushrooms, as once our whole family had.

The Jager boys' father, whose first name was, like mine, Manfred, was a remote, white-haired man, a dentist; his wife was dark and small and quick, almost like a child herself. As soon as we came into her house she gave us lemonade. She appeared cheerful and light-hearted, and kept saying that it was good for children to play. "Here everything is normal. Let's have fun, kids."

Dr. Jager played Santa Claus for us that year in 1941, but it was a subdued affair, an illegal gathering, since Jews were denied the right of assembly, and I don't remember much about it except that no children were taken away in a sack. It was not a Sinterklaas I thought of often.

Soon all the young Jewish men were called up for work duty in Germany. We knew that older men would follow, but my parents thought that the Nazis would not harm women and children. "Should I flee to England?" pondered my father. "But how can I leave my family? No, better to come up with a plan for all of us."

My father and my uncles discussed escape routes, poring over maps. They were working on a plan which would require us to travel through France. On the whole, our family preferred land routes to sea routes, which seemed more dangerous. One day Dr. Jager escaped on a small fishing boat to England. Six months later, his wife and children were seized by the Germans. When the war was over, he learned from the Red Cross that they had all three died in Auschwitz, and we heard in Curaçao that he had gone to Bilthoven for a short time but did not stay there.

But in 1944, during my first Curaçaoan Sinterklaas, we did not know that, or much of anything else, about the fate of those left behind in Europe. My own memories in Curaçao of Dutch Sinterklaas were always those of my brother's school in Bilthoven. And they were joined by the celebrations I read about. How marvelous it would be to do what the kids in my tattered Dutch books did. They were so wholehearted and eager. Maybe in the future I could have celebrations just like that, after we all returned to the Netherlands.

My geography teacher in Curaçao seemed pleased with my pleasure in the holiday and asked me, in his formal way, where I had "observed these festivities" the year before.

"In Suriname, in a refugee camp."

"And the year before that?"

"In Portugal."

"Oh. What did you do on that occasion?"

"We ate till we got sick. Everything was cooked in olive oil, which we weren't used to. We had come from France, where there was almost no food."

"Well, you've certainly moved around a lot," he said, sounding a bit confused. But he also congratulated my family for being so tradition-minded and said he hadn't expected us to be so very Dutch.

"My favorite Sinterklaas was the one I went to at my brother's school," I said.

"That I can understand," he said. "I too miss Holland. Sinterklaas isn't really Sinterklaas in this heat."

"I wish I could go back right now," I said, confiding who knows why in this teacher.

"Someday you will, after the war, and everything will be the same as it was before you left. You'll see."

"I hope so," I said dubiously.

"How could it not?" he answered, almost reproachfully. I wanted to believe him, but something gnawed at me. My parents did not think that anything would be the same. I wish I could feel as he did, but I knew that was easier to do in school than at home.

Now he confided in me. "Here in Curaçao, people are so wild. They turn everything into a riot. Sinterklaas is a party, yes, but it shouldn't be out of control. In Holland, we have fun that is disciplined."

In my Dutch books, children enjoyed themselves, but they were not loud or crazed. You never saw a kid throwing a rock.

After the teacher left, Mundi ambled over. "He's crazy. We're never allowed to do anything here. These Dutch people try to order everything."

"But Mundi," I protested. "No one restricts you."

"That's not true, Wolf. They control everything, these *macamba* teachers. You know, there's Carnival in South America and even on other islands. Why not here? I'm sick of all this Sinterklaas stuff."

As I got older, of course, Sinterklaas became a holiday for children. It faded, along with the aubades I had attended. I started spending more time with Mundi, and he and I would roam the streets, not exactly looking for trouble, but certainly willing to shout and scream at any opportunity. Mundi once dressed up as an African warrior with a shield. He drew admiring comments, and I was happy to be seen with him. "I made this costume myself," he boasted.

No point thinking any longer of how it had been in Holland, now that I was getting too old for childish holidays and anyhow lived in this faraway place. But sometimes I felt suddenly overcome with great yearning for that better time and infinitely more congenial place and thought that if I could not have a real Dutch Sinterklaas I might as well have none at all.

But now the biggest celebration was at hand. On May 5, 1945, Germany capitulated. "Unconditionally," the radio kept reporting. In Curaçao, a riotous storm of firecrackers, throbbing car radios, and sporadic dancing erupted. Mundi and I boarded a passing bus full of revelers. "No one pays today," they shouted to each new passenger. The bus stopped in front of a mass of people in downtown Willemstad. Two loudspeakers competed with each other, one broadcasting a Dutch voice, the other Papiamentu. No one seemed to be listening to either one, but some Dutch people had heard that now the war was over the Princess and the Prince of the Netherlands would pay us a visit.

At home, my parents were excited and restless. They hoped and they dreaded. The radio was never off. I did not think the news from Europe would be good, but did not consciously think about it much. The war was over.

"At last," said my father. "Maybe we will know now." Soon he knew.

But there was one more aubade. The royal couple arrived in Curaçao two years before Juliana's ascension to the throne. Preparations for the two-day visit had taken months. In school, we rehearsed special songs of praise. I felt more curiosity than excitement about the royal visit but had to admit that this aubade was the most beautifully orchestrated of them all. Mundi too was full of admiration for the event.

The 35-year-old Princess wore white gloves, and her handsome husband a white Dutch Air Force uniform, his slicked-down hair and fine features sharp under his military cap. Both looked good-natured and pleased with themselves when they descended from the Governor's balcony, and walked on a path of flowers strewn by old black women walking backward. The papers next day spoke of "prolonged jubilation."

Everyone came to see them. The parents of my Dutch friends stood in line for hours. They were waving orange flags. I was there with Dutch and Curaçaoan friends. Mundi was happy, as was my Dutch friend Peter.

* * *

Many years later, in 1969, I came back from America to the island to visit my father and stand at my mother's grave. She had been dead for ten years.

Curaçao was virtually independent now, but its capital lay in ruins, the result of a Black Power riot some months before.

In a small Chinese restaurant on the bottom floor of a bombed-out building, I saw a familiar figure, heard a voice I faintly recognized. It was Mundi. He was explaining in Papiamentu that the island needed a larger Carnival, a real procession. He would masquerade as an African king, an ancient from ancient times, when African kings still had power — why any Curaçaoans would want to dress up as rock stars or chorus girls he just couldn't understand. His lunch companions said little and looked bored. Insistently he drummed his hands on the table.

When I went over to him and spoke to him, he said, "Where have you been?" as if I had been away for a year or two, instead of almost twenty.

He was now a taxi-driver stationed in the same square where we used to serenade the Governor. He had grown stout and prosperous — ringed fingers, one of them a small diamond, a Rolex watch — but his swift smile was the same as ever.

I invited him to dinner. The main thing he wanted to talk about was the sacking of Willemstad in 1968. He had joined the strikers who marched into the downtown area and set fire to as many stores and businesses as they could.

"It was the best thing I ever did," said Mundi. "That time and the Carnival are the only times I've been alive. It was long overdue. We needed to liberate our island from the Man," he said, imitating Black Power talk.

"But Mundi, Curaçao was already independent, wasn't it?"

"Independent but not free. The foreigners were draining away our money. They still are."

"But you, you seem to be doing fine," I said looking at his Rolex.

"Man, I wear my wealth on my sleeve, not like the *Macambas* or the *Polacos*." Dutch people were called *Macambas*, a word of uncertain derivation dating back to slave times. The Jews, having mostly come from Poland, were always called *Polacos*, just as Filipinos were called "Chinee-Manila."

"There are some Dutch people here who don't have any money," I said.

"That just shows how clever they are at hiding it. These people don't laugh, they don't sing, they don't spend, I never know what they do — but they have power."

"Still?

"Still."

"But you, do you laugh and sing? You look pretty sober to me."

"You think so? Look at this cap I just bought." He took a felt cap out of a paper bag and molded it with his fingers before putting it carefully on his head. "We wear these to annoy the Dutch, the left-over Dutch."

"Do you remember the aubades we used to go to, Mundi?"

He laughed hard. "Yeah, that was fun. Almost as good as Carnival," and he suddenly moved his arms and chest to the side as if swaying to a dreamy rhythm.

"You wouldn't like the aubades now."

"You'd be surprised... Hey Wolf, what are you — a *Polaco* or a *Macamba*?"

"Now I'm an American, Mundi."

"How can that be? You seem to be a little of everything."

"I am."

"Wolf, when you guys were in the war, how come you didn't take a gun and shoot those Germans?"

"Same reason the slaves didn't kill the slave masters."

"Yeah, I guess so."

"I wish it would have been possible."

"Can you imagine: first slavery, then colonialism."

"C'mon Mundi, you know slavery was much worse. Colonialism wasn't so bad."

"Yeah, but I still don't know how we took it... We should have torn the place apart on one of these aubades."

"They wouldn't have let us."

He laughed, then said thoughtfully: "You know, it was magic that allowed us to get rid of the Dutch."

"Magic?"

"*Bruha.* Caribbean magic, African magic. You didn't know that, did you?"

I didn't. And Mundi didn't feel like explaining. So we parted company for possibly another two decades. He said I knew where to find him: that there was far more chance of my coming back to Curaçao than of his visiting me in America. He said that he envied me and that I was the Wandering *Polaco* or maybe the Wandering *Macamba* or possibly the Wandering American. Whatever.

Chapter 5. Comrades and Capitalists

Every other Sunday my father went to see his friend Tovarich. My mother first called him that, the Russian word for comrade, and the name stuck. Sometimes she said, "Max, Why don't you visit Tovarich today?" and then my father went off to see the friend he first made at the Curaçao Jewish Club over a year ago, right after the war ended. In all of 1946 or 1947, Mr. Frim was at our house only once; my father was embarrassed at our relative affluence and did not show it off to Mr. Frim.

The Club was a spacious old house with an imposing porticoed facade on a dusty street. Inside were several large, wood-paneled rooms where every evening loud, card-playing men and women bent over circular tables. During my eleventh year, I had played ping pong there, but as a family we did not often go to the club. Now my father wanted to watch the filmed newsreels about the war and its immediate aftermath in Europe.

In the half light of the largest room, the club social hall, gray, dark footage of heavy Russian tanks entering Berlin flickered high on a screen. The audience clapped. The war-time leaders stared from behind a table at Potsdam. Truman and Churchill received boisterous applause, but when a mustachioed, smiling Stalin emerged in close-up, one woman in the audience yelled that Russia had grabbed half of Europe. My father turned to the frail man with his hair cut so short he looked bald sitting next to him and muttered in Yiddish, "Some people are not enlightened."

I knew that "enlightened" was a special word. My father used it to mean that if someone showed you the right way, the socialist way, you became "enlightened." Mr. Frim responded by pulling his slight frame upward, and with a stern frown replied, "Yes, they do not have the knowledge; they need the right education to guide their minds." Mr. Frim's eyes swept over the room as if it were a mass meeting.

"'Why don't people understand?" asked my father, his head cocked.

"Because they have been hoodwinked, deluded. They are corrupted by luxuries. They don't read the correct material." And Mr. Frim displayed a small Yiddish newspaper, his green eyes visibly enlarging as he showed it.

"Yes, that's it," exclaimed my father, as if this were a revelation.

"Exactly," answered Mr. Frim. "People must be forced to think correctly."

Soon my father subscribed to the Yiddish newspaper *Morning Freiheit* from New York, which regularly spoke of the achievements of Stalin. Often my father would read us a passage from the paper and say, hoarse with controlled emotion, "This is truth."

Mr. Frim had arrived on the island of Curaçao with his wife and three-year old daughter in 1935, the year I was born in far-away Europe. In Poland, his wife had been diagnosed with weak lungs and her doctor had told Mr. Frim that he must find her a warmer climate. Like some of the other Polish Jews now on the island, he had set out for South America but did not reach the mainland. He landed in Curaçao and decided to stay. But unlike the others, Mr. Frim had done poorly. He owned a tiny candy store in a slummy section of Willemstad and lived in a stucco, mud-colored, two-room house nearby. The climate had not helped his wife, who died in 1941. Now Mr. Frim lived in the house with his daughter and spent his evenings and Sundays reading biographies of Marx and Lenin.

One Sunday my father suggested I come along. "It will be interesting for you, but remember, Mr. Frim and I discuss politics."

I did not think it would be interesting, but I wanted to see if Mr. Frim's teenage daughter was at home. She was a studious girl, who read hefty books in Spanish. She was much older than I, fifteen or sixteen, but maybe I could talk to her. The conversation between my father and Mr. Frim had nothing to do with me, with school, my friends, my hope for the future. It would be old people's talk, full of politics and sad Jewish things.

My father and I drove silently from our tidy suburb into a warren of dusty streets. The little houses stood so close to the street that their radios blared like amplifiers at a political rally. In front of Mr. Frim's yellow, sun-faded house, a listless dog lifted his leg against a spiny cactus.

The house was as small as I had imagined it but infinitely hotter. It seemed engulfed in steam, and the little open windows only let in more heat and noise. My father had brought along a box of cookies and two bottles of Manischewitz wine imported from America. Mr. Frim opened a brown tin of salt crackers that somehow smelled of fish and put them on the kitchen table. He poured me a warm glass of Coca Cola and made tea for himself and my father. Then he gestured me to sit at the tiny table in the cramped living room, where he and my father faced each other. Mr. Frim's daughter was not at home. My shirt clung to my back, and sweat trickled into my eyes. A fly buzzed around my ears.

Mr. Frim aimed a leaky Flit gun over our heads. He wiped off its round canister and rapidly pumped three or four times in several directions, while the insecticide was slowly spreading all over the little house. I inhaled with pleasure. I liked the smell of it, so much like gasoline.

Now Mr. Frim looked around him. "Do you know," he began, "that the Soviet Union lost more people than any other country which fought Hitler?"

It was hard to read from my father's face whether this was new information, but his excitement was obvious. Mr. Frim went on without stopping: "Is it any wonder that a devastated nation still has many hardships to endure? And, of course, the enemies of socialism use economic turmoil as a cloak to hide their own evil intentions." Mr. Frim stared straight ahead, his small face suddenly rigid.

My father strained for every word. On such occasions he listened without moving. It pleased him to hear what he already believed. "Yes, that stands to reason," he nodded, his eyes misting over. "How they fought for us!"

Mr. Frim wore a short-sleeved khaki shirt that might have given him a military bearing if he hadn't been so slight. The shirt was the same color as our chauffeur Emile's and even had epaulettes, but it looked less convincing on Mr. Frim's sunken chest. Still, Mr. Frim could have been a soldier or a spy, small and wiry enough to escape detection behind enemy lines. I had just read a Dutch espionage novel and tried to visualize Mr. Frim parachuting into darkness.

I could not picture my father in uniform. My own favorite war hero was my mother's brother, Uncle Paul, whose picture perched on our mantle: standing next to his camouflaged truck, smoking a cigarette in Normandy, patting his dog, he was handsome and nonchalant. I was said to resemble him.

Mr. Frim continued in his immobile, relentless way. "I'm not denying that the British and Americans fought too, but can we really claim that without the Red Army the fascist criminals would have lost? No."

Mr. Frim now took a saltine. He had not opened the box of cookies my father had brought.

Two large cockroaches marched in single file from the kitchen. Would they be followed by others? They climbed up the gray wall facing my father, who did not notice them and sipped his tea with careful little sips and spoke hesitantly.

Though respectful as before, my father looked pained, worry showing on his brown, serious face. "Is there still anti-Semitism in the Soviet Union?"

Mr. Frim smiled, as if he had anticipated this question. He cocked his head a little to one side. "How can there be? Think of all the Jews who have sat in the Politburo. Think of Kaganovitch, Litvinow. Besides, when religion is exposed as the superstition it truly is, how can there be anti-Semitism?"

My father looked relieved.

On the drive home, my father said, "Mr. Frim is a good man, a selfless man. It's people like him who build a new society. With them in charge, what happened in the war can never happen again. The communists would never have permitted the slaughter of the Jews. If there ever is a Jewish State, let's hope it'll be socialist."

I could picture Mr. Frim as a socialist leader in Palestine but even more as a commissar in the Soviet Union, always telling the workers what they had to do and why it was good for them to do it.

My father was musing about something, then spoke slowly. "Manny, everybody is excited because Curaçao now gets three different brands of soap from America. Even your mother is. Do you want three different brands of soap?"

"Of course not. What a question."

"Do you want two kinds of cereal?"

"No, but what is cereal?"

Oh, something American. I don't know exactly, but you see. you'd make a good socialist."

"Me," I protested, "I don't think so."

"Yes, you would, because you understand that one brand of soap is good enough. We don't need luxuries. Capitalist profusion is a waste."

I wanted to disagree with him. "If you lived in Russia, you couldn't even be in business."

"Yes, I could," answered my father, "but not for profit." He looked uncharacteristically self-confident.

"How would it be business then?"

"Well, I could manage a business, but the profit would go to the state."

This made no sense to me. After all, it was profit that made business exciting, and I had seen my father excited about business in a way that would surprise Mr. Frim. Still, if Mr. Frim was a commissar, my father would be a hard-working manager of a branch of GUM, the Soviet state-run department stores I had read about in our local newspaper.

My mother laughed at my father's socialism; she thought he was naive. And he laughed at her lack of interest, saying it was natural for a woman to concern herself more with immediate things than politics, with family rather than "things of the mind." As early as I can remember, I felt my father's explanations did not explain things. He often recited, "When this fist does not will/ then all the wheels stand still," but I never thought this old German socialist battle cry was anything more than a slogan.

He reiterated a few phrases about socialism, ardently wanting them to be true, thinking they would some day come true. His introduction to socialism had come in Germany, where he arrived from Poland in 1922 at the age of seventeen. A friend introduced him to the pamphlets of Karl Liebknecht and Rosa Luxemburg, and took him to mass meetings. Away from his parents in Poland, his belief in the rigorous practices of Judaism waned. Judaism now struck him as quaint and old-fashioned.

His growing business success in Germany did nothing to lessen his new-found political convictions. Some day, business would be phased out and the world would be a kinder place for it. Meanwhile, he was happy to be in Germany and happy to be a success. From my stamp collection I learned about the great inflation in Germany during his time, and I asked my father about it. "The Weimar Republic," he replied. "Good people, Jewish people, were in the government. But ten thousand marks for a pencil?" Socialism, he continued, offered stability, fairness and a refuge from anti-Semitism. "And remember, socialists fought the Nazis."

Mr. Frim and my father were probably the only socialists among the Jews of Curaçao. The others were amiable capitalists, eager to make money in their businesses. Few of them seemed to do anything but work. Politics or religion did not attract them. The island had a mere handful of observant Jews. My first view of a really orthodox Jew — other than my grandfather — was the occasional bearded man who came to Curaçao from Brooklyn to solicit funds for this or that yeshiva. I disliked those small, black-clad figures, their shuffling and mumbling, the way they tried to make me feel guilty. "Do you ever look at a prayer book?" one of them asked me while seeking a donation from my father. He kept tugging at his ear locks.

Communists like Mr. Frim also tried to make you feel bad but they were brave. I would not mind being one of those clean-shaven fanatics. They had fought Hitler; they knew how to use weapons. They too felt we were soft and given to luxuries, but they judged us with a righteous, manly anger. I would have liked to have been strong enough to fight the Nazis, like Uncle Paul, or at least be one of those pioneers who were building a new state in Palestine, armed young Jewish men with bronzed features, working next to young Jewish women in shorts.

Sometimes I would take my toy rifle out in the backyard and fancy myself in the Red Army, turning the tide at Stalingrad or entering victorious into Berlin, grabbing watches from the defeated Germans and putting them on my wrist. My Dutch friend Henny and I played war in my backyard, and I told him about the street fighting in Stalingrad: how every building had been bled over, and how even chicken coops served as shelter. We had a large chicken coop in our own backyard, in which the two of us crouched and ran and fought numerous battles, yelling, "Bang, bang, bang," while the chickens squawked angrily.

Slumping in the overstuffed green armchair near the radio, in the heat of our living room in Curaçao, I listened to one song after another popular in 1947: "Drinking Rum and Coca-Cola" had something to do with American soldiers stationed in nearby Trinidad during the war so recently concluded. Some of these soldiers had come to Curaçao on leave, and my friends and I tried to speak English to them and shake their hands.

Soon it would be time to go into town and help my parents in the store. I loved going into Willemstad but my father's business bored me. Being there meant hours of standing while customers slowly scrutinized shirts or socks or underwear. I could never find all the things they asked for, and if I asked the Curaçaoan salesgirls they gave me a pitying look and said they would help the customer themselves.

At exactly three o'clock on Saturday afternoon — the busiest time in the store — Emile pulled up in front of the house and honked once. His khaki chauffeur's uniform gleamed in the sun. He had created that uniform himself, and I wondered why he was so eager to display his servitude. Didn't such a proud, cheerful man resent being an underling? But no, he had even bought a matching khaki cap to go with his long-sleeved shirt and beautifully creased pants. "You don't catch us Curaçaoans wearing sloppy Dutch-people clothes," he told me.

Reluctantly, I turned off the radio. On the little pathway through the garden, the sun beat down fiercely. In the car, the leather seats scalded my legs and back. Emile smiled. "Ready to roll into the big city?" he asked and swiftly headed for town. But to my pleasure, he had one errand and stopped before a little yellow-walled house and pounded on the door. No one opened, but across the street a woman yelled in Papiamentu: "She's out, having a good time." At the end of the street, a man cupped his hands around his mouth, and Emile gestured back, his mouth shaping silent words, which the man answered. They "talked" that way for a few minutes, and then Emile turned the key. He was in no hurry, and neither was I. The delay gave me time to practice my whistling, which my grandmother had warned me against. "Only a Gentile whistles," she said.

The store faced a narrow, busy street. In the display windows, dozens of men's shirts hung on hangers. A woman's stocking clung to a dismembered dummy's leg. This afternoon there were few customers, and the salesgirls stared straight ahead. My father stood in the doorway, his short-sleeved white shirt wet around the neck. I suddenly noticed how gray he had become, at 42 much grayer than my friends' fathers. He surveyed the street but not as expectantly as usual. Today he was in a philosophical mood. "What is business?" he greeted me. "I ask you, what is business? It is exploitative, manipulative. Say you have twenty socks but no shirt. You'd be eager to get rid of some socks to get a shirt. That makes sense. That is barter. But what doesn't make sense is to have ten thousand shirts and sell them one by one."

"You like selling them wholesale, not one by one," I argued.

"Yes," he said, distracted. "Of course."

He knew perfectly well that it made sense to sell ten thousand shirts, but he wanted to make a favorite point: that the businessman merely bought in one place and sold in another — capitalism encouraging unproductive labor.

My mother looked relieved that she could go out for a while. "I'm going off to see Louisa while you men talk politics." I stood in front of the store and hoped that none of my Dutch friends would walk by. They knew we had a store, but I did not like to remind them. No truly Dutch person I knew had a store on the island. I wished my parents were professionals or colonial officials, and that my father was more like Mr. Zorgdrager or Dr. Voscus, real Dutchmen, not immigrants, men who talked to their families about sports or other Dutch things. Something foreign clung to business and commerce.

The street bustled with Curaçaoans. I watched a man and a woman gesturing at each other across the narrow street, mouthing words. All over the island people spoke to each other this way. They gestured silently over great distances, and their eyes lit up when something important or funny was mimed. "It's the jungle tom-tom," once declared my geography teacher. "These people have perfected a system of communication that's better than ours."

"We got it from Africa," said Benjamin to him.

"You did?" asked the teacher, surprised.

Mundi, my Curaçaoan school friend, ambled by. He had a funny, rotating gait, half dance, half walk. "Wolf, what are you doing here?"

"It's my father's store."

"Your father has a store? I didn't know you were *ciboyo*. "

I knew *ciboyo* meant 'onion,' but I didn't understand why Mundi called me that.

"All *Polacos* are onion," he said.

"Mundi, I'm not Polish. I'm Dutch. You see, we fled here from Europe. We're refugees."

"If your father has a store, you're *Polaco*. *Polacos* do business and eat onions."

"But we came from Holland, and we don't eat onions."

"Business is for *Polacos*," Mundi said flatly.

In Curaçao, my parents went to work for Mr. Altneu, who owned a run-down textile store on Herenstraat. Mr. Old-New, as he was nicknamed, was a slender elegant man, with a distracted manner. He did not like to work — and did not like the store — and enjoyed having people do the work for him. Neither of my parents had ever sold retail; they had owned a textile factory in Germany and a wholesale business in Holland. When Mr. Old-New went to Miami, as he was fond of doing, my parents were in charge. Soon they made themselves indispensable and became his partners. After the war, Mr. Altneu sold them the store and moved permanently to Miami and changed his name to Altman, which sounded more American.

My parents bought textiles at the lowest possible prices. Many of their customers were merchant seamen and their officers who wanted inexpensive goods. These were the *tripulantes*, as the crew of a ship was called in Spanish, and they did not buy a shirt or two, but dozens. They were amateur smugglers. Because Curaçao was a free port without tariffs, prices were low. In the sailors' countries of origin — Venezuela, Colombia, Brazil, Argentina — tariffs were high, so they smuggled these textiles into their home ports without paying duty and sold them. Some crew members had captains they feared, but often the captains and other officers did the same thing, only more so. It was not unusual for a captain to buy six dozen stockings and ten shirts.

Though my father did not speak Spanish, he called them *tripulantes*. He liked the sound of the word. "Who would have thought in Europe that we'd work with *tripulantes*?" he chortled. "Emile, please go to the harbor and see if any big ships are coming." I liked them too, those military-looking, cheerful men. Some wore white sport shirts with gleaming epaulettes sewn on their shoulders. Sometimes they came twice a week; then my father got really excited. "*Tripulantes*," he said, "here come the *tripulantes*. You're right," he told me, "about wholesale. It's the only way. Retail is dull."

My father loved the business but urged my brother and me to have professions or become government employees like the parents of our Dutch friends. Sometimes the store was like a family joke we all shared. My mother took a practical view of business but did not talk about it much. She could handle it, as she could handle almost anything. Her family was agile and adaptable; the Kornmehls negotiated with one and all, finding their strengths and weaknesses, and then charmed them into cooperating.

My father did not have my mother's gifts for human relations, and I could not picture him doing anything other than business. He was not assertive enough to be a doctor or a lawyer, I thought, not authoritative enough, not comfortable, especially among Dutch people. I had only seen him look at ease in old photographs, the last one taken before I was born, when he was a young entrepreneur in Germany surrounded by his employees. In that picture, he looked different than I had seen him look, more confident and relaxed as he stood beaming shyly at what he had created. In Germany he had switched from Yiddish to German, but he found it harder when we came to Holland in 1938 to switch to Dutch, which he spoke fluently but not well. Late in life he hardly made the effort with English.

It was during this time in Curaçao when I was twelve that I first dreamed a dream I would have many more times: my father had been called up into the army, the Dutch army, and he was fearful and helpless, so I went instead. The dream ends happily because I did well in the Dutch army, making friends with the other soldiers, who in the dream looked my age. No one saw anything unusual or foreign about me. My father could not possibly have assimilated into this Dutch setting; he was too foreign, too Jewish. The last time he felt at home was in Germany. From 1922 to 1932 he was a happy man, comfortable among the Germans, eager to have others share in his well-being, and he thought that if some day the world turned socialist, everybody would be as happy as he had been during that period.

"A general always plans the next battle," my father was fond of saying. And in the newly arrived Salvation Army couple, Captain and Mrs. Loddum, he sensed a promising, happy battleground. I liked seeing him excited. He seemed more a father then, less a melancholy presence. "This campaign has to be carefully executed," he declared.

The Salvation Army ran the Seamen's Home in Curaçao, which had a profitable canteen with a rapid turnover of goods. Captain and Mrs. Loddum were youthful and energetic, neither of them older than thirty-five. They loved the island at first sight. Two days after their arrival, Captain Loddum lay out in the sun on the beach at Piscadera for a whole day and kept saying loudly that he had expected the island to be hotter; this weather was really quite moderate. My mother went over to the bulky newcomer and warned him of the harshness of the sun.

"Thank you, kind lady, but I don't think it'll have any effect on me. I have a rhinoceros hide."

He spent a week in the hospital recovering from third-degree burns, but he never lost his enthusiasm for the sun, the island, and his new life. I liked his energy and enthusiasm. And the Loddums became my parents' friends.

For some reason, he was Captain Loddum, but his wife, also a captain in the Salvation Army, was Mrs. Loddum or Vera or Captain Vera. He was always in uniform, while she rarely was. He told my mother that he had ordered a military tie from America, because the regulation tie from the Salvation Army was shoddy-looking, pathetic. I liked Captain Loddum's uniform, his muscular build and broad shoulders, though his handlebar mustache made him resemble an old photograph. When no one was looking, Captain Loddum had the habit of rapidly clipping his mustache and nose hairs with small, silver scissors.

As the friendship with the Loddums grew, my father became increasingly livelier. "Whatever they need in that seamen's canteen, we can supply it. Shirts, socks, ties, ladies' underwear, everything… why should they buy from others what we can deliver more cheaply?" he asked. When I saw the canteen, a large side-room off a cavernous hall, I was startled to see our own store's merchandise displayed on mannequins stared at by gesticulating, loud men. The *tripulantes* were serious shoppers.

"Capitalism forces us to look productive, but we're just middlemen," said my father.

"But you enjoy being a middleman," I said.

Now he enjoyed masterminding the conquest of Captain Loddum and making a profit off him. My father thought himself a strategist, but my mother courted the Loddums. She was gifted at conversation, and she laughed more. While my father lapsed into long silences, she sparkled. She was eager for friendship, hopeful with each new contact, as if making up for some lack, some emptiness I sensed but could not define. She liked the Loddums, or at any rate liked having people to talk to. And she liked the captain's joy in his surroundings, so different from my father.

For his part, Captain Loddum loved to talk to my mother about the pleasures of his new existence. Running his hands through his bushy hair, he moved his head toward her, the muscles in his neck throbbing, his sky-blue eyes fixed on her. "We have the canteen, yes, but we are our own masters and we have this beautiful island and warm people, good friends, like you, Bertha — and Max, of course."

"And in Holland...?" asked my mother, who sometimes talked wistfully of returning to Europe.

He seemed to love to say my mother's name. "Bertha, you can't imagine what it's like in Schiedam, how dreary."

"But that's only twenty minutes from The Hague," laughed my mother.

"Yes, but then you're in The Hague, Bertha," roared Captain Loddum. I wished my father could laugh like that.

The captain moved his muscular frame closer to my mother. His thighs were enormous, though he was not fat. "I had to get out, Bertha. I couldn't breathe." And he touched his throat and stroked the handlebars of his mustache and patted down his mass of curly hair.

Mrs. Loddum looked pinched, worried. She flushed easily. Though childless, she had an affinity for small children and animals. At her house, my brother and I watched her make a large hoop with her arms, which her cat jumped through. She would do it again and again. I liked her but for some reason felt drawn to Captain Loddum.

Captain Loddum continued: "After the Liberation, I rushed to England, but two years later it's still like war over there. Shortages, rationing, people standing in long lines. Not for me." Unlike most of my parents' Dutch friends, Captain Loddum rarely said "we" or "us." "You can't even get a cup of coffee with some decent cream. These English people are shell-shocked. They can't pick themselves up."

"And in Holland?" asked my mother again, this time turning to Mrs. Loddum.

"It's like this," started Captain Loddum, but my mother kept facing his wife, as if to draw her out. Mrs. Loddum deferred to her husband. "Oh," she said, "what do you think, Frank?"

"Holland," said the captain, "Holland is always Holland. Too many people, especially too many Dutch people. Too many know-it-alls. Too many scolds. The best have always left our land of mud and drizzle. And now... Now some stragglers are returning, trying to make some fast money. I tell you, if I were not in the Salvation Army, I too would feather my own nest."

His wife looked at him, her reddish skin seeming to redden even more. "Ah, Frank, you know we have elected this life, for so many worthwhile reasons."

"Yes, my dear. So true. For us it's not business but service."

My mother looked at my father. It was obvious she wanted him to say something but he sat still, his eyes lifeless. It embarrassed me that he often fell silent, and I wanted to jump in for him, to say something in his place, to speak for him. But my father felt that if you do business with people, you do business; you don't really have to go and talk to them also. Besides, he could let my mother do it for him.

Instead, Captain Loddum spoke. "Things were pretty hard for us over there during the war."

Now my father bolted upright as if just awakened. "For you," he said, turning a question into a statement. "In the war."

"Yes, during the hunger winter of '44, '45."

My mother explained to Captain Loddum, "We wouldn't have survived till then."

Captain Loddum cast a long look at her. "Bertha, I can't imagine how anyone would want to kill someone like you."

She blushed but looked composed. For a moment she appeared to see into him in the way she often took pride in doing, like the wordless understanding of the Curaçaoans over long distances.

He answered her gaze, and then my mother said, trying to sound lighter, "Oh, well, here in Curaçao, there is God's plenty."

"I'll say. We have black people, brown people, white people. Poles, Turks, Jews. That little guy who owns the candy store, where's he from?"

"Poland," answered my mother. "A refugee who got out in time."

"God has willed it so," said the Captain and looked around him, breathing in as if he were inhaling the scenery.

"Glad we're all here," said my mother now nodding at my father again to say something. My father didn't notice.

"I'm so glad, Bertha." Captain Loddum half stood in front of her as if blocking her way. "You know what we should do one of these days? Go dancing, that's what. Just the four of us."

"Yes," said my mother in that tone that I recognized as meaning "No." I was starting to use this way of speaking myself with loud or argumentative friends. Like my mother, I too made friends easily and felt it necessary to be diplomatic.

Mrs. Loddum stood up and said, "Frank, time for us to go."

I knew at the time that Captain Loddum was flirting with my mother but only later could I see that she was encouraging him, flattered by his attention, though also eager to have the business transaction go smoothly. My mother often had mixed motives, as I did, and do. I suppose it's one of many things I learned from her.

"It's wonderful," exulted my father. "They're buying everything from us. That little canteen of theirs just vacuums up merchandise. Can you believe what's happening? We own the means of production. They order like crazy." He sounded happier than I had seen him in a long time.

"True," said my mother. "Some sailors don't have time to walk into town. But they do have time to buy at the Seamen's Home."

"There's no stopping the *tripulantes*: they have a few hours. They buy."

"God knows what they do with all that stuff," said my mother.

"We know what they do with it. They sell it back home for twice the price they paid. That's what."

"And the Loddums: how do you suppose they square all this with the Salvation Army home office?" asked my mother.

"They don't."

"You don't think they do?"

"No, besides, Gentiles aren't afraid of anything," said my father pensively.

"Maybe you should give the Loddums a big present," I suggested.

"Oh, people like that shouldn't be bribed. They respond to kindness," laughed my mother. "They're not really business people."

"But don't they like to make money?" I asked.

"I guess not. But they do like the pleasure of business."

"They do?" How could these Dutch people like having a store? I thought.

"Yes, they do like business," said my father. "But they have to turn the money over to the Salvation Army. You know, they don't even get a salary. Just an allowance, pocket-money."

I pondered that. So it was possible to get excited about business without making a profit. Maybe my father could have enjoyed being a department store manager in Russia. Did the Loddums operate a kind of GUM? But then, why would my father want to take advantage of that? Because he did not believe in the Salvation Army as much as in socialism?

✻   ✻   ✻

One Saturday at closing time, I insisted I did not want to go home but to see my friend Henny Zorgdrager.

"Why not have dinner first?" asked my mother.

"Because I don't want to hear anything more about the Salvation Army or *tripulantes*."

"That's what we live from," said my father quietly.

I felt ashamed. Of course we did.

"The child is nervous," soothed my mother.

"I'm not nervous," I almost shouted. "I hate nervous people. That's why I'm going to see Henny: his parents are never nervous."

Feeling foolish and hungry, I went off. Henny was Dutch, and his father was a colonial administrator. Unlike my parents, Henny and his parents and older sister were always doing Dutch things, this time playing Monopoly. I was invited to join in. Mr. Zorgdrager's cheeks glowed; his eyes stared at the board. Tugging gently at his tie over a crisp, military-looking white shirt, he explained how much you could learn from this game about commerce, trade, and also financial planning. "These are things we should know about, even if we don't engage in them ourselves."

I rapidly lost at Monopoly and Mr. Zorgdrager exclaimed, "I would have expected you to be good at this, Manny." He looked at me probingly. "Your father is a merchant, isn't he?"

"Yes," I replied.

"It's just unbelievable," exclaimed Mr. Zorgdrager. "How many merchants can this little island support? And most of them are Jewish."

"Like the Lebanese in Africa, remember, Tonny?" said Mrs. Zorgdrager.

"I remember it well," replied her husband, his thin blond hair seeming to fly up from his scalp, and he now started to tell us about the swimming pool of their house in Lagos, Nigeria, where he had worked as an executive for Shell Oil. Then he returned to the subject of the Lebanese in Africa: how they owned most of the businesses there. Suddenly he wheeled around. "What will your parents do if some day the Curaçaoans take over all the businesses?"

I did not know what to say, so I answered, "A general always plans the retreat," quoting one of my father's sayings. Mr. Zorgdrager gave me a puzzled, worried look. "My father does not want me to go into business," I added. Mr. Zorgdrager looked surprised. He did not think of me as a Dutch kid, like Henny. It was not even likely that Henny did. Though I wanted no part of business and thought of myself as Dutch, it was obvious that commerce and refugee ways, and being Jewish, all clung to me. The Zorgdragers really had no idea about me. And if I told them about my father's socialism, they would be truly bewildered.

I quickly went home, put on a record of a Puerto Rican song about "the trumpets of my tropical land." Too bad there was never any Dutch music. Then I turned on Radio Curaçao and read one of my Dutch novels. It was all about a young man who became a mercenary in Africa and later represented a large Dutch firm in Singapore. Soon he met a beautiful woman who came into his room "naked as a second Eve." Maybe I would work abroad and have many adventures. But that involved doing business. Instead, I could go to Palestine and fight to help create a new Jewish State, or even better: join the Palestine Brigade that was rumored to be operating in Germany, taking revenge — kill a few Germans every night, then disappear. Now the radio started making American sounds, about cruising down the river and taking a slow boat to China — all things I could do in the future. I could even be one of the *tripulantes* on such a ship, but I wouldn't bother smuggling shirts and socks.

Chapter 6. A Small Emotion

Mikve Israel, the stately synagogue built in 1732 by Portuguese-Jewish refugees from Europe and Brazil, towered over the narrow streets of downtown Willemstad, the capital of Curaçao. Its white-trimmed, orange-yellow gables were visible from many parts of the town. In 1947, the tourists, absent during the war, started coming back in great numbers to see the oldest synagogue in the Western hemisphere. They circled its massive yellow walls, then entered through several porticos into the courtyard. The Americans usually wore white baseball caps and bulging nylon shirts, the women cotton skirts or slacks. They looked strange to me, so pink and gray and old.

On one side of the courtyard, in a little prayer house across from the synagogue, my older brother and I sat every Sunday for what we called "Rabbi Lessons." Rabbi Isaac Morenos, a fine-featured, dark-browed Dutchman of Portuguese descent, strained to teach a handful of us children the rudiments of Hebrew. Once in a while, a tourist snapped a picture through a wide-open window, the camera a few feet from our faces. Suddenly, my friend David — now a prominent gynecologist in Geneva — rose from his seat, chest out, eyes bulging, upper lip protruding, in an unforgettable imitation of Tarzan's Cheetah, gibbering, whining and making rapid scratching gestures under his arms.

The rabbi, wiping tiny beads of perspiration from his fine brow, asked, "David, why did you do that?"

"Rabbi, they were distracting me from Hebrew."

"Oh, well, good. Yes, I am a little tired myself of these interruptions."

Why were we there? My parents had long ago fallen away from religious Judaism, but I was to be bar-mitzvah soon — and then there was my grandfather. His devotion knew no bounds: neither the war nor his wanderings had lessened it. He remained incorruptibly himself, that is to say, Jewish. Only his white suit was a concession to his new tropical home. As a young man, he had left Poland for Austria and then Holland, but his language remained Yiddish, and he carried with him the ways of the shtetl. A traveling salesman who had roamed all over Europe in the early years of the century, his practice was always to look for Jews wherever he found himself, whether in Salonika, Prague, Vienna or The Hague, and to head for the local synagogue.

Oddly, he did not try to impose his rigorous Judaism on us. He knew we drove the car on the Sabbath, but said nothing. He knew we did not keep kosher at home. On the other hand, since we did not wish to offend him, we parked the car around the corner from his house when we came for the traditional Friday night dinners.

Because my parents worked long days, every day after school I went to my grandparents' house. One afternoon my grandfather announced to my grandmother, "We'll have an important guest from America Friday night."

Tightening the bun of her gray hair, my grandmother, a compact woman of sixty-three, answered: "Good, I'll cook chicken."

My grandmother invariably cooked chicken, whether there were important guests or not.

"He is," announced my grandfather, taking off his straw hat and rapidly flipping a black skull cap on his bald head as if it should not be uncovered for even a second, "a young man who keeps strictly, strictly kosher, and since he has to travel around these Caribbean islands he sometimes goes without food rather than eat anything unclean."

"How do you know that?" asked my grandmother.

"That's what I heard from a Jew I spoke to this morning."

"Why does he want to eat here?"

"Because he has been told ours is among the most kosher households on the island," replied my grandfather proudly.

"Is he a Yeshiva student?"

"No, a businessman."

"Does he collect for a Yeshiva, then?"

She referred to the bearded, black-coated men who came to Curaçao to collect money for religious schools in far-away places like Brooklyn.

"No, no, he deals in socks and shirts, like me, but on a grand scale. So this Jew told me."

Next Friday night, the seat of honor close to a wide-open window was offered to a clean-shaven, fleshy, black-haired man in a cream-colored tropical suit. Mr. Finkel did not seem bothered by the heat and kept his bulging jacket on. To our surprise, he spoke no Yiddish. In nasal American, he said, "Hi, bruiser," to me. He asked my brother if he was going to be "a fighting man."

"You betcha," said my brother, who had been reading American detective novels and had recently started on True Police Cases.

To my parents Mr. Finkel tried to talk about baseball. I could tell from the way she furrowed her brow that my mother was feigning interest. He kept saying something about Hank Greenberg, to which my father nodded as if he were listening. My brother and I looked at each other. The guest ate his chicken greedily and my grandmother looked pleased. My grandfather gave him the guest's honor of reciting the Prayer of Thanks but he said his "Jewish" was a bit rusty, and anyway he had to catch the plane to Miami.

My grandfather — through me — asked, "But how can you, on the Sabbath?" In Vienna, he had once walked himself to the hospital with acute appendicitis because even illness was no excuse for driving on the Sabbath.

The guest smiled broadly. "It's an emergency." After he left, my grandfather got up to stand at the little table which faced east and started rocking and bowing and mumbling a special prayer for him and for all American Jews who knew so little of Jewishness. He then told the story of how five years ago, he and my uncle had organized Friday evening prayer meetings in the prison in which Franco had put them in the autumn of 1942 when they crossed illegally into Spain over the Pyrenees. "Some of the men were chained to each other, but I told them that way they could pray together." And he suddenly laughed, his blue eyes mild and good-natured.

"Chained together?" asked my mother.

"Yes, but look, we didn't know it yet, but we were the lucky ones. Franco let us go."

"He wasn't doing Hitler's work yet," said my father.

"Yes, but we prayed well there. Good thing we Jews don't need a synagogue to pray. We don't always have one available."

We were talking about this when there was a knock on the shuttered door. A large black man in a pale blue suit introduced himself as Police Inspector Martina.

Always impressed with authority, my grandparents and parents in a flurry of activity waved the visitor to an easy chair and brought out cold drinks and a piece of cake. Two important guests in one evening was unusual.

The inspector took out a large red handkerchief and patted himself under his chin, then loosened his tie and mopped up under his shirt. He sipped at his drink.

"Have you," he asked, "entertained someone here?"

"Yes," answered my mother, who in such circumstances always spoke for the family.

The inspector wrote for a long time in a small black notebook he pulled out of his coat pocket.

"How would you describe him?"

"He was heavy-set, short," said my mother.

"Let's speak precisely. Was he a fat, young man?"

"Yes, he was."

Again the policeman wrote at length in his book. Finally he looked up and announced:

"Then you have played host to Kid Tiger."

"Kid Tiger... What's a Kid Tiger?" asked my grandfather.

My mother's usually animated face looked blank. The inspector continued, "I have reason to believe that the dangerous gangster Kid Tiger was pretending to be a religious Jew."

"But why?" asked my mother.

"We have a theory — that he wanted to present himself as a devout Jew before swindling some of the rich Jews on the island. But that is just a theory."

I could see the corners of my mother's mouth turning up, trying to suppress a smile. My father looked vague as the inspector continued to talk:

"We received a long-distance call from the American police, the FBI if you please, asking us to arrest forthwith this dangerous criminal if he came to the island. Then we found out, through internal sources, that you entertained him."

"But he may still be at the airport," said my mother now smiling broadly so she would no longer have to suppress that laugh.

"Too late, too late," sighed Inspector Martina, "the bird has flown," and he grimaced contentedly. "Good-bye, birdie. The FBI will have to do what it has to do. Why should we arrest him anyway? He hasn't done anything to us, has he?" And he chuckled.

"How did that man know to come here?"

"That is a question the police cannot fully answer yet. My visit here is just for identification and verification."

When the Inspector was gone, my grandfather asked, "So was that guy Jewish or not?"

My mother answered, "He was pretending to be — or maybe he was."

"Still, he must've been — otherwise he wouldn't pretend to be."

"Yes, only a Jew would come up with such an idea."

"Even Jews aren't Jews any more," said my grandfather.

"Well, you can't judge by him," said my grandmother soothingly.

"He didn't even know Hebrew."

"Maybe he wasn't Jewish."

"He sure looked Jewish."

"In America many people look Jewish, even if they're not."

"First Hitler takes six million — then the remaining Jews can't be relied on," said my grandfather.

I wanted to talk about Kid Tiger and what a strange thing had happened to us, and I felt sure my mother did too, and laugh about it also, but now she looked serious and spoke little. My father said that strange things happen in Curaçao because it wasn't a normal country. Once you left Europe you had to contend with "jungle conditions."

Next Friday evening, after services in the synagogue, whose high ceilings supported by majestic mahogany pillars allowed a hint of coolness, the fifteen or so worshipers, scattered in a sanctuary that could easily hold two hundred, went as usual to the little meeting house across the courtyard. The rabbi's brother who had recently arrived from Amsterdam was to give a talk before the blessing of the wine. He and his immediate family had survived the war by living in a storage cellar below a farmer's stable for three and a half years. Every night after the farmer put fresh straw over the trap door and they heard the farm animals tramping overhead, the whole family felt secure. He and his wife seemed emotionally less damaged than their children, who were in school with us, a boy of fourteen, who often stared abstractly into space and a twelve-year-old girl in little girl dresses.

Mr. Morenos was a lawyer but he had studied for the rabbinate at one time. Less delicately featured than his brother and rounder, he stood very straight and beamed. "Now that I see all of you here, I am reminded of a little exchange in the Talmud, yes, a little Midrash. One learned Jew turns to another and asks, 'What is better than prayer?' And the other, even wiser Jew, replies to him, 'Many things are better in the eyes of the Lord than prayer.' 'Such as?' 'Such as people coming together, quietly, reverently, contemplatively.' And that is what I see here with you." He started stroking his cheeks and patting the back of his head nervously. His voice shook a little, and my brother and I glanced at each other.

"And that is what I see here tonight." A large tear trickled down his cheek. "Forgive me, I feel a small emotion coming on."

Again my brother and I looked at each other, struck by the phrase "a small emotion." Mr. Morenos wiped at his cheek. Across the room, my friend David was mischievously making ape faces.

"To see all of you here, to see Jewish life flourish here in such abundance, such profusion, such luxuriance," he said, gazing blindly at the handful of people who surrounded him. "I could not help but think of that passage in the Talmud. This is what gives me a small emotion."

He dabbed at his cheek again and sat down, overcome. It wasn't clear if he was going to speak again. For a few minutes, no one said anything. Even David kept still. The air in the little house was humid, oppressive. In the courtyard, camera-laden tourists and staring Curaçaoans looked in, as they did every Friday night. I felt constricted, confined. I wanted to be with my friends, have adventures, go sailing, drift away from this island. When would the service finally be over?

At last, the Rabbi thanked his brother and said a few things about the upcoming Passover festival: "Remember to start ordering your Passover food. You know, it is written, when Passover approaches, ordinary, everyday food must be thrown into a river. But since Curaçao has no rivers," he paused humorously, "we could, of course, throw it into the sea. However, in this time and this place, we can also hide it." He then said the blessing for the wine, and the handful of people dispersed.

My whole school sailed on a Dutch frigate for a three-day trip to the neighboring island of Bonaire. The ship steamed past my grandmother's house, which faced the sea, just when I opened the first of many sandwiches she had packed for me. Watching the expanse of blue and green from a windy deck I dreamed of some day going to sea, the first Jewish sailor. A friendly Dutch marine, his young eyes looking bright, told me he would join the merchant marine when his military tour was over. My favorite teacher, Mr. Gos, reminded me that Charles Darwin too had sailed the seas.

I admired Mr. Gos. He was so utterly Dutch, so unworried, so un-Jewish. Now he set up an easel on the veranda of the main bungalow where we stayed. Sitting up straight, his head seemed to shine under a white cap. He said he welcomed interruptions. Once he asked me as he was painting, "Wolf, what goes on at a Jewish bar-mitzvah?" Two kids stood around when I answered in a few words and one asked me, "Hey, are you Dutch or Jewish?" Just then a local tourist official came to give a brief talk on scuba diving in Bonaire. For three days two hundred boys and girls swam, saw the island's few sights, and looked at flamingos in muddy lakes and deserted inlets.

Other teachers organized a dance in the main building of our campground. The only one I danced with was Gos' daughter Trix. Her freckled face wore a pleased expression and maintained that throughout the dance. That is the Bonaire memory I remember best. After our return to Curaçao, Gos invited me to come out swimming with the family next Sunday. Somewhat intimidated, I sat on the back seat with Trix, while Gos and his tall, blonde wife

Ellen were in the front. She wore shorts, which until that time I had never seen on a grown woman. Her voice was sharp and she kept up a running commentary about the grand but dilapidated old houses we passed, "Look, that one looks Neo-Greek, how is it possible!"

"Late nineteenth century, no older," smiled Gos and drove fast into the scrub brush countryside of Curaçao. Suddenly he swerved to avoid a young donkey who ran across the road. When it happened again, he started to laugh loudly. "I want to paint those marvelous creatures. Their grace, their style. My God, Curaçao is beautiful. What colors."

I had never thought of the island as beautiful. Hot, weird, strange, backward, or even safe, benign, harmless — these were words used in our household, as they were in many Dutch households. Gos' enthusiasm was extraordinary.

"Ellen, let's grab one of those donkeys."

"But how can we?" exclaimed his wife. "They may belong to someone." She scratched her long, sharp nose, but looked amused at her husband.

"Manny, you ask someone in Papiamentu, would you?"

Soon we saw an old black man in a torn straw hat trudging along the road. Gos stopped the car.

"Are those little donkeys wild?" I asked. "Or do they belong to someone?"

"Wild, they're so wild when they're young," he whistled through his sparse teeth.

"Do they belong to anyone?"

"Belong? What do you mean belong?"

"Does anyone own them?"

"No one can own a young donkey."

"Can we take one home, then?"

"You can. But donkey and white man don't get along."

"But is it OK to take one?"

"Sure, but you have to put salt on its tail first." And he guffawed, rubbing his scraggly white stubble.

I translated what he said. Gos was undaunted. "I love the way these people talk. I'm going to learn Papiamentu, so I can talk like that."

After a few minutes of further driving we saw a small donkey walking peacefully along the side of the road. No bigger than a large dog, he seemed to be strolling. We all got out of the car. The donkey stood still. Gos' wife put two sandwiches on the back seat.

The donkey glanced at the food. At first he seemed uninterested, then suddenly he reached forward, his baby eyes innocent and soft. He ate a bit of the sandwich, pulled his head back, and chewed. Then he reached forward again, and Gos gave him a huge shove from behind and swiftly closed the door. Trix started to laugh and said, "Lock the door, Dad. We don't want him to escape."

Her mother shouted too. The whole family looked happy. I was skeptical.

"Now where are we going to sit?" yelled Ellen. I was as conscious of Trix's soft side against mine on the front bench of the Chevrolet as I was of the donkey's rancid breath. Since our necks were exposed to the creature, I expected to be bitten, but instead the donkey in a whoosh of rapid activity kicked swiftly and purposefully at the left car door. Gos looked around and swore. Within a few seconds, the door was dented. He stopped the car and we got out. To my surprise, Trix and her mother were doubled over laughing. With difficulty, Gos pulled open the smashed back door, and the intelligent beast fled at a gallop into the bushes.

That night, my father was speechless. Finally he asked, "Why didn't they just leave the creature alone?" I answered that they wanted to own one, probably because Gos wanted to paint him, and he said, "The patience, the calm, the tranquility . . . the unbelievable peace of mind of those Gentiles. Can you imagine any of us, after what we've gone through, running after a donkey?"

I wanted to be like Gos, who seemed so comfortable, so at home in the world, such an enjoyer. For a few weeks, I cast my books aside and, sporting a white cap, started to paint. I had never shown any talent for drawing and found it hard and unsatisfying. Soon I gave up sitting under a stinging sun trying to reproduce what I couldn't reproduce. But indoors I attempted to render color — not with more success, but in greater comfort. Maybe indoor pleasures were best for me.

"All of you," said Gos in class one day, "we are blessed to be living in this time, when so many declamation artists are visiting us from the Netherlands." Indeed, the war's end loosened numbers of performers, people who traveled to small Dutch towns and recited poetry, did sketches from longer plays, or spoke long monologues. Every few months such an artist arrived in Curaçao, and I attended all their performances, wishing I lived in the Netherlands.

Starved for entertainment, starved even more for Dutch events, cultural and otherwise, Dutch people turned out in droves. It was in this wave of speakers, entertainers, lecturers, that in 1947 we came to hear one man, widely advertised as a Resistance hero, but now an academic who studied the activities of Dutch diplomats during the war. An owlish, balding man with a censorious expression, he tugged at his bow-tie and told a group of comfortable colonial officials in the meeting hall of a luxurious beach club how tirelessly Dutch officials struggled to resist the Nazis. With slow relish he recounted how in wartime Lisbon one Dutch consular official had thwarted his German counterpart by pretending to be German on the telephone and barking out some confusing orders. The audience chuckled appreciatively.

Suddenly an un-Dutch voice rasped out. "I was in Nice in '42, and what did the Dutch consul tell me? To go to hell." He was an acquaintance of ours, a man with a gray face and tiny hands, who had traveled the same escape route through Europe as we had but had arrived on the island just recently. I remember thinking that he should have waited for the question period. Small, excitable, he was almost spastic with rage, "The consul told me to go to hell."

The audience grew still and embarrassed. The speaker, in a generically patrician Dutch manner, said, "Sir, the relevance of this?"

Now sounding more foreign than ever, the man yelled, "The consul in Nice, in '42, he told me he would call the authorities if I did not leave his office. Because of him, my wife is dead."

"That is a large assertion," said the academic puffing out his chest. "Before you make such claims, you should be in a position to substantiate them."

"It's a charge I'll make till I die."

"What nationality do you have, if I may ask?"

"I am Dutch now."

"Were you Dutch then?"

"I had my first naturalization papers at that time."

"But you were not Dutch yet, were you?"

"I was about to be naturalized when the war broke out."

"And your wife?"

"She was Polish."

"Well, then, that explains it; it's easy to see why our Dutch diplomat couldn't give your wife the requisite documents. She was not Dutch. But the consul you malign apparently gave documents to you, even though you were not fully Dutch yet. If anything, you owe the gentleman much thanks for coming to your rescue." And he turned to an audience in the manner of an attorney who rests his case.

The little man seemed to slump in his chair, and the visiting academic explained with the magnanimity of victory to the audience at large:

"You may not have fully grasped the significance of this exchange, but our Dutch consuls simply could not give exit documents to those who were not citizens. How could those people expect that? First we had to help real Dutch people, young men who were trying to reach England to fight the Nazis. Then we helped genuine Dutch families. Next we tried to do something for the refugees, Jews, others, who had somehow gained the Dutch nationality, in some cases just achieved that nationality. And then there were the others, Poles, Rumanians, stateless ones, poor unfortunate souls; but what could we do? One consul I interviewed for my study spoke of hundreds, even thousands of people, all of them talking to him at once, speaking gibberish. We could do nothing for them."

"Nothing," screamed the man hoarsely, "nothing? I went to Sally Noach in Lyon, and he gave me papers. But my wife was caught without papers by the Vichy criminals and deported."

"Sally Noach," said the visitor, now flushing red, "that man was an impostor. He pretended to be a diplomat but he wasn't. He wormed his way in with genuine diplomats and then just passed out documents as if they were toilet paper and as if he, as if he, mind you, was a diplomat. But he was a zero. That man didn't even ask people if they were Dutch."

"He saved my life," yelped the man in the audience, but few people even heard him, and the Chairman of the meeting was already rising "to thank our distinguished guest for enlightening us on a not oft-remembered chapter of our recent history... And I should note," he added, "that out guest, in his modesty, did not wish to mention his own crucial role in the Resistance."

I felt ashamed somehow, and as the applause swelled I looked around, hoping that no one from school was present in the hall. This unappealing man was deeply familiar to me. He would have been comfortable at my grandfather's table. I turned around again and, to my grief, saw Gos sitting in the back of the hall, his wife chatting with another blond-haired woman. It was going to be harder for me now to convince him that I was an ordinary Dutch boy. At least my friends from school were not here. I wished the little man had nothing to do with me, but he did; as did also my grandfather praying and facing east, and the rabbi's brother in the Synagogue.

* * *

Not long after these events, Inspector Martina came to my parents' store, looking cheerful in his suit and Panama hat. My parents had befriended him, and he enjoyed coming in for a chat:

"We got another bulletin from the FBI, and guess what? That man wasn't Kid Tiger because Kid Tiger is in prison. They got it bulloxed up. The real Kid Tiger is much older."

"Then who was the man?" asked my mother. "Was he innocent?"

"Certainly not," said the Inspector. "He was a cell-mate of Kid Tiger, and he learned from the great criminal, from the Master Swindler. But he was not half the man Kid Tiger was. The real Kid Tiger is in his fifties, speaks many languages." Martina read from a printed sheet in his hands: "English, Polish, Russian, French, Yiddish and Hebrew." The Curaçaoans, great polyglots themselves, admired that talent in others.

When told, my grandfather was pleased. "The real Tiger spoke Yiddish? And Hebrew?"

"Yes," said my mother.

"I'm so glad this man, this impostor, wasn't Jewish."

"Well, we don't know that for sure."

"But we know the Tiger is a Jew. How else would he know Hebrew and Yiddish?"

"That's true."

My grandfather rubbed his hands and stroked his little white beard. "Probably," he mused, "the real Tiger would have been able to say the Prayer of Thanks."

So this Kid Tiger wasn't who he claimed to be. People aren't always what they seem. I liked that; it was a cheering thought.

Later I thought I might tell the story of Kid Tiger to Gos, who would certainly enjoy it, but I decided against it — too many things I would have to explain, and did not want to go into. Too many small emotions I did not want to raise.

Chapter 7. Ever More Tropicalized

In 1945, the year the war ended, I was ten years old, and my greatest pleasure at that time was to go out with the whole family. I cherished such occasions and tried somehow to create more of them.

Every Sunday my parents, my brother and I went out to lunch at 'the Chinese,' as Dutch people always said. You didn't eat "in a Chinese restaurant" or "Chinese food" — you ate at "the Chinese."

The restaurant was a large, low-ceilinged room in downtown Willemstad. One fan labored directly over our heads, its enormous blades seeming to slow when you looked at them. My father sat down with a sigh and looked around him, "Here it's not hot." He wiped the sweat off his forehead with a large handkerchief. My mother always looked cooler.

He glanced indifferently at the menu and said, "At the Chinese you can only eat steak," and ordered Tenderloin Steak for all of us. Looking back, I'm surprised that my mother, my brother and I went along with it so agreeably.

But he also always ordered one Chinese dish.

"Give," he said distractedly to the waiter, a bald Chinese man with a nodding, bobbing manner, "give too one Chicken Chong."

"Yes," the waiter bobbed and nodded, "yes, one Chicken Chong. Yes, Chicken Chong."

"But Papa," said my brother once or twice, "there is no Chicken Chong on the menu."

"They know how to do it," answered my father, misunderstanding the point. "They can make Chicken Chong here."

Probably it was Chicken Chow Mein we were served, but I never much cared what that dish was. It was good enough for me, as long as we were all together. For years, this ritual was followed, and my mother, though not at all docile or demure, said nothing. She must have felt that it was a satisfactory ritual, why bother?

My parents worked in their store every Saturday till late at night. Sunday was our only day together. Before having Chicken Chong we went swimming at a beach called Piscadera, a Dutch-run sports club on a beautiful coral reef bay. Most of the swimmers were Dutch civil servants, but there was a sprinkling of refugees like ourselves and a good many Curaçaoans here as well. In the changing room, my father sailed to exactly the same locker every time, and my brother and I did likewise. Outside, my parents greeted their friends and customers, while my brother and I talked to our school friends.

Over Chicken Chong my father reviewed the highlights of the morning. "That boy with the crazy hat, who is he?" One of my school friends, then maybe twelve, wore an American sailor's cap.

"Oh, he is the son of the Police Chief."

"You mean Klooter?" asked my mother, who was good with names.

"Yes."

"Those big shots, those important people, they can do anything they want," my father commented wistfully, abstractedly.

He was in his early forties at the time and tended to lose interest in the middle of a sentence or stare straight ahead of him for long periods of time. His long face could instantly become immobile, his eyes expressionless. My father's thoughts were on the past, on his losses, on our own narrow escape. We had gotten out, yes, but only one of his six brothers had survived. He tried to help but they were in Poland, out of reach. Unlike my mother, he found little joy in the present.

At the time of Chicken Chong, we all went to a comedy show in the Jewish Club of Curaçao. The comedian, a lithe Jewish man from Argentina, told jokes in Spanish, in Yiddish; he did magic tricks, he sang Polish-Jewish songs about Friday night in a little town called Belz. His lone accompanist was Rachel, a twelve-year-old girl I had started to notice lately, who played the piano while he did his magic tricks. At the beginning of these, he dramatically turned to her and demanded, *"Musica, maestra!"*

The audience, starved for entertainment, mainly Polish and Russian Jews who had lived in Curaçao since the early thirties, applauded heartily. They had come to the island by way of Peru or Panama or Venezuela and knew enough Spanish to understand his jokes. My father looked blank, frozen, distant, his eyes expressionless.

The comedian now called, in a fit of self-mockery, for the *Desfile de Estrellas*, the Parade of Stars, and he and Rachel marched around the room to great applause. My father's head followed them as if he wondered where they were going.

After this interlude, the program was entirely in Yiddish. It began with a skit about a Jewish immigrant in Argentina rounding up cattle with the gauchos. My father looked at the stage and sat motionless. Next the comedian told about a Jewish survivor from Europe coming to the US and being questioned by Immigration:

"Do you want to come to the US?"

"Yes, sir."

"Are you a Communist?"

"No, sir."

"Do you want to go in the Army?"

"Oh, sir."

The last line was a pun on the Yiddish *Oo-ser*, which means something like "Hardly." My father smiled wryly.

Next, the hard-working comedian acted out a story my father had told us a dozen times. It was about the Polish Jew who shares a train compartment with a Polish officer. The Jew is in the top bunk and complains, "Oy, I'm so thirsty."

The Pole rises from his bottom bunk, gets a class of water, and gives it to him. "Shut up now and sleep."

After an hour or two, the Jew again sighs from his top bunk, "Oy, I'm so thirsty."

The Pole, awake again, curses him out, "Here Jew, here's some more water."

When the Pole is asleep again, the Jew starts complaining loudly, "Oy, I was so thirsty."

My father was now making sounds. At first, I thought it was laughter, but then it changed to a high whinny. His face looked strained, unnatural. There were tears on his cheeks. I expected it to be over any minute, but the sound continued and did not lessen and people started looking. I thought he might be crying but he wasn't. It sounded as if he switched from a kind of sob to laughter, but the high-pitched noise persisted for several long minutes. In the half darkness of the hall, I looked at him, but now his face was turned away.

"That was a good story," my father said the next day to Davido Naydorf, a Polish Jew who had lived on the island for decades. "The more you hear it, the better it gets." Every other Saturday night Davido came to visit. He was a lonely man because his wife, who couldn't bear the heat of Curaçao, lived in Miami. There she spent most of the year with Davido's brother.

My parents tended to pick up loners. There was Mr. Mishel, who had applied to the colonial authorities for an accent on the second syllable of his name, a slim, fastidious man, who repeated ritualistically that "watermelon contains a lot of water." There was also a Jonas Bonaparte, whom everybody called Napoleon, a slight man with a blurry face and little glasses. Napoleon was fixated on fish, their variety, behavior, beauty. In better times, he would have been a scholar, but he, like Davido and Mr. Mishel, considered himself lucky to have escaped Europe in the thirties and was in awe of our flight a decade later, after the Nazis had already invaded Holland.

"Davido," said my father, "is a good man but he has no idea what we went through in Europe. He has become tropicalized."

"But, Max," said my mother, furrowing her brow, "how could he know? How could anyone?"

"Yes, how could he?"

"And that ulcer of his," she continued, "he must be very sensitive."

"Yes, yes," answered my father, "the bowel is the barometer of the person."

One of the many ways my father imposed reason and regularity on the world was to repeat certain sayings that intimated order. With the extermination of the Jews never far from his consciousness, he used these phrases and invested them with an almost magical wisdom. I see this now as a sort of Talmudic summing up, a way of creating predictability in an unpredictable and vicious world. Nor were his sayings always solemn. Looking at some of the ways the Dutch colonial officials around him prospered during their stay on the island, he proclaimed in Yiddish: "From eating small noodles, you don't get a large behind."

When his boss in the small wholesale business was put in prison for keeping two sets of books, my father pronounced, "You can't dance with one rear end at two weddings." That's what Mr. Perlmutter had done: he had danced with one *toochis* on two weddings; he had been too slippery, too agile, too shifty.

Every afternoon for three months, at precisely five o'clock, my father and I carried chicken soup to the Willemstad jailhouse inside an old military fort facing the glaring Caribbean Sea. The jailer was a large, jovial black man, who always greeted us with the same question, "Chicken soup for Mr. Perlmutter?" He seemed to have all the time in the world.

"Yes," replied my father, each time happily surprised by this question, "For Mr. Perlmutter."

"I will see to it that he gets it. Mr. Perlmutter shouldn't have to do without his soup."

"How is Mr. Perlmutter doing?" asked my father.

"Mr. Perlmutter has all the comforts of home," grinned the man, wiping the sweat from below his tight khaki collar and adjusting his broad belt with its shiny holster. Under his short sleeves were two perfectly bleached sweat stains.

"Can we give that guard something?" asked my mother when we got home.

"Sure," said my father. "Let's send him a present for his wife."

My parents always assumed that men had wives, that everybody who was courteous or did a favor should be rewarded — that friendliness worked, though of course only in normal times. Friendliness did not work with Nazis, nor could they be bribed. Our friend Mr. Kommer in Amsterdam had naively tried to give money to the Gestapo and was seized and deported in 1941. But, on the other hand, Vichy French officials could be and were bribed, and some people were always more pliable than others.

But while pliability, maneuvering, even slipperiness, had been a necessity in the war and were still part of my father's own makeup, he disliked the trait. Necessity had forced him into carefully befriending a Dutch policeman, who had tipped us off in 1942 that the German occupiers were about to deport us. But in normal times, so much better not to have to be calculating. He admired the genuinely Dutch Jews who were more conventional, more "solid," less inclined to being roundabout or devious. He wanted my brother and me to be straight and educated and Dutch. We were. My father believed in conventional, ordinary pleasures, though he did not understand them.

To my excitement, our whole family went to an evening of high school drama. Adding to my pleasure was that it took place in a small theatre, a newly renovated old house on the outskirts of town. Large numbers of people stood on the brightly painted verandah and looked through the wide-open doors and windows. The program began with *tableaux vivants*: fellow students I hardly recognized in breathlessly still and acrobatic poses. Boys in supple, elegant clothes stood motionless near girls in exotic, diaphanous gowns. Each pose was silent but meaningful, and some were actually announced as representing "Harmony," "Humanity," or even "International Peace."

"Isn't that nice?" asked my mother to rouse my father.

"What did you say, Bertha?"

"I said isn't that good, what they're doing?"

"What are they doing?" asked my father.

Then the play. Our friend Sam, the rabbi's nephew, had the lead role. He was a short, olive-skinned boy who arrived on the island after the war, which he spent hidden away in a cellar underneath the stable of a Dutch farm. Emotionally, Sam was odd, given to sudden mumblings, his glittery dark eyes remote. Even when he was normal, which was much of the time, he stood too close, as if confiding in you. He occasionally talked to himself, though my brother said that "he made a lot of sense when he did."

Sam was the star of the show. Without having to act overmuch, he played a retarded boy who shouted things like, "Yes," "Perhaps" and "Eighty-eight." The role was perfect for him. His squat figure jumped around the stage as if he had found a way to overcome gravity. At the end of the play, he got most of the applause. I was happy for Sam, and envious.

But my father remarked afterwards, "Sam shouldn't have done that."

"Shouldn't have done what?" I asked.

"Well, it doesn't look good."

"What doesn't look good?"

"I mean for the other people."

"What other people?"

"You know, the others," said my father slowly.

"You mean the Gentiles?"

"Yes, they were all there."

"But what did he do wrong?"

"He made a fool of himself."

"But he was acting, Papa."

"Yes, yes, maybe, but he was a buffoon; people remember that."

"That was the role, don't you see?"

"Yes, folly sometimes wins — but it's still folly."

And he wandered off, not wanting to belabor the obvious.

Sometimes it was a relief to be at school, surrounded by kids in this new Caribbean world. The boy who sat next to me in class was a handsome, brown-skinned lad from Suriname. Edmund was a story-teller, a mimic, a talker, with smooth natural ways about him and an unflappable, mature manner. "Manny," he said one day, "let me tell you something." He knew I loved his stories. "This Chinese man back home in Suriname had a grocery store. I went there every day."

"Why?"

"I'll tell you. I went into that store every day to hear the man and his wife speak."

"What was so odd about that?"

"She kept looking at him and saying, 'Leo.'"

"Who was Leo?"

"It was part of a chant she had for him. She'd say, 'Leo, Ootahn Seen Leo.'"

"You mean always?"

"Always. That's what was so good about it. Always."

"You mean you'd come in the store, and she'd be in the middle of that song?"

"That chant, yes, always."

"Is that what they would say to each other all day?"

"All day. Like this," and he stood up very quietly, seriously, his wavy hair impeccable, and put his face close to mine. "Leo, Ootahn Seen Leo!"

I started to laugh. "Were there more words to it?"

"Never, no. Always the same words. 'Leo, Ootahn Seen Leo."

"Did you ever know what they meant?"

"No."

"But they must have meant something?"

"Maybe they didn't mean anything."

"Why did they do it?"

"I don't know. Maybe they liked the idea of it, the regularity."

I thought of the way my father used slogans and sayings, political slogans and Jewish sayings, to create order.

Whether it meant anything or not, Edmund started to chant, first slowly, then more insistently, "Leo, Leo Ootahn Seen Leo," repeating it in the same languid, plaintive way, once in a while turning it into a wail, sometimes forming a question, then making an answer with exactly the same words. Other kids started listening, then joined in. I did too, happy to be part of this life now, this Curaçaoan life, and soon the whole classroom was chanting until a red-faced Dutch teacher burst into the room and shouted, "What kind of tom-tom ritual is this? Wild creatures who can never be quiet!"

Edmund was one of the few kids who was soft-spoken and never swore, but everybody else did, especially in the native language Papiamentu. I knew all the bad words, but couldn't make myself say them. For months I rehearsed sounding out the words and then slowly started to say them in an ordinary speaking voice. It got easier every day. I also practiced making the sign of the prick, middle finger stiff between bent index and ring finger. It seemed impossible to brandish this gesture publicly but finally I succeeded.

I had a sense even then that there was something playful about the way Curaçaoans used profanity: "You're not only a prick, you're a water prick," yelled my friend Mundi after I flashed him my newly learned sign. "And then you're a prick on water."

"Both of you are so beast."

"No, you're beast, beast, beast."

"To say the least, you're a beast. Your head's in a whirl, but you're so beast it's not for a girl. You wouldn't know what to do with one, Manny Cayman."

A song, Sindbad Cayman, Sindbad the Alligator, had become Manny Cayman, and so for a while I was Manny Cayman. Why?

Because Sindbad and Manny had the same rhythm. It was so easy to get a new identity here.

"They call this old man 'Boy,'" laughed my mother. "Who can understand it?" But she sounded intrigued.

"That's his nickname," I said, glad I could interpret this Curaçaoan habit to her. "His real name is Boo-boo. I know him."

"Boo-boo... Boy... Everything is really crazy in this country," said my father, who remained indomitably European despite the enormity of what had so recently happened there.

Davido Naydorf took my brother and me to the outdoor boxing matches in the Curaçao stadium. In a corner of the stadium, the boxing ring was a brightly illumined square. We were always in the third row. Those close to the ring screamed the loudest. I looked forward for weeks to these excursions and soon had my own favorite, a tall, lanky boxer name Pantera Negra from Cuba. He beat Young Tiger, Zorro, and a hapless Belgian who wilted in the humid heat of a Curaçao evening.

Davido wore a light-weight cream sports jacket to these events because, he said, they were special. He said that the fights were good for his ulcer; they stimulated him but did not upset him. Hobbies and pastimes were always helpful and should be indulged. All around us, black, white, and brown people came by and slapped him on the back. A sultry, chocolate-colored woman, her hair in ringlets around her face, her dress damp from the heat, said admiringly, "Hey, Davido is wearing his jacket."

He held her hand a brief moment.

"Are these your kids?" she asked.

"No, mine are in Miami."

I too started wearing a jacket. In a photograph I saw the other day, Davido holds a thin cigar. My brother and I look smug and serene. The crowd around us is shadowy. "You know," said my father, "Davido is totally Caribbeanized."

I told my father about Pantera Negra.

"When two men fight, a Jew grabs his hat," he said.

These were exciting days. Unannounced, we got a visit from a young man with whom we had fled Europe. Charles was an American soldier now, looking smart in his uniform, his forage cap perched high on his brown curly mop. He seemed to bounce with every step. Last time I had seen him was during the long voyage of our escape from Holland, in 1942 in our hotel room in Nice, then still unoccupied by the Nazis. He had pounded on the door of our room, having just come upon a fellow refugee who hanged himself. The man had gambled away his escape money in the beautiful shore-side casino. Now Charles was in US Army Intelligence. He and a buddy impressed my brother and me by sounding just like the movies: "OK, guy, let's get in the back." My brother and I imitated that American sound for months, saying it just the way he did and moving the back of our hands rapidly over our mouths, as we had seen Americans do in movies.

American GIs were popular on the island, especially black GIs. Many Curaçaoans engaged them in conversation and slapped them on the back. Soldiers of all kinds were coming through. My 24-year-old uncle Paul, who had been in the Dutch Army in Exile, The Princess Irene Brigade, visited us from Holland. Under Canadian command, these five thousand young men landed in Normandy and fought their way into Belgium and the Netherlands.

He appeared in uniform before the Jewish Club in Curaçao. The whole family was present for his speech. I was excited and proud of my uncle, looking so cool and confident. He mentioned the invasion briefly, but so great was the desire in those days to talk about something else, anything other than the war, that he went off into a lengthy discourse on the plight of Indians on their reservation in Florida. I was restless and beginning to regret not being with Davido at the boxing match. Maybe I was becoming ever more "tropicalized." Pantera Negra was fighting tonight. Also there was a moonlight picnic organized by the Jewish Club. Would Rachel be there?

I left the island in 1951 to go to Brandeis University. Our family was now spread out over different countries, and my childhood dreams of doing things together were long in the past. Eight years after I left Curaçao, my mother died. My father retired to San Francisco in 1970. Much as he tried, no amount of regularity could keep the chaos at bay. His routines continued to please him, but they were ever more engulfed by the ever-present memories of his past. And he was disturbed by what he felt to be a wild and unpredictable American culture. Every Saturday night he went to the same movie theatre because it had good seats. Around the time of my divorce he wandered into "The Rocky Horror Show."

"You know, this was just like Curaçao. People were on their feet and shouting at each other. Then they yelled and threw things at the screen. I had rice on my jacket when I came out."

*   *   *

Because so many of us left the island, it was hard to keep up with high school friends. No school reunions that I know of were ever held. Long after I came to America, I started searching, but the news was always elusive: Benjamin had been a cab driver in Rotterdam, Frank an engineer in Geneva but had moved, Carlo disappeared off the coast of South America.

I did find out that Edmund became Prime Minister of Suriname. He was among the last democratically elected rulers before the military coup in that South American country.

And Sam, the rabbi's nephew? One day in the eighties, his reincarnation turned up in my Survey of English Poetry class at San Francisco State University. Sam's double: squat, potato-nosed, the same thick hair, only gray now, the same intimate expression, the same intensity, the same mumbling. Mr. Piddler was an eager, intent listener but appeared to hear nothing. "I worked in industry for a while," he told me in that standing-too-close, familiar Sam-like way, "but I'm now wondering whether to take up poetry and make a career in that field."

After Mr. Piddler appeared, I asked my brother, who lived in Boston, if he knew anything about the real Sam. Yes, he did: he couldn't quite remember all the details but Sam had been found dead in a tiny hotel room in Amsterdam just a few years ago. The Dutch have a name for that kind of oppressively small room — a "suicide room."

Chapter 8. Mundi and the Coming Autonomy

My Curaçaoan friend Mundi laughed at me every time he saw me go to the Willemstad Public Library. Mostly the books I borrowed were about Holland. By reading about things Dutch I felt nearer to a life I often fantasized about, blending memory with daydreams, while I read of boys' adventures in the Dutch countryside, camping in the heather of the Netherlands, playing soccer in small Dutch towns. These books reminded me of Bilthoven, where I had been happy until our abrupt flight from Holland in early 1942, almost two years after the German invasion and now almost five years ago.

"Not enough," said my brother, shaking his head seriously. "You're taking out only four books." He was fifteen at the time, I twelve.

"These books by Karl May," intoned the librarian, a middle-aged refugee from Hungary, who was known on our island as Little Rat because his nose twitched incessantly and he had a busy, snuffling manner. He wiped the sweat off his forehead with a rapid sweep of his handkerchief. "Just like back home in Europe. You boys are good Dutch boys, always reading books by Karl May." His hands swiftly scratched in check marks on our cards.

"You know where it would be great to be an Indian?" asked my brother, his curly mop standing up with excitement.

"In America?"

"No, silly, in Holland. There everybody knows about cowboys and Indians."

Mundi joined us as we walked from the library back to the schoolyard. He liked me because I sometimes did his homework for him, which he claimed he "had no time for." "You guys are water pricks," he said in Dutch, but the key word was spoken in Papiamentu. His copper-brown head gleamed under a fresh haircut. "Why don't you do something, sing or make noise or bother some girl? Or would you rather just read about it? Have an adventure — be a Curaçaoan for one day in your life!"

"There's nothing to do but read in Curaçao," said my brother, sounding almost like a teacher, one of our Dutch teachers.

"That's why you guys are so dumb. Let me explain what a water prick is."

"No, don't bother," scowled my brother, but Mundi had spotted a friend and was already gone.

"Why did you say that?" I asked.

"I don't want you to be around that guy."

"Why not?"

"He is a wild kid." "Wild" was one of my father's favorite words, a word I disliked.

"Don't tell me what to do," I yelled.

"Why shouldn't I? You're my little brother. I have to protect you from types like him."

"You don't have to. I don't want you to."

"I do. He'll get you into trouble."

"At least he has fun. I wish I were like him. I don't want to be protected anymore."

On a square in front of the Maduro Bank, a sound truck was parked, and two or three brown-skinned, official-looking men in white dress shirts and dark ties were checking the equipment. The bank was a stately, turreted building, flying several flags I did not recognize. This kind of mass meeting was new in the colony, which had experienced little political activity before 1947. In the shimmering heat, a small crowd gathered, some people talking and laughing, others making those gestures that frequently took the place of language, cupping their mouths but not uttering a sound, voicing messages with their hands and arms to friends on the other side of the square. There were few white people, and they either stood quietly in the shade or did not pause but hurried on their way.

Mundi and I stood watching. He had grown quiet, his face intent. At last the loudspeaker rumbled, and a voice, warming up the crowd for the main speaker, harangued the listeners in booming tones about the coming autonomy, the end of the colonial period, and the need for leadership. At last, the voice introduced a small light-skinned man and several in the crowd yelled, "Doctohr, doctohr." The slight, bearded man smiled mysteriously at the crowd and made the "Silence, please" gesture with his little hands. He was Dr. Moises da Costa Gomez, the prominent politician who would lead the island into autonomy.

"Doctohr" wore a dark suit with a vest and showed no awareness of the heat. He lectured this crowd in mild, pleading tones about voting and the greater independence of the representative body, but the people did not respond until he chanted, *"Nos ta manda, nos ta manda"* — we're in charge. Then a long-pent up noise resounded. People repeated the chant, screamed, laughed, and whistled; some even cried. Mundi screamed too, but he was making a face while he did.

"Sometimes I think Doctohr is *pendejo*," Mundi said. 'He talks too much; he's not strong."

"What would you rather see him do?" I asked.

"Stand up to the foreigners."

"Isn't that what Doctohr is doing? Trying to push the Dutch away?"

"No, not just the Dutch. The *Polacos* too."

I was alarmed. "What do Polacos have to do with this?"

"I'm telling you. They have the money. We're not talking about Dutch white people here. We're talking about *Polacos.*"

"Dutch people have the power, Mundi."

"I don't understand *Polacos.* They eat onions and don't drink beer." He wrinkled his nose as if he were mentioning something distasteful.

"Why do they bother you, these onion-people?"

"They come to Curaçao and make money."

"So do others, Mundi."

"Yes, so do others, especially the white people. I mean the gray people."

"No one stops black people from making money like the *Polacos.*"

Mundi looked away. "Sometimes I like *Polacos* better than Dutch people. They speak Papiamentu. They're easier to be with than the Dutch. But they get rich."

"Will there ever be a cool evening?" asked my father and cocked his head as if he had just made a joke.

My mother said nothing. She was used to these flurries from my father. We were still at dinner in the small dining room off the kitchen. The maid had gone home early.

"I was at a rally today, with Mundi," I said.

"Oh, Mundi, Mundi," said my father, his eyes cloudy in his brown, leathery face. "I knew a Herr Mundt in Chemnitz once."

"No, no, this is Mundi, you know, the Curaçaoan boy. I think his real name is Sigmund."

"Oh," said my father, "I don't think Mr. Mundt's name was Sigmund. No, I'm sure it wasn't."

I was annoyed at my father's inattention. "Mundi's name is Sigmund," I said loudly but did not really expect him to hear.

"Mundi? Oh, yes. Mr. Mundt was Jewish, of course, but he so wanted to be a good German."

"He did?"

"Yes, in those days, the good days, 1929, 1930."

"And this Mr. Mundt?"

"Oh yes, Mr. Mundt. He was an athlete in our Jewish Club Maccabi."

"So this Mr. Mundt?"

"This Mr. Mundt, this Mundt. I have to remember now. Yes, this Mundt, this Mr. Mundt had won a trophy for running."

"Really?"

"Yes, a trophy, and then he ran in a race to become city-wide champion and won second place."

"He did?" I asked, surprised.

"Yes, and the paper announced that the Jew Mundt had won Second Prize. He was proud of it and showed it around."

"But wasn't that before the Nazi time?"

"Yes, it was. But still, that's how they did things over there."

"Would never happen here. My friend Mundi…"

"Well, it is better that way here. But those were good days. Your mother and I were just engaged. I had a good business, friends. We had a good apartment. Then suddenly everything gone, everything. Isn't that right, Bertha?"

"Yes, Max, but Manny …"

"What happened to Mr. Mundt?" I asked.

"He had a chance to go to Switzerland before the war, but he couldn't bear to leave Germany."

"What happened to him?"

"Murdered in Treblinka."

My mother had been listening quietly. Her pale blue eyes were fixed on my father, but suddenly she said insistently but diplomatically: "Manny was telling you about the political rally he went to, Max."

"Yes, tell me."

I had lost interest in telling the story. My father just would not listen. "Oh, it wasn't much," I said. "Just announcements about the coming autonomy."

"Everyone is talking about it," said my mother. "Everyone. Louisa had a discussion about it at her house — eight Dutch ladies."

"I'm all for autonomy," mused my father, "but let's hope the autonomy won't affect us. We don't want to leave just yet. But, of course, if we can find a really good country ..."

My father often initiated conversations about where the "good" countries were. They seemed to revive him.

"I mean good countries, safe countries, sensible countries," he said, "where they leave Jews alone, where you can live a solid life, where the government is strong but fair. Yes, America, yes, though it's far too capitalist."

Either my mother enjoyed the topic also or just liked seeing my father livelier than usual. "Australia?" she asked. "Gerda from school in Germany lives there, and she has a good life." She smiled brightly at the recollection of her friend from school.

"Even New Zealand," said my father dreamily. "That country is far from trouble, far from Europe, even farther than Curaçao."

"Maybe Santo Domingo will work out," threw in my brother. "Manny, get the atlas: let's find other places."

I got out the atlas and my father looked on.

"I want to go back to Holland," I said.

"You know that your uncle Paul is thinking of leaving Holland and going to Ireland," said my father.

"Either Ireland or Australia," laughed my mother. "But really, Max, Curaçao isn't so bad." And then wanting to include me, she asked, "What do you think, Manny?"

Despite all this talk, my parents made no preparations to leave. They were prospering in their textile store and settling in. They decided to install air-conditioning in the bedrooms of our house. We were put on a waiting list, and I found myself ever more eager for it. When it finally arrived, two dark-skinned Curaçaoan men in khaki uniforms with "Carrier" stitched on their pockets installed huge boxes in my parents' bedroom and in ours. From then on, I could spend every available moment in my room reading. The steadying roar of the machine put me in a kind of trance, and the unaccustomed cool transported me to places I read about in my books. With the windows sealed and the curtains drawn, the tropics outside receded, and I was back in the Dutch countryside. The dial was set to Very Cold, and lying under a blanket I read by lamplight. In my books, small children were starting school and playing with their friends, as I once did. Their older brothers went bicycling or camping. All through 1947 and 1948, my twelfth and thirteenth years, I read these books.

I would return to Holland. On this over-heated island, I daydreamed of cool, green days, myself in a long rain coat, a bicycle to go from here to there. My friends would be Dutch, and perhaps like the Zorgdragers or the Voscuses, but not so stiff. That life was easy to picture and even easier to feel: the overwhelming sweetness of those memories and that house in Bilthoven, my parents still laughing, and my brother and I free to live the life all the other children lived.

The autonomy for the island continued to be talked about, and slowly, surely, some small changes became apparent. Curaçaoans went into politics in greater numbers and became ever more visible as bureaucrats and officials. Once in a while there was talk among my parents' Dutch friends that soon no European would be welcome here and that "they" were taking over; but that still seemed a long way off.

At times I looked forward to becoming ever more Curaçaoan. I practiced my Latin American dance steps; I spoke Papiamentu as much as possible; I dreamed of finding a Curaçaoan girlfriend. But at school I was always reminded of my early childhood in Holland. The teachers and the books spoke of something familiar to me, while becoming a Curaçaoan took effort. And I never really believed I could succeed at it.

At choir practice in school, we sang a sad song about a frog on the bank of a Dutch river, between Delft and Rotterdam, who sits on a clod of mud with an infant frog on his knee to whom he talks of the death of its mother. I thought of the coolness of those Dutch rivers set into dazzlingly green beds. The boys sang heartily, pronouncing Dutch in their Curaçaoan accents: "'God darn it,' said the little frog. 'Has the stork done that? Was he the murderer of my mother?'"

Between endless choruses of this song and "A shark celebrated his birthday by inviting all creatures from the sea," Mundi whispered, "Hey, Wolf, come to my house for lunch."

"Don't we have to ask your mother first?"

"No."

Mundi had dropped his best friend Ricardo because he had "cut my ears," Papiamentu for stealing his girlfriend away. Mundi was thirteen, his friend Ricardo fourteen, the girl, Miranda, a slattern who was known to be "hot," fifteen.

"How far is your house?" I was worried about getting back to school on time.

"Far, far, far," answered Mundi, and we started walking across the wooden pontoon bridge connecting the two busy banks of downtown Willemstad. On both sides of the Anna Bay that split the town in half, gabled houses in different shades of pastel glowed in the sun. Despite the heat, crowds of Curaçaoans stood, laughed, and jostled on the narrow walkways of the bridge. I felt the sun singeing my hair.

"My house is different from yours," said Mundi, looking at me .

"Yes, I know that," I answered, still wondering whether we would be late for school.

"This bridge," said Mundi, repeating a story I had heard from other Curaçaoans, "was built by an American. People without shoes, poor people, were allowed to cross free of charge."

"And now it's free to everybody," I answered.

"Yeah, Dutch people did some good stuff. If I had money, you know what I would do?"

"What?"

"I'd go to Campo Alegre every weekend."

"You mean you've gone?" I asked, wondering if children could possibly be admitted to the island's famous brothel.

Mundi's house on the outskirts of Willemstad was tiny, with a huge refrigerator in the living room. A few wooden chairs stood against a wall, but no table. His mother, a worn black woman in a yellow dress, looked at me and said something in Dutch which I couldn't understand; her phonograph boomed like a jukebox. She spoke again, yelling this time, "You're the Wolf-man Mundi talks about. Tall, skinny, with glasses like an owl. Do you want a coke?"

Mundi shared a little room with three brothers and a little sister. We drank our cokes standing up near the refrigerator. Soon his father came in and, hardly looking at us, changed his clothes in the living room. His white undershirt was soaked against his copper skin. All the while, his wife yelled over the music in Papiamentu, "Why are you going out now?"

"I told you," he shouted back, "I have business to do."

"What business do you have?"

"You wouldn't understand. I have to see a man about money."

"You don't have business with a man. Yours is with a woman."

"You see why I don't like to stay here, woman? You're lucky I come around at all."

"Don't come here just to change clothes." I was uneasy and looked at Mundi, who cut himself a slice of salami and slapped it between two slices of white bread. Then he did the same for me. He didn't seem bothered by his parents' argument, but I wanted to leave as quickly as possible, to get back, to hear Dutch, to be in school, which felt safe. I decided not to tell my parents and my brother about this visit.

* * *

As the autonomy fever grew, the island erupted into many fiestas. Even our school got caught up in the celebrations. Mundi and I went to a dance with several hundred kids from different schools throughout the island. Mundi danced every dance, and I stood watching.

Suddenly he asked: "Wolf, do you want to go with me to a *balia di tamboo*?" He held his oval head to one side when he was being sly.

"You mean the forbidden dance?"

"Yes, forbidden, one of these weird Dutch words. It just means Dutch people are scared of it."

"Well, I want to go, but that *tamboo* dance is not happening anymore, is it?"

"It's illegal, but that means nothing."

"Really?"

"Wolf, you're such a fool. Why do I waste my time with you?"

"OK," I said, with a little jump of anticipation. This was the sacred dance I had heard whispers about, a kind of voodoo rite where goats were sacrificed and men and women danced half naked. I had wanted to see the dancing ever since my friend Wilmoo told me about it on the day he showed me some pornographic photographs, men and women doing unspeakably wonderful things together, the women's gleaming round flesh inviting and receptive.

"There's one after sundown near your house tonight," said Mundi.

"Near my house? No, that can't be."

At seven, after dinner, Mundi and I walked down an asphalt road that soon narrowed into a dirt road into the shimmering, dusky countryside. We walked for a good hour past large-armed cactuses and little huts scattered messily around. Goats wandered freely in yards and often on the road as well. As soon as the sun was down, the night became blacker, more menacing, than I thought possible. How different a walk through the countryside would be in Holland, how cool the air, how much more inviting!

Mundi guided me to a small hut behind a prickly cactus hedge and whispered, now looking frightened himself, "This is as far as we can go. We'll hide behind these bushes. If they see us, we will have caught water," and he shook his fingers rapidly up and down the way Curaçaoans indicated big trouble.

"Oh, what could happen?"

"I don't know, but they don't like white people here, so keep your white ass down." In the excitement, Mundi's stiff, crinkly hair was starting to look damp and flatten out.

From our hideout we saw men and women going by, chatting amiably, bantering in the steamy night. As many as twenty crowded into the tiny room. Some of the men carried lightweight jackets over their arm, while the women wore airy cotton dresses, their bright colors contrasting with dark shiny skins. The windows and door of the one-room hut stood wide open, so we could see into a tiny living room, its walls a startling orange. At first a drink was passed around, probably rum, and the talk became louder. Then a throbbing drum became audible. "That's the *tamboo*," said Mundi. "Magic; it defeats the spirits."

In that part of the hut we could not see, women's voices clamored and made laughing sounds. We saw them when they came back to the front of the room. They had changed into long strips of yellow paper, which looked as if they had just recently been shredded and pasted onto the women's naked bodies.

The *tamboo* now started up again, and the men and women approached one another teasingly. They writhed toward each other and then backed off. Slowly the strips of paper began to melt in the heat of their bodies, which seemed to radiate toward me. One man and woman held each other close, his hands firmly on her buttocks. The other couples barely touched, but they seemed to move ever closer. I hoped to see all the paper strips melt away, but a kind of acrid smoke was now obscuring our vision. I could hear a low, soft moaning, and the incessant throb of drums.

"Is this religious?" I asked. "Where's the priest?"

"He's inside. He wants to see naked ass too," answered Mundi.

"Where are the goats?"

"We don't kill animals here. They do that in Haiti."

I looked at my watch. Not even nine o'clock yet. I was feeling brave. "Let's try to look through the window. They can't see us, Mundi."

"Wolf, don't be dumb."

He seemed suddenly tired in a way I had not seen him before. "The spirit has got me, Wolf. I shouldn't have brought a white boy along."

"You bet," I said. The spirit was giving me a lift. I was finally having a Curaçaoan adventure.

The dancers were writhing, locked in tight embraces, their bodies merged into each other.

"All that smoke," said Mundi feebly. He slapped his hands on the side of his head, as if he were knocking something out of it.

"No smoke out here in the open air. Come on, let's get closer."

"You go closer," hissed Mundi, his eyes looking watery.

"I will." And I walked forward, waving away a swarm of mosquitoes that had settled on my arm.

"Watch out, prick. I should never have brought you here. When I see this dance, I am angry at all white people."

"You idiot. What do white people have to do with this dance?"

"They took it away from us," brooded Mundi.

"No, they didn't," I said, annoyed. Mundi wasn't wild, I thought, he was just unreasonable. "Look at these people here."

"Look at what?"

"Nobody took anything from them," I said willfully. "Besides, the Netherlands is the world's finest colonial power. We learned it in school."

"Learned what in school?"

"I mean, compared to the British and French, the Dutch helped and educated the native population," I said, mouthing one of our text books.

Before I could see it in that darkness, Mundi's fist shot at me. I felt a numbing pain in my left upper arm, and in a sudden rage I grabbed the collar of his white shirt and pulled it tight around his chest. I didn't care if he or anyone else came back at me; I was furious. He looked surprised but not frightened. The sweat pouring from my forehead, we stood for a long few seconds and glowered at each other in the moist, unseeing night.

Even Dutch people frequently said Curaçaoans were generous. Mundi was no exception. He bore me no grudge, but our friendship cooled and I started seeing more of my Dutch friends, Henny and Peter. One afternoon I mentioned to Mundi, "I'm going to Henny's house."

Mundi's mouth curled: "I don't like him. He's a real *macamba*, not like you."

"You talk to him at school."

"I know, but he's a real Dutch *macamba* with a green *macamba* ass."

"I'm going to see his rabbit," I said, afraid of sounding younger than my thirteen years.

"I don't give a shit about his rabbit. And I never want to see those parents." Here Mundi did a stiff-legged, rigid-armed walk in imitation of Mr. Zorgdrager, a formal-looking Dutchman, who was Chief of the Bureau of Population Statistics.

"They're OK," I answered. "What do you have against them?"

Mundi made a fist and lightly pounded his forehead. "Wolf, you don't understand; your head is hard. His people brought us over as slaves."

I felt relieved. At least Mundi wasn't talking about *Polacos*.

Mr. Zorgdrager was frequently home during the middle of the day. In his house, he always wore a white dress shirt with a colorful tie; in his office, he also wore a white dress shirt but with a subdued blue or brown tie. He greeted me cordially, bending down a little, his head tilted to one side.

"Well, Manny, you've come during a moment of drama."

"Is Henny home, Mr. Zorgdrager?"

"He is indeed, but the aforesaid drama also claims his attention."

"Should I come back another time, sir?"

"No, come in. Teenee, the rabbit, has been diagnosed with cancer. The question before us is whether to put her to sleep."

Henny looked red-eyed. Mrs. Zorgdrager, who was not bothered by the heat, wore a long-sleeved house-dress with plastic sleeve protectors reaching to her elbows. Smiling, she asked, "Would you like a cup of hot tea, Manny?" She smiled and spoke at the same time, which created a soft hissing sound.

"Yes, please, Mrs. Zorgdrager."

Tea was taken at a small round table under a pretty indoor awning near an open window of the dining room. I was careful not to spill tea on their crocheted tablecloth. Mr. Zorgdrager sat with his back to a wall mirror, so that when I looked at him I saw him twice.

"You see," continued Mr. Zorgdrager to Henny, "Teenee would be better off if she were put out of her misery."

"But she's still alive," answered Henny with tears in his voice, "and frisky. Why put her to sleep now?"

Mr. Zorgdrager turned to his wife and beckoned her to speak. "What do you think, Mother?"

"I think we might wait a while to see how she's doing." Something about this comment reminded me of my own mother.

"Well, a diplomatic compromise," answered Mr. Zorgdrager with a little chortle.

I was surprised by the attention his parents paid to the rabbit and the way they listened to Henny. They seemed to lose themselves in events, as if they were children and not grown-ups. Though my mother tried to pay attention, my father did not, and neither of them seemed at ease the way these Dutch people were. True, I sometimes had to laugh at their Dutch formality, but I envied Henny. His father had time for him, and both parents had energy for the children and each other and seemed carefree. I understood why that couldn't be so in my family, who had gone through such worry and pain during the war, but I wished it could. And I wished my parents could share some of my pleasures, but of course they couldn't. So I enjoyed being at the Zorgdragers and felt a comfort in their presence, however strange their formality.

The telephone rang. Mrs. Zorgdrager turned it over to her husband. "Anton," she whispered urgently, her smile wide and tense. "The governor's secretary. The governor himself wants to speak to you."

Mr. Zorgdrager sprang up from the table and sprinted to the hall and swiftly donned a white sports jacket, then ran back and picked up the receiver. "Yes, your Excellency ..."

When he came back to the table, he looked as cheerful as before. "The autonomy question, always the autonomy question... They'll never be able to run this show on their own, no, out of the question." He paused and then lightly pounded the table. "They will never be able to sail the ship of state."

Mrs. Zorgdrager frowned. "Then we'll just have to go back to Holland, won't we, Anton?"

"Yes, because I assure you they'll make a mess of it. Today I saw some of those black fellows with caps, heavy woolen caps, if you don't mind, passing out leaflets. Can you imagine wearing a heavy cap in this climate?" And he touched the thin knot of his tie and quickly patted his neck dry.

Mrs. Zorgdrager smiled and made little hissing sounds: "Well, Tonny, we could request early retirement and settle down in Zeist or in Apeldoorn. That's what Jan and Kitty will do when he gets his pension from Shell Oil."

Her husband turned to her: "You know, some people retire in Spain, but how can they leave their own country? How can people who are Dutch, truly Dutch, leave Holland in their settled years?"

"I wouldn't like it one bit," said Mrs. Zorgdrager. "No, give me my home, my people, my language. I'll take the rain."

The towns they mentioned — Apeldoorn, Zeist, De Bilt — were a few kilometers from where I had lived as a small boy. I remembered white houses with large gardens, and I could easily picture the Zorgdragers living there and, with a little more difficulty, picture myself too.

I looked at Henny, who was now bright and clear-eyed. His older sister Anya, a tall, long-limbed girl of seventeen, walked in from her room with a magazine. She wanted to be a stewardess. "Hi, Manny... Mom, Dad, I read such a great story in my magazine from Holland. All about a KLM pilot who landed his plane in a tree."

Mr. Zorgdrager beamed. "I want to read that article when you're through with it ... Those are men, those KLM flyers; they can do anything. Manny, have you ever flown in a KLM plane?"

All the Zorgdragers now turned to me, as if my answer mattered more than anything else possibly could. Fortunately, I had been on a KLM flight, the one that took us from Suriname to Curaçao four years ago, in 1944.

"Ask Manny about Israel!" exclaimed Mrs. Zorgdrager.

"Yes," said Mr. Zorgdrager. "Manny, is it *de jure* or *de facto* now? Have all the important countries recognized the new state? The former," he explained to his family, "is the more valuable endorsement. It demonstrates a government's approval of the new country."

"Well," I said, happy to contribute, "the United States has recognized it *de jure*, but a lot of other countries still only *de facto*."

Mr. Zorgdrager nodded, took off his glasses, and cleaned them thoughtfully with a crisp white handkerchief. He was still wearing the jacket, which made his image in the mirror more imposing too.

"The Jews and the Arabs are both Semitic peoples, aren't they?"

"Yes, Mr. Zorgdrager."

"Pity they should fight each other... Still, wasn't that wonderful, the way the Jews gave the Arabs a thrashing? I always knew you people were clever, but I didn't know you were brave too."

How could I want to be here with the Zorgdragers and yet feel so uneasy? I yearned to be like them and belong to a family like theirs, but I really couldn't. I could speak their language, but I was different. They lived in a world at a huge distance from my parents. And were they comfortable with me? Or did they see me as alien and strange? I did not know, and I did not know if any Dutch people could ever accept me fully. Perhaps in America refugees could find a home; in Holland, or in Curaçao, they could not.

That night, in my air-conditioned room, I pondered it some more, but the cold lulled me into reveries of Holland, a country to which the Zorgdragers later returned, though I did not. I stayed in Curaçao after the advent of autonomy and once even told Mundi I would never leave. It was one of the few conversations I had with him just before my departure to America in 1951.

Chapter 9. A Jewish Word

For me, the major event of 1946 was winning the Neerlandia Prize, the award for best student of Dutch in my high school.

I was eleven years old in 1946, and still liked all things Dutch, even our special ceremonies at school. On the day I won the Neerlandia Prize, when the Dutch National Anthem had been played and we had seen a tableau vivant of Queen Wilhelmina returning in triumph from exile in England to the Netherlands at the end of the war a year ago, the principal got ready to announce the winner. He stood up, tugged at his black tie and ran his fingers through his gray hair. Now, his red face cocked to one side, his horn-rimmed glasses blinking in the stage lights, he spoke my name with a flourish. I walked quickly to the center of the stage and shook his hand, and with a crooked smile, he handed me a book and said, "Cherish this." Then he announced that the Neerlandia Prize winner would declaim a poem.

I stepped forward and recited an old Dutch classic I had prepared:

> He gazed and said,
> Farewell, oh mother,
> never to return, never more.
> And over dusty roads she saw him go,
> and wept her bitter tears —

till one day a leprous drifter
came after many years
and knocked on her door,
and from too great joy
she had no further tears.

Ear-shattering applause, as much from pleasure in the performance as relief that it was over — the boys were excited and restless. For this occasion, girls were present too, though they sat with their school on the other side of the auditorium. Black, white, and brown children filled the hall. Back in my seat I was clapped on the shoulder by several boys. Curaçaoan children especially liked the poetry but wondered at its strange contents. The kid sitting next to me asked, "A leper, man, a leper came to the door? Is this some kind of Dutch thing? Are there lepers in Holland?" My friend Mundi grinned. "Wolf, why does the mother first let him go, then welcome him back? Dutch people never make sense."

The principal now leaped forward. He was an energetic man, with a large, gray forelock, who spoke his words lustily: "This great language of ours ennobles these youthful voices. Let us not forget that you, the audience, are ennobled by the words you have heard recited. When language is shaped into poetry, when words become music, all of us stand in awe, all of us feel consummate pride. Let us hope that the day won't come when Dutch will cease to be spoken on these beautiful islands. The flag, the crown, the mother-tongue — these protect and strengthen us forever. Now we shall sing 'Sturdy Boys.'"

Sturdy boys, stalwart lads,
Don't stand idling over there.
Have you all your wits about you
And your senses fully in your care?

I thought of Holland, the sturdy boys with their wits about them — I had read about them often and wished to be one of them. Not the timid, fearful boy also present in the song, Jan Dullard, who walks around dreamily in his slippers; but Jan Courage who chooses the "rigging" and the open sea, proud of his country and his bravery — perhaps I could have been Jan Courage if we had been able to stay in Holland. Here on this island, in this murky heat, I was beginning to doubt whether I had it in me to be the Dutch sailor boy, considering my refugee circumstances and Jewish family. We had fled, we had lost our home, we were weak; above all we were different. Did Jan Courage have a grandfather who bowed to the east?

I had longed for this prize, dreamed of it, worked for it. The award would prove how Dutch I was — not like the Yiddish-speaking refugees with whom I felt little kinship, like my grandparents, who were utterly different from what I wanted to be. Even my Dutch-speaking parents had been born elsewhere. Though I was a refugee, and always had to explain that we were "naturalized Dutch," I was at least Dutch enough to win a language prize.

The more I could be like other Dutch children here, the more I could leave the worry and anxiety, the unseemly insecurity of being a Jewish refugee, behind me. I remembered the bombardment near our house in Bilthoven, remembered our flight to France with its sudden panics and sudden departures. In Europe, for several years before our arrival in Curaçao in 1944, I had not been allowed to mingle with other children. We always had to move on, and I had always been urged to be careful. Feeling the tension in my parents, hearing that the time was not right for games or fun, I longed for an ordinary life, as normal a Dutch childhood as I could have outside of Holland.

In Curaçao, I made friends with a number of Dutch boys. Peter and Henny were eleven also, and Henny especially had an enviable family. His father and he were building a guitar together, something I could never imagine doing with my father. Their next project would be a sailboat. Being around them made me happy — and a little envious.

"You did this well, Manny," beamed my mother, who could smile and look serious at the same time. My father, sitting in a large chair, looked at a space above my head and spoke dreamily: "You can never go wrong with education. You boys need to study for a profession, because business people are always vulnerable in a war."

"Yes, I know," I said.

"Business people," continued my father, looking as if he were thinking this thought for the first time, "we're just maneuverers. We move things around, that's all. We buy, we sell. We're not productive. If there's a war, or if the government suddenly turns against Jews, then there is nothing we can do. But if you have a profession you can always go elsewhere, even if you have to flee your own country to do it." My father's eyes looked distant, the sort of foreign, faraway gaze he always had when he was being serious.

I did not need convincing. I did not want to be in business, nor did I like maneuvering, "turning," "shifting," as my father used to call it, translating from the Yiddish *drayhen*, turning.

"Yes, yes, that's true," I said, wanting him to stop.

"A Jew has to turn," he continued, "there is no other way. If a Jew doesn't maneuver, he is lost. Look at us during the war; the way we got our papers, the consuls we bribed, the forged documents, the borders crossed illegally, pretending we had all legal documents. How could we ever give a straight answer to any question? Where would we be now if we had done that? Dead in Auschwitz, without question."

"Max, everything you say is true," soothed my mother, "but don't upset the children now."

I could not imagine this being said in the home of any of my Dutch friends.

"Yes, of course," answered my father, "but I'm just making the point that without a little maneuvering, we could not have survived. Tell me honestly, Bertha, what could we have done without money, forging, bribing?"

"Anyway," said my mother, "Manny has won the Neerlandia Prize. He won't have any need for maneuvering."

I knew that winning a prize, looking forward to a school trip, talking about school, were trivial things when measured against bombs falling, families deported, or children ripped from their parents. I felt ashamed for thinking about having fun, but did not like being burdened by what my parents felt and by what I had experienced as a child.

So when I envied my friend's film projector, I asked my parents for one.

"You want a film projector? Why?" asked my mother, puzzled. My father had not heard.

"I do," I persisted, ever more uneasy. "I do," I said, no longer wanting it.

"What attracts you to it?" My mother seemed amused and a little disconcerted, as if I had just reverted to earliest childhood. She looked at me indulgently, the way you would at a small child who craves something foolish.

My cheeks burned, and I thought of everything my parents had gone through, and how silly it was to crave a film projector. I stammered out something.

"Well, we'll get it for you," said my mother.

After a week of playing with it, I lost interest, which revived a few years later when it helped me get the girl across the street to come into my room.

I concealed pleasure from my parents and also pain. Nothing I could feel, no bewilderment or fright, could possibly match theirs. My father's anguish about his mother and six brothers, dead in Auschwitz — their fate now finally known a year or so after the war — was overwhelming. Whatever I felt was small compared to that.

Maybe all feelings should be concealed, I thought. Dutch people always said not to be too expressive. Any emotion almost was a kind of excess.

Friday evening at my mother's parents' house: my grandfather, a small, graying man of sixty, walked into the house wearing his straw hat and worn white suit, carrying his sample case. He wiped the sweat from under his hat and swiftly put on a little skull cap, then stroked his short white beard. He kissed me solemnly, and while my grandmother went into the kitchen said to no one in particular, "Before I do anything, I just want to say a Jewish word."

He walked over to a corner table of the small dining room and faced east, the direction of the Roxy Theatre next door and Jerusalem. Barely glancing at his black prayer book, he swayed and shook and muttered almost inaudibly for half an hour, then chanted a sort of finale and sat down.

My grandfather began doing in Curaçao what he had done as a young man in the Austro-Hungarian Empire, in the early years of this century, before he settled in Holland: he sold to small retailers all over the countryside. Now on the island he was buying goods in town and driving in the scorching heat of the scrub brush countryside to the sorts of shops that were frequently nothing more than an open window in someone's house. A black face would look dreamily out of a rectangular opening flanked by tubes of toothpaste and cans of food.

To these shopkeepers, he quickly learned to speak a mixture of Yiddish, Dutch and Papiamentu, which they seemed to understand perfectly. Sometimes he sold buttons, sometimes yarn and thread. Frequently he wrote down in Yiddish what the small shopkeepers required for next time. I once read in his little notebook, "Man with porcupine beard and funny goat in front of house — wants three dozen buttons."

I enjoyed my grandfather, his good humor and warmth, and accepted his rituals, though alien to me, as dignified and good-natured. He did not force them on his family the way rabbis always tried to do, asking whether you had prayed or observed this or that rule. He was mild and gentle, and when he prayed in his dining room he shook and swayed, and kissed the prayer book when finished. He appeared happy in his rituals and afterwards looked refreshed and smiled.

Unlike my grandfather, rabbis and other religious people made me feel uncomfortable, as if I had not done enough or were doing the wrong thing. I always wanted to be out of their presence as quickly as possible. Above all, I did not like the way they insisted on the difference of Jews. They seemed intent on separating me from others, from the people I really enjoyed, the Dutch people who were living the kind of normal life I craved. The rabbis' stories of persecution and anguish filled them with a perverse pride.

At Sunday school in the little meeting house in the courtyard of the stately synagogue, Rabbi Morenos stroked his cheeks when he mentioned the martyrs, who followed a different path and listened to God. And so, naturally, they were martyred. He would stare off in the distance, his head in his fine hands: "Whether in England before the Expulsion, or in Spain during the Inquisition, they were persecuted and very few escaped with their lives."

Suddenly I thought, I was one of those who had escaped with my life. How was it possible? Most had not. Jewish history always made me sad. But Judaism also made me cross: the way rabbis explicated passages during synagogue services, the hairsplitting interpretations, the constant recourse to the sages — I found it oppressive. And then the outlandish ideas: foods that contaminated each other, meat and milk, or a fleck of yeast at Passover.

"Here, here's a spot, a mite of yeast," I said to my brother. My brother's curly mop of hair gave a shake of surprise.

155

"What are you talking about, Manny?"

"Now all the food has to be thrown away," I shouted and started lifting imaginary crates of food toward the window.

"Don't be a jackass," my brother said. "Have some respect."

"Respect," I yelled, "for what?"

"What are you getting so upset about?"

I swallowed my irritation. I did not want to be upset. But, honestly, those strange customs! Truly orthodox women shouldn't wear their own hair but had to cover it with a wig, and you could see the ugly border between their own hair and the wig, a funny webbing where the wig had been attached.

"Why do they do that, Opa?"

My grandfather said that he liked my questions and answered patiently. "So as not to provoke lust in a stranger's eye."

"But then, why not shave their hair? Why would they put a wig over it?"

"Well, you know how women are," he said mildly. "They want to look pretty."

I did not know how women were, but I wasn't persuaded by his answer: "Couldn't a stranger feel lust toward the woman with a wig?"

"Well... I'll look in a Jewish book for the answer — maybe the Talmud."

"Why would the Talmud have the answer?"

"Because the sages wrote it." He stroked his little white beard patiently.

"Sages again! I just think this is all so stupid."

"Hush, don't say such things." My grandfather looked startled. "These are the very wise Jews who lived a long time ago."

"Would those sages be wiser than our present-day sages?"

"Maybe we had some sages, but Hitler killed them. Now you're asking questions no one can answer. Some things God doesn't want us to know. Do you think anyone can really explain what happened to us in the war?"

As on other Friday evenings, I was trying to stall a moment I dreaded. We were sitting in relative darkness. "Manny," he said, "please call the kid downstairs."

"Oh, can't we wait a little longer?"

"No, it's dark now. Go."

Downstairs lived a large family, a small Venezuelan father, a large Curaçaoan mother, with an ever-larger brood. My grandfather paid their twelve-year-old boy Carlito a few coins for turning on the electric lights on Friday night. He was the "shabbos goy," who, not subject to Jewish laws, could keep the Jews from violating them. Every time Carlito saw me at school, he wiggled his index finger to remind me of that light-switching activity.

My grandmother did not wear a wig, and I never heard my grandfather complain about that. Before they had married, she declared that she wouldn't: her own hair, she said, was "good enough. And if someone objects, let them not look." My grandmother's independence of mind was legendary. "I am observant, I am a Jew through and through, but my father told me, 'Think for yourself.'" She pulled the bun of her graying hair tight, stood up very straight, and looked at us fiercely.

My grandfather always wore a white linen suit and a straw hat. His assistant and driver was a black man named Virgilio, whose lanky left arm with its silver bracelet dangled casually over the car door. On the island it was rumored that Virgilio was my grandfather's illegitimate son. Virgilio did not mind the rumor. He was phlegmatic and dutiful, with a wry sense of humor:

"If the old man really was my father, I wouldn't drive for him, now would I?" I heard him say to two young women, servant girls of the neighbors, who looked admiringly at his strong arms polishing my grandfather's gray Dodge. Esmeralda wore a pretty flowered dress and a white kerchief, her beautiful black face cheerfully smiling, while Yolanda looked on with

157

teasing eyes. We were all standing in front of my grandfather's house. They were speaking Papiamentu, which my grandfather did not understand, though I did.

"How do I know? He might exploit his son," replied one of the women.

"But wouldn't I be rich?" asked Virgilio with a broad grin, his hand deftly touching her elbow.

"Maybe you are rich but hide it like the white people." Yolanda grinned, her eyes sparkling mischievously.

"My riches are on my body."

"Let's check his money, then; he says it's on his body," said Yolanda to her friend and reached over to him, her long bare arm gliding over his shirt and patting his back pocket.

"Who said anything about money? I say my riches are here," and Virgilio made a caressing downward gesture, his fingers lightly touching his beautifully creased tan slacks.

My grandfather now came outside, wiping the inside of his hat with his handkerchief, then his forehead. He knew about this banter and never tried to inhibit it. Only when Virgilio created a little shrine to a Saint on the dashboard did he stop him, though he failed to notice when his driver fastened a Mercedes insignia onto the hood of the Dodge. Finally, my grandfather said in his half Dutch, half Yiddish, "Come, Virgilio, we have to drive to Canario."

Virgilio stood awhile to assert his independence in front of the two women, and Esmeralda started chorusing again in Papiamentu: "White people say we when they mean you... you drive to Canario is what they mean."

"Esmeralda, you're crazy. White people don't say what they mean because they don't know what they mean." Virgilio had that Curaçaoan mock-indignant look, which meant he was enjoying himself.

Yolanda pulled at her kerchief, her round, brown cheeks gleaming. "White people know what they mean but they're not going to tell you, black man."

"Well, they might not tell me, but I can read their pale faces," muttered Virgilio under his breath, looking at me, because he knew I understood Papiamentu. Carefully holding the back door open for my grandfather, he intoned, "Good-bye, ladies, may we meet again, hopefully under compromising circumstances."

I found this Curaçaoan rapid banter between men and women exciting, especially at twelve and thirteen. It gave me pleasure in a way I couldn't fathom, a thrill I did not fully understand. It had something to do with adult life. I envied the Curaçaoans, the way they could be so fluent and uninhibited and make each other laugh, but I never thought that I would have that gift. If you were not Curaçaoan, you couldn't talk like that. So it left me out. And since I could not become Curaçaoan and did not want to be Jewish, I could work toward becoming more Dutch, study the language and history. And surely I would return to the Netherlands someday, either with my parents or on my own.

I especially liked our Dutch cultural outings, which, in the aftermath of the war, benefited from visiting performers who were thought to be educational. One young Dutch woman sought to involve her whole audience in her performance and had us all recite, "Whose Dutch blood flows through our veins." Next she declaimed Resistance poems by the martyred poets of the recent war, one of them written in a cell just before the poet's execution, "Two meters long, two meters wide." She walked into the audience of the little theater in which our whole school was congregated, looking at us directly, leading us in the refrain. Then performing a Dutch classic, she wailed, "Constantine, little Constantine," the heart-rending poem of the seventeenth century poet Vondel about the death of his young son. I liked her forceful manner, her poise, and planned to imitate her at home when nobody was around. But my mood soon changed, because in the back rows a low hum of Curaçaoan voices echoed her, half-mocking, half-participatory. "Constantine," they moaned, "Constantine died, man."

She heard it but seemed unfazed, her dark bangs against her skin as cool as if she were in her own temperate setting in the Netherlands; she recited poem after poem, concluding with a recent one about poetry: "In poems you bring into breathless being/ What in the world streams by and merely fades ..." Yes, that is what I would do, though it was not clear to me what that meant. I would be a poet, a Dutch poet. Meanwhile, the participatory voices had grown louder, echoing certain words she spoke but interspersing others. "In poems, stupid, in poems. Constantine died in poems, man." Now the principal, red-faced, ended the proceedings. We got a tirade from him after the performer left, "Insolent idiots, have you no conception of how to behave in public?"

Outside, my friend Mundi was critical. "These Dutch people just speak their lines; they stand there going 'And so he said... And so I did.' We have poets too, much better ones. In the countryside. Those people sing, they chant, they dance. They're wild, they're savage, they speak magic. They're still from Africa, you know." And suddenly he climbed on a pillar in the schoolyard, and, writhing like someone possessed, he started emoting in Papiamentu.

"Watch out, Mundi. There's the School Commissioner in that black car. He's supposed to come today."

We ran into the classroom. Our teacher, knowing of the impending visit, seemed tense. His handsome, lined face looked gray. He buttoned and unbuttoned his white jacket. Under his arms, two dark sweat stains were spreading. Within minutes, the Commissioner, an old, white man with a round bald head and thick glasses, walked in. We all stood up.

The Commissioner moved slowly, clumsily to the teacher's desk and whispered at him for a while. The teacher looked startled, reverential, then whispered back questioningly.

We all sat down. Now the teacher cleared his throat portentously and announced: "As you know, the Commissioner of Education represents the Queen on this soil. At least in matters of education he represents the Queen, by way of the Minister of Education, whom he directly serves." The Commissioner looked solemn but said nothing.

"You might say he represents the Crown. At any rate, he has come here personally to inform me — as well as the other teachers — that The Hague has ordered that henceforth in the secondary schools of the Kingdom, Spanish shall be on the same level with German as the fourth required language, after Dutch, English, and French. From now on you may choose one of these two and your choice will fulfill the fourth language requirement."

The Commissioner turned to the students and looked hard at all of us. He seemed to be searching for someone. He looked at me significantly, then turned to the teacher and asked audibly enough: "Are these the refugees?"

"That boy is, yes, sir."

"One of those stateless wonders?" He scratched his beard indifferently.

"No, I think they obtained the Dutch nationality." Our teacher looked deferential but stubborn.

"Lord knows how."

"I think they got their naturalization papers in the war."

"I didn't think The Netherlands was in a position to give final papers during the war," the Commissioner said sarcastically, looking suspiciously at the teacher.

"Maybe not, sir."

"Oh well, some people always have a way of maneuvering, if you see what I mean."

"I believe I do, sir."

I felt the blood rush to my ears; "maneuvering" — it was the same words my father used. I hated to hear it from the Commissioner.

When I was fourteen, my grandfather had the first of a series of heart attacks. His angina symptoms had started in the Spanish prison where he had spent the winter of 1942. Now, seven years later, his weak heart was beginning to give out. He knew his days were numbered, and he spent even more hours praying at the little table that faced east in the dining room. Ever more frequently he interrupted himself to "say a few Jewish words." After one of his prayers he sat my brother and me down at the large square dining table and tugged nervously at his white beard. His face looked haggard but his eyes seemed steady, determined.

"You boys should never forget you are Jews."

Neither my brother nor I spoke.

"Always try to lead a Jewish life," he continued, plucking at his little white beard. "Above all, marry a Jewish girl."

I felt sad, but his words had little to do with me. I did not want to lead a Jewish life.

"And don't ever forget," he said, still stroking his cheek before he half rose from the table to kiss us good-bye, "don't ever forget what happened to our people in Europe."

It was the only one of his last wishes I heeded whole-heartedly.

During the next several months of his sickness, he never referred to that conversation again, and I barely thought about it. I did not doubt that he would die soon, but it was hard to imagine his absence from that house with the wide-open windows, where he had stood so often facing the east, while the dim sounds of the movie house next door wafted into the room. Sometimes during his prayers I thought I could hear my classmates laughing in the movie, but I never felt the desire to be with them, except once when a rare Dutch movie had come to the island.

My second Neerlandia Prize came in 1949, three years after the first, when I had just turned fourteen. It no longer had the significance for me of the first one, but I now saw it in more practical terms as a way to get to a Dutch university. The ceremony was as elaborate as ever, and the certificate looked as florid as before. Some things had changed in Curaçao in three years: rumors of autonomy and even independence were in the air. With anti-colonialism sweeping the world, Holland was beginning to lose its hold on the island. The Commissioner of Education had returned to the Netherlands, and no successor was sent.

At the prize ceremony, the principal sounded defensive: "Our language is the key to order and stability. Even aside from the fact that Dutch is admirably suited for literature, for science, for knowledge, it is also the language of precision and order. European tongues possess that characteristic, but Dutch is a primary example of reason in words, rationality made accessible. And may I add: a good thing Dutch is taught so well here. Lord knows what would happen on the island if we were not present to impose the language and the good sense that goes with it."

I was beginning to hear how stuffy he sounded, so earnest, so full of "white piss," as my Curaçaoan friends said about the Dutch, mimicking their arid sonority and well-chosen clichés. But I still admired them, so confident and poised, while the Curaçaoans who mocked them seemed flamboyant and unserious, and the Jews battered, melancholy, and always, always sad.

I continued to study Dutch and read as many Dutch books as I could find and continued to dream of some day returning to the Netherlands.

Shortly after my grandfather's death, the Neerlandia Prizes were discontinued. With the island's autonomy looming, the officials decided that a prize for Dutch could no longer be justified. Some day Dutch in the schools would be replaced by Papiamentu. When colonialism ended, there would be no reason to continue the colonial power's language. It was the beginning of the slow end of the Dutch language on the island, though my own passion for what was not quite my mother tongue persisted for years to come.

Chapter 10. The Dance School

In 1948 when I was thirteen, a ballroom dancing champion from The Netherlands came to the island and in a flurry of publicity opened a dance school. Articles in the newspaper proclaimed this yet another bounty for the colony from the mother country, which now after the disastrous war years was beginning to find itself again. First came the new DC4 from KLM inaugurating a direct route between Amsterdam and Curaçao, then the new brewery — and now the "Dance School De Beer" for children. Within a few weeks, virtually every child I knew was enrolled in this school. There were many different classes for children, and they seemed to meet all the time.

Frank de Beer was a trim, florid-looking man in his thirties. Like many Dutchmen, he was flax blond and a bit pink from the new-found sunshine of the tropics. An animated, small man, he walked, moved, and gestured like a dancer. Every step he took was either long and deliberate or short and deliberate. He insisted that in each dance all the boys should ask all the girls to dance. When we had approached within three feet of the girl of our choice, we were supposed to bow deeply, and ask, "May I have this dance with you?"

The rule was that the girl was not permitted to decline, which still did not mean that the boys could dance with only the girls they wanted. If someone else approached her first, just a second before you did, this then required a swift move to another girl who had not been approached yet, also with a bow. Mr. de Beer explained that such jockeying shouldn't cause embarrassment. "If the young lady of your choice is no longer available, you walk firmly, decisively, gracefully, up to another young lady." Despite his pleas for dignity, there was a certain amount of running to the girls several boys wanted to dance with. Some boys would have to bow three or four times before they were able to find a partner. The girls had to nod and smile but not bow back.

I looked forward to the afternoons in that reddish-colored house with its gingerbread trim, the two white-washed rooms with their parquet floors giving onto a breezy veranda. And it felt good to do something with girls without having to talk to them a lot. Mr. de Beer would play a record, and you had to decide quickly what dance was appropriate, make your deep bow, and start dancing. Despite the pressure of these decisions, I liked the school and its atmosphere. It was serious business, but we learned to dance.

Mr. de Beer's favorite dance was the Bote, which he pronounced in his Dutch way *boatay*. Sinuously you stood on one leg, leaned all your weight on that side, and then slowly, sensuously leaned on the other. The aim was to create a flawlessly fluid hip motion, Mr. de Beer explained. He said it was the basic Latin American step and that all the others, the rhumba, the guaracha, the mambo, the merengue, were all based on it.

"Mr. de Beer," said my friend Mundi, a superb dancer, "I've never even heard of the Bote." Brash though he sounded, Mundi was actually being more deferential than usual.

'Well," said Mr. de Beer mildly, "we learned it in Amsterdam, and it took us right to the championship. Latin American dancing is very big in Holland right now."

He demonstrated the step all over again. "Gently, smoothly, this must be lithe and controlled," said Mr. de Beer to our class of twelve- and thirteen-year-olds, his ever cheerful voice commanding attention. When the record stopped and we were done with our partner, he made us bow again from the waist and escort the girl all the way to the exact spot against the wall where she had been standing. Another bow and, "Thank you very much for this dance."

Mr. de Beer's brother Nico, light on his feet, roamed the hall, smiling, encouraging, cajoling. Taller than his brother, he had the same flaxen hair but a heavier face. Nico was a stickler for posture. When the brothers introduced a new dance, they would often dance side by side, next to each other, one more supple than the other, and both extend their left arm to hold an imaginary woman with their right. Sometimes Mr. de Beer would whirl around his assistant, Nellie, a redhead with an upturned nose, her colorful skirts twirling.

Curaçao was a dancing culture, but this was something new. The Curaçaoans did not need to be taught to dance, but of course many Curaçaoan children enrolled in the school. Mr. de Beer was lavish in his praise for their talents but never condescending to the others. He especially stressed the gravity of these occasions, their dignity. And he enjoyed having us all watched by dozens of leisurely staring Curaçaoans, men, women, children, all of them peering through the louvered porches around the veranda and occasionally whispering comments through the shutters. Mr. de Beer, fresh from Holland, could not understand some of these hissed remarks in Papiamentu from staring boys as the girls swished by, such as, "What delicious legs, what sweet thighs, what a luscious little ass," accompanied by a strange slurping sound made with indrawn breath.

Though there were not many Jewish children in Curaçao, they tended to be segregated from each other. The newcomers, to which I belonged, were the smallest group. More numerous were the Jewish kids born in Curaçao — children of Polish immigrants who had arrived in the thirties. Then there were Curaçaoan Jews, long-time residents, descendants of Spanish and Portuguese Jews. Most of them belonged to the Jewish Club, but I never felt at home there: they found my background odd and unsettling. Nor did I want to meet with their incomprehension. But here in Mr. De Beer's school, we all came together.

One of my dance partners, Annette, was in the category of the just-arrived. She had a rather resolutely Dutch manner, brisk and purposeful, and was a laconic dancer, her pigtails flipping briskly from side to side. Her father, Dr. Goedhart, picked us up in the afternoon. We envied him because as a doctor he was not bound by rationing and received new tires for his car, whereas three years after the end of the war we still drove on tires that had been inserted one into the other. Dr Goedhart was a kind, small man who somehow never pushed his car seat forward, so he could hardly see where he was driving. If he drove by, you saw just a hat reaching for the steering wheel. Despite his innumerable kindnesses for the island community, he was made fun of for his chicken phobia. There had been reports of Dr. Goedhart freezing in his tracks as he approached the house of one of his patients who had a chicken coop. When he walked through downtown, sly Curaçaoans made clucking noises to each other.

Annette was bold and took after her mother, a tall, aristocratic beauty, with a distant manner. Unlike her father, she was not going to be led, not on the dance floor or anywhere else. I tried but she insisted on moving her arms up and down and pulling me this way and that. Once in a while, the proximity of her body persuaded me that I liked her, and I started saying whispery things to her about the dance; but she gave me a hard, silent stare. She appeared to dislike all weakness.

"How can a doctor be afraid of chickens?" my father asked.

"Some people are afraid of snakes," said my mother, "why not chickens?"

"Are there snakes in Curaçao?" wondered my father.

Every Saturday night I practiced all my steps. I had the radio on and danced the Bote as if I had a partner, with my left hand

167

out and my right arm encircling her waist. I sang with Radio Curaçao, *"Aunque ya tú no me quieres, yo sé que algun día, tú me darás toda la felicidad,"* "Though you do not love me yet, I know that someday you will give me all happiness." That is what the future, and marriage, would bring, a life of total happiness. It would be just as good as the distant past in Holland before the war spoiled everything and replaced pleasure with panic and happiness with dread. I could see the little house in Bilthoven, and in front of it my playmates, a round-headed boy and a girl who could not pronounce the name of the dog they had recently taken over from the Dutch people in whose house they lived. The family had come from France to Holland because they thought Holland would remain neutral. I helped her say 'Hector,' which she pronounced "Ector."

Both children were lost in the war, my parents said, using the word I found so odd, lost, as if they had been endlessly misplaced, as if they could still return some day when in fact they had been incinerated. In that little park across the street we rode our bicycles, the girl always looking over her shoulder at me, as if seeking approval or guidance. She always rode tentatively, questioningly. A music-induced wave of yearning for that idyllic time broke over me, and for a moment I reeled, the mist coming unstoppably to my eyes. My future bride would understand this in me, would appreciate it, love it. How could it be otherwise?

I continued dancing, almost grimly, concentrating now on how I would create that happiness, wondering which one of my classmates would be part of the future I fashioned. Slowly the pictures of the little children and the barking dog suffocated by the burning cloud dimmed, and I saw instead myself and someone else, the two of us as adults, dancing, our arms around each other, the way it sometimes happened in American movies, especially when the evening breeze was said to caress the trees, tenderly.

My brother was studying in our bedroom. My parents were out. I had the living room to myself, its overstuffed chairs lately acquired by my mother, who got no aesthetic appreciation from her male household. It was time for "Radio Curaçao Presents... By Special Request," and I listened for the song that invariably emerged, requested by "Wilfried for Mary," or "Chrisma for Enrico," or "Johannes for Carlita," a haunting French song that had first come out in 1938 and was popular again in the forties, "*J'Attendrai*," 'I Will Wait,' sung by Tino Rossi, the divine Corsican, the other Corsican, as he was known in France. My imaginary partner and I were still; we held hands and looked at each other with longing and joy. Such happiness wiped everything else out; that's what happiness was for. "Yes," I said to her, "I will wait for you, all the days of my life."

"*J'attendrai*" was never part of the repertory of the dance school. Mr. de Beer was not fond of the foxtrot and perhaps wanted to discourage close dancing.

Soon Gloria started coming to our class. She was born in Curaçao a few years after her parents arrived from Poland in the early thirties. Auburn-haired, small, vivacious, Gloria knew all the dances but was frustrated that Mr. de Beer didn't teach the Jitterbug. She wanted to be an American bobby-soxer and go to proms and sock-hops. At fourteen, Gloria had seen all the American movies that came to Curaçao and modeled herself on Esther Williams, though she was a bit round for the part. Her fondness for things American was matched by her patience: she had once read the English-Dutch dictionary from cover to cover. We traded movie magazines and she swooned over John Derek. In the Jewish Club, she sat at the piano and sang again and again, "I Love You — For Sentimental Reasons... I hope you do believe me; I'm giving you my heart." Through the amazing immediacy of the years I can still hear her accent, "Santimantal reasons..."

Painfully aware of being a year younger than Gloria and not having seen many American movies, I copied out the words she sang. The only way I could think to approach her was to have her check the English. "Not 'santimantal meeting,'" she said irritably. "'Santimantal reasons.'"

After dance school, my friend Alex was always hungry. He was born in Curaçao of Turkish-Jewish immigrants, so both his Dutch and his manners were exotic to me. His brother was caught in the local brothel and his picture appeared in the newspaper. Alex's mother had packed an enormous sandwich, which he squashed between his two large hands, sometimes even leaning on it with all his weight. Then he scooped half of it into his mouth and chomped vigorously while talking.

"These girls drive me crazy," he said, his round face sweaty from the exertion. "They won't rub up against me."

"Why should they?"

"Because it's dancing, *pendejo*, don't you know that's what dancing is for?"

"That's not what Mr. de Beer thinks," I said pedantically.

"Who are you, Wolf, some kind of fool? You're thirteen years old now. De Beer doesn't know what passion we South Americans have. Have you ever seen a bolero where the man and the woman stand so far apart from each other as we do in that school?"

Alex had a point, but I was reluctant to accept it. "The de Beers know a lot about dancing," I said.

"And you know nothing about girls. Girls are just as hot as we are." His round face was now glowing, and his short hair seemed to stand up on end, making him look younger than thirteen.

"Do you really think so?"

"I know so," said Alex expansively, his hand flattening his cheek bulging with food. "You know, I'm not going to marry a Jewish woman."

"You're not? Why not?" I asked.

"So people will know that a Jew can make a Gentile woman happy, that's why. But first I'm going to Germany, to Berlin, to study gynecology."

"Gynecology?"

"Yes, because I can never get enough of women."

"And why Germany?" I asked, this time genuinely shocked by Alex.

"I'm going to fuck all the women there. And they'll be grateful."

"Why does it have to be there?"

"It has to be there. There first. Then I'll fuck my way through the rest of the world. Wolf, you're growing up now. From now on, no more games, no more kid stuff. There are more important things: in future it has to be all fucking." He used the Papiamentu word for cleaning, one of the many that described sex. "*Limpia.*"

"Alex, why in Germany?" I repeated.

"We begin there," he said, not answering the question. "Promise me, don't ever say 'Oy' again, don't ever listen to anyone who says that. Never, never again, never, never."

I didn't even know that with his Sephardic background Alex knew the Yiddish word "Oy" and was about to ask him, but Alex never really answered a question. He was a born ranter. "You know how to be Jewish?" he said, grabbing my collar violently. He still smelled of the sandwich he had just devoured.

"I know," I said, "*limpia, limpia.*"

"Yes, and go to Israel. Get Middle-Eastern girls."

It was not to be. I didn't go to Germany or to Israel. Neither did Alex. He went to South America and somehow got into the furniture business in Colombia. Years later I heard he was in jail in Peru.

The latest arrivals were the Franshorsts. In their forties now, they had married right after the war. They had met in Bergen-Belsen, and even at thirteen I could instantly tell that their survival had something to do with an indestructible constitution. Mr. Franshorst had been a butcher, Mrs. Franshorst a sales lady in a department store. They were both red in the face from the tropical sun beating down on their pale skin.

For some reason, my mother adopted them. She spent every other evening with the Franshorsts and gave Mrs. Franshorst blouses and sundresses from our textile store, and they laughed when Mrs. Franshorst tried them on. My mother also doted on their child, a beautiful dark-haired boy of three. Often she would smile at them because the Franshorsts were not very genteel, saying things like "I eat like ten horses." They were not blunt exactly but blurted out what came into their minds, as if they had not been in polite company much.

The Franshorsts adored their child. Mr. Franshorst would move his large horse face close to the child's belly and say, "Eddie, Eddie, the hippopotamus is nuzzling you," and the child pealed with laughter. Mrs. Franshorst gazed at Eddie with awe and wonder.

I saw Eddie several times, and, while I enjoyed the child, I felt a growing unease in his presence. A fist of foreboding squeezed my heart the more I saw him. What if this child were stolen, killed, or lost, the way so many children had been just a few years ago in Europe? He was too precious, too much in jeopardy. "People should always have more than just one child, but the Franshorsts were not able to have more," my mother explained, with that serious, melancholy look she could get. I changed the subject, pretending that I did not know what she meant, and that I wasn't interested anyway; but I knew exactly what she meant: this child was a fragile entity, a beautiful being easily removed, the Franshorsts' sole chance for happiness. I was all too aware of how dangerous and threatening the world was and could not enjoy the Franshorsts' pleasure in their child. I was too afraid.

Half conscious of turning away from such thoughts, I became fanatically curious about the future, eager for the present. In back of me was a dank, heavy mist; before me, an airy plain I wanted to cross. At the far edge of this plain stood a beckoning row of trees. What would lie beyond them? I wanted to hurry to those views, those fields and skies. Perhaps I would settle in a small town against a green hillside, with music, laughter and the ever-palpable presence of love. Suddenly, on this plain stood Melda, a girl in one of my classes, whose presence distracted and excited me. I now lived in my crush on her.

Melda was thirteen, a clear-featured, brown-skinned beauty with lovely black hair, and a small, thin nose. Her kind of coloring was most desirable on the island, not pale, not black, but glowing-brown, honey-gold. She looked directly at me in dance school and one afternoon whispered, "Ask me to dance." The large white room seemed to shimmer, and I was dizzy with wanting to, dizzy with her glamorous presence. Her father represented the island of St. Martin in the local Parliament. We danced the Bote under Mr. de Beer's watchful eyes, and she said over the music, "I like talking to you because you have so much sense."

I wished she could see me in a more romantic light but I didn't know how to bring that about. Maybe if I stayed her friend, she would someday give me "all happiness."

When she spread out her arms and sang, to no one in particular, "I want to go on a ship and be towed out to sea," I did not say anything. I felt that if I said I would tow her out to sea, I would somehow have to make good on that promise, would really have to try and do it. So I said nothing.

My classmate Carlo was not so cautious or so literal-minded. He picked it right up. "Let's build that ship together."

"Sure," said Melda with her hand on her pretty hip, "Let's see you do that."

"I've got the wood all ready," said Carlo, making an unsubtle pun on *palo*, Papiamentu for both 'wood' and 'prick.'

"You have the wood, but do you have the hammer?"

"My hammer is ready at a moment's notice."

"Let's see if you have the muscle-power." And she kneaded the biceps on his upper arm and rolled his short sleeves up higher.

Carlo let her feel all she wanted. Soon they became a couple.

Disappointed, dejected, I could not conceive of how I could do without Melda. I continued to think about her, to picture her, to imagine her speaking to me. She saw I was wounded but was too happy to think about it. We still talked, and I hinted at my infatuation. The talk lessened. Soon I decided to pursue Annette instead.

The dance school lasted almost a year. Then something odd happened. The daily Dutch newspaper ran a series of articles on Mr. de Beer. The headline on the first article proclaimed, "Dancing 'Champion' Really In 37th Place." There had been 38 contestants in the competition Mr. de Beer claimed to have won. This information was repeated in subsequent articles, and each time it sounded more ominous. At first Mr. de Beer denied it but then there were more serious charges.

It seemed that right after the war, the de Beers had a dancing school in the little town of Amersfoort and then fled with all the cash to another town. How this could have remained undetected for any length of time in a tiny country like Holland was never clear, and the charges struck me — an avid newspaper reader even at thirteen — as strangely vague. Whose cash did they take? What is it they made off with? It then developed that the editor of the paper, the father of one of my classmates, had in the early days of the school withdrawn his child and demanded a full refund, against the rules. At least so Mr. de Beer charged. But the damage was done. Two months later the de Beers left Curaçao for the Netherlands. I don't remember many other examples of investigative reporting in Curaçao. And no other dance school was started while I lived on the island.

I kept missing the school for years. I regretted losing it as much as I now regret not knowing what Melda looks like or to whom Gloria is married. Most of all, the school was not only a place to dance but a refuge from thoughts that jarred and feelings that could overwhelm a sunny day with darkness. And I continued to need such a refuge because a few months after their arrival, the Franshorsts' little son Eddie died of amoebic dysentery.

After that, it was especially difficult not to think about the Franshorsts. But I succeeded better in those days than I do now, when I sometimes can't get them out of my mind at all.

Chapter 11. Emile and Yahnchi

Sometime in the late forties, when my family was beginning to feel settled on Curaçao, our modest import-export business began to thrive. Suddenly there were more employees, and one of them started calling himself my father's chauffeur. He wasn't exactly: he was just a young man who carried things in and around the business and occasionally drove the family car; but one day he appeared in a khaki uniform and then bought himself a rather military-looking cap, and from then on Emile was our chauffeur.

He was tall, elegant, very dark-skinned. Though thin and unathletic, he moved with lithe self-assurance and grace. When he laughed, which was often, he would take off and wipe his rimless glasses and then quickly put them back on his fine oval face. Sometimes he drove my brother and me to school in downtown Willemstad, and he was quiet and thoughtful. He preferred us in the back of the polished '48 Plymouth.

Occasionally, when our family was having lunch, he would use the phone in the living room to call his latest girlfriend. I would hear a murmuring, happy sound, and when I could make out the words, they were inevitably intimate and reassuring. I could glimpse him through the doorway speaking into the receiver, quiet and self-contained, the words fluent and sure. *"Tin cos cu bo'n po bisa na palabra,"* I heard him say insistently, caressingly, in Papiamentu. "There are things that just can't be said in words." But clearly he thought everything could.

Words, music, dance — they were all over the island. Talk for talk's sake, the pleasure of it, people dancing out the words, gesturing to each other across the streets, from house to house; but Emile was somehow distinct from the other talkers, more urbane and suave. Nor was this exactly what the Curaçaoans called *pleita*, pleading, the language of courtship and sweet talk. That was more overt, more strenuous, with a desire to overpower; you told the woman that since you had seen her eyes you had been unable to see anything else, that you were in distress because of her, because of the way she made you feel. Few women would allow themselves to be courted without this undulating, rapturous language. The man's pleading was the essential prelude to her giving in and surely as great a pleasure as the aftermath, possibly for both. But Emile's brand of it was more polished and subtle.

As were his other gestures. When he drove the car on a narrow street in the old colonial town, its steep-gabled houses looking like a jaunty, sun-crazed Amsterdam — with any number of streets barely broad enough for one-way traffic — and the driver in back of us started honking, he would not get out of the car and start arguing with the other driver; much more likely he would slow down a little more and with his left arm and hands make a languorous overflying gesture, so that the impatient driver would know that he could only pass by soaring over our heads.

At about the same time, we had a servant girl, who like many of the servants in Curaçao came from one of the poor English-speaking islands. Helen was from St. Kitts and lived in a small room with her own entrance in the back of our house. She was young, talkative, and homesick, her plump body occasionally growing still and dreamy. She and Emile were friends; he treated her cordially, almost paternally, though there was a certain banter between them; but her heart belonged to another English-speaking West Indian, a serious, tough-looking electrician who came around on weekends. When she became pregnant, we all expected them to marry, but to my mother's somewhat anxious inquiry, she replied, smiling, "*Mevrouw*, my veil isn't ready yet." My parents in their own mild way repeated this to some of their Dutch friends, who thought the story was typical of the "mentality" of the West Indians and passed it on to their friends, who no doubt gave it the sort of hearty, raucous laugh I would hear in the hot, tropical evenings, from the porches and balconies where tall red-faced men and sturdy blonde women drank whisky-sodas brought by their servants from Nevis and Montserrat, from St Kitts and Trinidad.

I see now, and I think I vaguely thought then, that her answer was a sly put-down, that there might be a certain amount of black laughter about this retort on other balconies and porches. On the other hand, the subject of marriage was serious enough for Helen to one day drink half a bottle of Lysol, from which she recovered only because my mother rushed her to the hospital. The police in those paternalistic days quickly found the young man, and shortly after they were married.

Not entirely a happy ending, because he soon hired on to a large freighter and was never heard from again.

Now it was Yahnchi who came to be noticed. He too had worked in the business for some time, but he was no Emile, who through sheer force of personality had risen to a kind of prominence; Yahnchi was a *loopjongen*, an errand boy, the lowest in the office hierarchy. He didn't exactly run errands, he walked them, quietly, slowly, his stocky short body concentrated in effort. *Loopjongen*, a Dutch word that had been assimilated into Papiamentu, was always pronounced with a certain derision, or that's how it sounded to native Dutch speakers who could never quite get used to Curaçaoans pronouncing their language, with its accents always in the "wrong" place, somehow turning Dutch into something no Northern ear should have to endure.

My father had recognized that this boy (he was seventeen at the time) had possibilities. I was only three years younger than

Yahnchi, but I could see both the eager child in his face and the resigned old man. His brown eyes would twinkle and then grow dull. Yahnchi did not have initiative, but he was steady, faithful and liked hearing my father say things, such as, "In our business, we don't deal with luxury items, like at Carvo's." I heard him repeat this in Papiamentu to other young boys and even to some girls who came around looking for work. "These are the *tripulantes* coming," my father would say, smiling at his own use of the Spanish word for crew, as sudden hordes of South American seamen came to do business. Emile would be standing serenely on the street, slyly eyeing a switching skirt; but Yahnchi was with my father, in back of his office, facing formidable rows of shelves, heavy with shirts, loaded with underwear, for men, for women, for children, for giants, for dwarfs, and echo, "Yes, these are good for the *tripulantes*."

Someone, somewhere, decided that Yahnchi and Helen should be together, in what I see now as a last gasp effort at colonial politics on the personal level. The large nations had to determine what was best for the smaller ones. Order and stability had to be maintained. The unity of the household had to be ensured. If they married, Helen would then be able to stay on the island as a permanent resident, Yahnchi would have a mate. He was a far cry from the handsome electrician, but he was steady and would be an adequate provider. A divorce from the electrician could be easily arranged. Alas, it didn't work out that way: Helen and her little daughter returned to her island, while Yahnchi soon after married a local girl, who in due course bore him eight children.

Emile had kept aloof from the situation. I heard him say that Yahnchi was a sorry figure, who didn't know the first thing about life or women and certainly should never have married so young; but he continued to treat Yahnchi courteously, warmly. He himself had a new woman in his life, a tall Aruban beauty with a reputation for haughtiness. Marriage, he said, was out of the question, but this was serious, the big event. Emile wooed her on the phone and I heard him saying in the early days of their affair that "only experience can make a man savor fully someone so different, so precious." Emile never stopped wooing after he had won his women. The calls continued: it was the time of the great popularity of *"Bésame Mucho,"* and he and she played on the theme of *"Como si fuera esta noche la última vez"* — 'as if tonight were the last night' — though he told her it was always as if they kissed for the first time. Unfortunately, it was also during the height of the great popularity of *"Perfidia,"* and he said to me he would be devastated if she took up with another man. When she did — with a handsome Arab-Curaçaoan named Ricardo Fuad Ramirez whom everybody called Calypso, because at fourteen he had been sent to boarding school in Trinidad for a few years to mend his hell-raising ways — there were no more phone calls.

It was the only time I saw him lose his cool serenity. He said he might go out to sea but felt it would take him longer to forget his pain if he could not meet new women. His soothing voice almost ceased; he grew somber, and his ever-quiet manner now became motionless, frozen. He exchanged his chauffeur's uniform for ordinary street clothes, as if returning to civilian life. When he spoke at all, he was restless, fitful, impatient; the island, he said, was a prison, the islanders foolish and simple and the Dutch people incapable of living.

He donned his uniform one more time, a few months later when he drove me on my first date. He told me that it was an important occasion and should be treated seriously. He hoped I was excited. Dating was not done American-style on the island: boys and girls were not trusted alone together. On the other hand, chaperoning, as it was still practiced in Venezuela on the nearby mainland of South America, was also growing less common. Either we met each other in secrecy or we went out semi-publicly, but never were we left alone.

I was now almost fifteen. Our high-school dances were held at an elegant club, a converted old plantation house, one of many that dotted the island. Parents drove their children, chauffeurs too were everywhere, taxis arrived ceaselessly; for this occasion, nobody, not even the poor, came by bus. Emile, somewhat restored to good spirits, joined the other chauffeurs. All stood watching.

The principal, a stiff, gray Dutchman, was incongruously fond of school dances, but he insisted that they always proceed the same way. They would begin with a Polonaise, which had to be tinkled out on a piano, barely audible here in the lush garden of Club Chobolobo. With the utmost gravity he took the arm of his tired-looking wife, and the two of them marched at the head of the procession, followed by the teachers, and then the student couples. Everyone had to join in the procession. We, Curaçaoans and Dutch, natives and colonialists, residents and refugees, black, brown, white, all adhered to the ritual, and walked gravely, reverently, through the gardens, through the dance floor, through the parking lot in front of the old plantation house. All the parents and chauffeurs applauded, and Emile, looking directly at me, gave an impish smile. My date was my dance-school partner Annette, a shy, dark Dutch girl wearing pig-tails and high heels, who said almost nothing all evening and barely smiled even when someone else came over to ask her to dance.

After this procession, the principal always decreed that the band play a Viennese waltz, which in turn was followed by a fox-trot. His white mane flying, his red face cracking, his feet stamping, he seemed to be doing a polka — and his wife looked in pain. But he was happy; he had imposed a design, an order, a pattern on these dances, and we never mocked him for it. However clumsily, he was in his way an aesthete.

The ritualistic part of the evening over, he lost interest, and the band played the mambo, the guaracha, the bolero, all those dances that the Curaçaoans did without even sweating, while the Dutch boys and girls were almost instantly and very visibly soaked through in the moist tropical night. Almost no one missed these dances. The future director of the bank, a handsome, heavy-set boy, danced with a Spanish beauty, his pelvic thrust both unabashedly macho and yet somehow mincing. A weird, constantly chewing fellow — nicknamed Cheetah — did the rumba with an angular, sweating Dutch blonde. She had just arrived from The Hague and looked incredulous. Many years later Cheetah would set the radio station on fire. A hoydenish, handsome Curaçaoan, named Inocencia, later to become Miss Antilles, was embracing a tubercular-looking waif. Even the class gay, a strapping, tall, red-haired fellow who delighted in theatrically and ironically calling out, "Oh, sir, I'm present," whenever the roll was called and everybody else merely said "Yes" or "Here," was dancing rakishly with a cheerful-looking, bespectacled Chinese girl, who would become a famous cancer-researcher in the Netherlands.

Emile was watching me from the other side of the shrubbery, encouraging me, smiling approvingly when I changed partners. I wanted very much to please him but did not quite know what I should be saying to these girls. Sometimes Emile seemed to smile broadly, approvingly. I tried to make small talk to Annette. My somewhat stilted remarks and observations were answered with a simple "Yes" or "No." Suddenly, inappropriately, I murmured, "Being here with you is something I have longed for." She looked cross and turned away, her pigtails flipping hard. If she had said something in response, however bland, I would have started believing my own words.

I fell silent and fantasized about someone who looked at me raptly. Surely the future would be kind. We danced in heavy silence, Emile still looking, and I now embarrassed. I felt I could be much freer if I were somehow anonymous. I was happy to think that elsewhere there would be no staring parents or over-observant chauffeurs. I longed to dance right into one of those American movies where even high school kids danced cheek to cheek.

The principal left first, as he always did. He saw himself less as host than as guest of honor. Next, the teachers left. The parents and chauffeurs outside too retreated; they would come back later to pick us up. But nothing changed with the authority figures gone: no rowdiness, no necking, just the continuous, strenuous dancing. At about midnight, some small urchins from the shacks surrounding the Club started mimicking the dancers in the parking area, but they got carried away by their art and ended up dancing seriously. Then the band packed up and it was over.

Soon after this event, Emile left my father's employ. In Curaçao, when somebody switched jobs, it would look to all outsiders the way a couple splitting up often looks to us now. First there is a period of estrangement, which only the parties involved may know about. Suddenly, if you haven't watched them too closely, you see them with someone new, and not too long thereafter they have reengaged themselves, recommitted themselves to another. A dance of realigning and recoupling takes place. There are slow changes, sudden reappearances — and then everything is as before, though not quite. And the reasons for this may well be the same: the circumstances are limited, the opportunities finite; only a kind of reshuffling is ultimately ever possible.

So Emile was now seen in front of Credenza and Winkler, Inc., the distinguished jewelry store that advertised in The New Yorker. He wore a white uniform with yellow braids, and his responsibilities were probably much as they were for us. I talked to him one early morning, and he was friendly but distant. He said that he was saving up money to go to America or Japan, because there "men did not talk to their women" and he thought he would stand out and be valued. He always chose his words carefully, and that's what he said, valued. But he needed money, which this new job would not provide. That was a misfortune, he sighed. Not long after this conversation I heard that he had been arrested for selling a small amount of what in that those days were called stupifiers, that is to say, narcotics.

And now, Yahnchi took over in my father's business; he was no longer loopjongen, errand boy; now he was driving the car, slowly, carefully, as was Yahnchi's way. In this too he was remarkably like my father, who prided himself on being cautious, painstaking and methodical, but who appeared to others as slow of speech and movement and overly deliberate. Long after I left the island to go to college in the United States, Yahnchi continued as my father's chauffeur. He never wore a uniform, and he didn't spend much time looking after the car, but he was a reliable and comfortable presence in the business and almost a companion to my father, who, as everyone on the island said, "treated Yahnchi like a son." And when my father retired many years later, he gave Yahnchi the old, still very elegant Plymouth that Emile had spent so much time polishing.

Chapter 12. 1948

During the late forties, in the beginning of the Cold War, my father was once again making escape plans. "You need a country to jump to, if you have to. You just can't rely on any place remaining good."

Much to my regret, my parents were reluctant to return to Europe. Life in Curaçao was temporary, of course, but Europe seemed too dangerous with another world war between the U.S. and Russia almost inevitable. Ever since we fled Holland, I wanted to return there and resume the life the war had stopped.

Before the war, in 1940 in Holland, we had a visa for Bolivia and Peru, but my father hesitated. "What will we do there?" I was five years old, but he showed me both Peru and Bolivia on the wall map of our dining room in Bilthoven, then checked the annual rainfall in an atlas and was appalled by how dry it was. He continued to worry about the wisdom of this move, mulling it over, but when the Germans invaded Holland in May of 1940, it was too late to go anywhere and we were trapped. Never again would he make this mistake. And never again would he feel secure. The war had proved that all security was an illusion. Now, after the war, there was still no reason for complacency. "You've got to have a country in reserve."

Wanting to be somewhere else was always approved of in my family. You would not willingly leave a really good country, like the U.S., unless things turned bad for the Jews, but since most countries were not good, you couldn't be blamed for wanting to be elsewhere. But just wanting *things* was a different matter. Yes, money to help you remain safe, maybe a good house; but to actually want possessions was a bit foolish. We Jews should not be enamored of our possessions; we did not have the security to hold on to them or the comfort to enjoy them. As to hobbies, they were good to have, but Jews could not have the peace of mind to take pleasure in them.

On this Caribbean island where we had lived since 1944, when the war still raged in Europe, we were safe, but my parents were acutely conscious of preparing an escape if another one was needed, of procuring "papers" to go elsewhere, of trying to get the necessary documents, whether for flight or the more mundane reasons of making a living — work permits for the island, a genuine Dutch naturalization for all of us instead of the provisional naturalization papers we had during the war. Documents and papers were an important part of our daily conversation — visas for safe places, papers for good countries, countries friendly to Jews. The stories about those who did not have luck or papers, who had remained behind, echoed through our house. The Romeels, Mr. Remak's family, my father's brothers — what became of them?

"You realize," said my father, pacing through the house, studying his hands, holding them up against the harsh electric light in our living room. "No one will ever come back. No one."

"Yes, that's so…"

He looked at me without seeing me. "But do you know what that means? That means no one, no one."

I knew all too well. I never wanted to talk about the ones left behind, those who were "lost," who had "disappeared," or "never came back," but I often thought about them as well as our own escape. It seemed improbable. How is it we had survived?

He continued, "Therefore it's always a good idea to have one country in reserve, one place to flee to."

"Let's look at the atlas," I said eagerly. I liked the prospect of travel and adventure but did not want to dwell on his reasons for moving. And if we could not go back to Europe, then I would settle for a life of restless movement. I wanted to go anywhere less Caribbean and more European, less hot, less confining, more in accordance with my childhood memories of Holland; and if I found such a place, perhaps that could be the country from which I would not have to escape?

In 1948, my father took me along, as his interpreter, to the Dominican Republic, to see if we could get "the requisite papers" to settle there. He contacted some Jewish refugees, who visited us in our hotel in Ciudad Trujillo, the capital. In the garden of our hotel near the city's Colonial Zone, the adults spoke in German, while two teenage girls and I talked to each other in English and Spanish. Among the huge, potted plants in the hotel garden, I looked anxiously at my father. Usually it was my mother who handled new acquaintances, but my father was holding his own: the conversation seemed animated and I could make out words like "safety" and "government" and "security." The local family had fled Germany just before the war, and the adults talked in an occasionally conspiratorial, whispery manner.

Their reports, said my father later, as if he were issuing a bulletin, were "not negative." He was "cautiously hopeful." But his mood changed when we took a small bus into the mountains and, along with other glum-looking passengers, had to show our papers every thirty kilometers at police checkpoints. My father had not realized what even at thirteen I knew: that in the Dominican Republic a monstrous dictatorship prevailed. On the radio at home in Curaçao, I had heard the Dominican announcers proclaim after each program, "In the year of the Benefactor, Our Great Leader Trujillo."

Which of the two benefactors was that, the dictator Rafael or his brother Hector, who was announced on Dominican Radio as being equally beloved by the Dominican people?

My father looked worried at each passport control and rapidly lost confidence in the Dominican Republic. "Well, maybe New Zealand would be better — or Costa Rica. I've also heard good things about Medellín in Colombia, but do any Jews live there?"

"Yes, let's try Medellín," I said. "It's at an altitude, but not so very high."

"We can look elsewhere. There must be some good countries. What about Mexico?"

"Mexico has problems," I answered, enjoying my sudden expertise.

"When we're home, we should draw up a list: a realistic list." Still excited about looking for new venues, he told me a favorite story of his:

"Have I ever told you the story of the man in Poland, who was so poor and cramped that he went to the rabbi for advice?"

He had, many times, and I knew the story well. But he told it again. The rabbi urged him to bring in a goat. That made matters worse. Then the rabbi urged him to take in a cow. Again, worse. Next the rabbi suggested he remove the cow. Much better. Finally, the rabbi recommended the goat be removed. All was now well.

My father laughed, a soundless laugh. He closed his eyes, shaking his head lightly. I had heard the story ever since I was a small child and understood it even then: something bad looked pretty good after you experienced worse. I had liked hearing my father tell the story, since he enjoyed it so much, but now it annoyed me. Always absorbing the blows and learning to like what you had to put up with, what was so great about that? I wanted things to get better; I wanted to change my circumstances. Besides, adjusting to painful circumstances was the very thing that always got Jews in trouble.

Flexibility was good, and I liked being diplomatic, just like my mother, and accommodating, just like my father; but it was a whole Jewish way of being I wanted to leave behind. It led to weakness and the greatest number of victims ever. My father told another story. "A Jew in Poland returned from a short trip. Back home, he told his wife, 'I met such a nice Pole. He was so nice to me.'

"'What was so nice about him?' asked his wife.

"'He didn't beat me.'"

Most of my father's stories and sayings were Jewish. I much preferred to hear him talk about his golden age in Germany in the twenties, his business success, his German employees, his socialism, his membership in a Jewish sports club — that time before Hitler when Germany was civilized and orderly, unlike Poland. But now after the war, he reverted to Jewish sayings and stories of the little Polish ghetto in which he had lived till his seventeenth year before going to Germany to make his fortune. Those German days of cosmopolitanism were gone, and the fright of the war returned him to small-town-in-Poland ways, which was easy to do in Curaçao — people knew each other, talked about each other, told little stories.

I wished my father felt more at ease with Dutch people or they with him. Maybe if he were more at home among them he would not look so hard for another country. But he did not understand the Dutch and was not comfortable dealing with them. I felt I knew better than he did how the Dutch colonials thought and felt in Curaçao. I spoke the language without an accent. My father's Dutch was foreign, though fluent. I liked my school and my Dutch teachers, and my friends were Dutch.

Soon after our trip to the Dominican Republic, our whole family walked in a funeral cortege through the narrow streets of Willemstad for one of the Jewish refugees. A Dutch policeman saluted as we passed. My father looked up, startled but impressed. I felt embarrassed. "Did you see that, Bertha?" he asked afterwards. "They did not care who it was, Jewish or Christian. The police here aren't bad."

My mother smiled, her cheeks suddenly round and girlish. She rarely corrected my father overtly but showed her disagreement.

"No, Max. They're not bad, but that salute is just something they do routinely."

If only he were more like the fathers of my Dutch friends, brisk, fluent, in command of themselves, not always so anxious. But how could he be like them with his Jewish refugee background? I felt ashamed for even wishing it.

One Friday night several years ago at my grandfather's house, my father said, "This Ben-Gurion is a great man. Let us hope for the best in Palestine." My grandfather looked up from his prayer-book and said, "Let us hope he is a man of God too."

"Where was God when we needed him?" sighed my father quietly, not quite wanting my grandfather to hear. And he would turn mildly to my brother and me: "Well, we have to fend for ourselves. Here in Curaçao, it's no different from anywhere else. Even here you have to fudge and maneuver."

Uncle Paul did not maneuver. From his landing place in Jamaica in 1943, he volunteered for the Dutch army in exile, which trained him in Canada and in England and landed him in Normandy in the year we arrived in Curaçao. He fought the Germans every inch of the way and was cheered with the other liberating Canadian forces in May 1945. Decorated for bravery by the Queen, he resettled in The Hague. But in 1948, Paul and his wife Melitta, and their little son, moved to Australia.

So even Uncle Paul wanted to be somewhere else.

"Manny, don't be old for your age. You have to learn to be a child," said Mr. Gos, my Dutch teacher.

It was easier to be an adult than a child. Ever since I was ten years old, I had read the daily newspaper from front to back. After I got home from school, with any luck it was already there, stuck into the grillwork of the gate. If it wasn't, I would start looking through the window of the front door every few minutes. Now at thirteen, I was better informed than anyone in the family, I thought: my father would look at events through his own lenses, my mother wouldn't read the whole paper, and my brother would be so busy with his homework that he would often skimp on the paper. As for my friends, whether Curaçaoan or Dutch, their interest in the news was slight.

Greedily I read the paper. Such crimes as there were on the island were crimes of passion. Surprisingly few robberies took place. Murder was almost unheard of, except for the occasional knifing after a party. The news I read with the most interest was international; Holland was reviving with help from the Marshall Plan; President Truman looked sure to be defeated; sporadic fighting took place in Palestine.

After the paper and before starting on my homework, I read magazines: TIME, LIFE, a Jewish magazine with recruitment posters displaying clean-featured young men and women sailors: "Jewish Youth Join The Navy." A warship plied the waves in the background. These were the fighters we should have had during the war. If only Palestine could've been strong enough to take on Germany. Why could nothing ever be done?

I thought with a familiar dread of the vast numbers; surely they were just as deserving as we were. Why could I never get used to what had happened? My only escape lay in avoiding it. And yet I wanted to know, and was in fact absorbed in the daily events of the world, always unfolding for my benefit. Oddly, these events distracted me from the past.

Like school, the news was a pleasure to me; it took me away from something heavy and nameless that weighed on me, a sadness I always felt but never fully understood. After all, we were safe and the war was over. What else was there? But how to account for the luck of some and the catastrophic misfortune of most? How to explain our own good fortune?

The Red Cross and the Jewish relief organizations, like the JOINT, brought further bad news of those relatives, including my father's family in Poland, who had not managed to flee. They had neither luck nor papers.

191

Fortunately, we never talked about any of this in school.

✻   ✻   ✻

"Scottish people are rigorous but dour," said our teacher, a tall, blond Dutchman who had come to the island a few years ago, right after the war. He taught history and French, but he loved to talk about national characteristics. The Curaçaoan kids egged him on in this; they saw it as Dutch behavior, naive and over-confident, unaware of its own narrowness.

"Now take the French," Mr. van Dam said as he folded his long legs under him on the teacher's desk. "The French are sensitive, good-natured, but they can be suspicious. Of course, they pride themselves on their logic, but I never found them very logical."

"And the Dutch?" asked a stocky Curaçaoan kid, older than his fourteen years. "We talk about the Dutch all the time," he added.

"Oh, do you?" remarked the teacher, with little apparent interest in how the Curaçaoans viewed his countrymen. He exhaled. "The Dutch are precise, reliable, calm, sober people. They may lack romance, but they're still adventurous. Solidly so."

"How can they be sober and adventurous?" asked another kid, now wanting to get into the game.

"They plan their conquests carefully."

"Sir, do you have views of the Spanish?"

"Spanish people are passionate — but cruel. Maybe it's their passion that makes them so."

And he talked about bullfights, and also that in Dutch we call a strange or difficult man a *sinjeur*, and how that word must have come into being during the Eighty Years' War between Holland and Spain.

"Poles, what about Poles?" It had now become a game for the kids, and the teacher did not notice.

"Well, Poles are loud and boorish, and they don't always wash when they should." Suddenly he looked around, perhaps realizing that Jews were called Poles in Curaçao, and he quickly added, "So it is said anyway."

I enjoyed these discussions. They were a diversion from the more difficult subjects and filled me with happy thoughts of travel and the future. Like everything at school, it spoke of adult life, of freedom, and even of fun. I knew the teacher's characterizations were superficial, having myself seen very different kinds of Poles and French, but on the whole I thought they had something valuable, especially for the Dutch, with their infinite calm, their quiet repose. Would we be as calm if no calamity had befallen us? Doubtful. I wish I could be as confident, as self-assured, and tranquil, as Mr. van Dam.

The celebrations in our Jewish Club about the birth of the State of Israel were muted. Everywhere danger threatened the new state. Arab armies invaded from the north, the east, the south. It was not clear that the Jewish state would be able to survive.

"The danger," I lectured my teacher Mr. Gos at school, "is that the Egyptian army and the Jordanian armies will join together, say, in Be'er Sheba or elsewhere in the Negev desert."

Mr. Gos beamed at me; his bald head shone in the sun. "You really know about this, don't you?"

"Well, yes," I replied.

"And you take it to heart?"

"Of course."

"But don't worry too much. Next week is another school trip to Bonaire, and I want you to enjoy it."

He had such an air of quiet, that man, such contentment, like so many Dutch people.

A few weeks after our celebration, it seemed clear that the Jews — or the Israelis, as we now called them — would win the battle of Palestine. One of my Jewish classmates talked about moving there and got all excited about all the planes they would have to take to make the trip. "We'll fly via Bermuda," she said.

"Wouldn't you rather move to Holland?" I asked.

"No, we're going back to our ancestral home."

At the Jewish Club, a young woman from the Israeli Army gave a fiery speech in rapid English. Her "R"s were Germanic, or was that a Hebrew accent? I didn't listen to what she said because she cut so striking a figure in her military garb, half soldier, half Campfire Girl. When it was all over, some of the Club members sang "Hatikvah," the new national anthem.

"What did you think of this Yael?" asked my mother with just a hint of disapproval in her voice. She patted the hair on top of her head while she spoke.

"I don't know," answered my father slowly, distantly. "She's strong, like a goy."

"Well, yes," said my mother, sounding unconvinced.

"Was she really in the army?" I asked.

"In the Haganah," my father said proudly. "The army that defeated five Arab armies. How is it possible?"

"Women fight next to men," said my mother. "They wear a uniform. They handle weapons. They can defend themselves and go on the attack. If only..."

"These Jews are different from the way we were," my father answered her. "What could we do? Who had a weapon in Europe? Who could even use one? We were scared, frightened beyond belief. Yes, maybe the Partisans fought in the woods, but most of us..."

"Sometimes I think," said my mother, "that we all went too quietly."

"But Bertha, where would we even have found guns? Where could we go? We fled in the night. And lucky we were. The rest were taken."

"But back to this Yael," said my mother. "Why does she have to wear shorts? Here in Curaçao where everybody is decently dressed, even the Curaçaoans."

"Especially the Curaçaoans," I interjected.

My mother laughed a hearty, gratifying laugh. "You're right. Curaçaoans have a real flair for clothes. You never see them disheveled. Even when they're poor."

"Sometimes the Dutch look sloppy," I said, encouraged by her agreement. "But they don't care. You have to give them that."

"All true," said my mother, "but shorts? Who wears shorts around here? Yes, on the beach."

I had liked Yael in her shorts but couldn't help agreeing with my mother. Didn't she know that everyone stared at her legs? Every time I had seen her, she had worn the same outfit: khaki shirt, very military, long-sleeved, but her shorts were provocative, seductive.

Days later, Yael walked into our store. She wore a skirt and a kind of halter top, as if she now decided to switch the area of attention. A bare midriff was rarely seen in the downtown streets of our Caribbean town.

"Shalom, shalom." Since we spoke no Hebrew and she no Yiddish or Dutch, the conversation continued in English and German. Yael was troubled by something; she was frowning and looked annoyed. "These Curaçaoan Jews give generously to the cause. But it's clear they don't understand anything," she sighed bitterly. "What nonsense they talk. 'You beat the Arabs,' they say. 'Here, here, take a thousand guilders. Now go away.' They think beating the Arabs is a one-time, simple thing. They don't know; they don't want to know."

My father looked up. "One time? You mean this fighting will go on and on?"

"Of course," said Yael sternly, and took a cigarette from a small case in her shoulder bag, which raised her halter top a bit and revealed the little curved rims of her tanned breasts. "It's not just the Arab armies; it's the people who had to leave their homes."

"Can't they go to Egypt and TransJordan?" I asked.

"Yes, of course. They can go there. But do they want to go there? Or will they come back as fighters, guerrillas, assassins? We cannot let our guard down for a second."

"Here I thought we won," said my father, "but now ..."

"Well, we did win," said Yael, puffing furiously on her cigarette, her sunburned face stiff and scowling. "We did. We won the war. We can't be victims anymore."

"No," said my mother. "Never."

"We will never run away again."

"I hope not," said my father dubiously.

"Now it's someone else's turn," continued Yael. "Besides, if you have a conscience, it will be held against you." She unstiffened as she said this.

"But tell me, Yael," asked my mother, "Are you a Sabra? Where were you born? Judging by the way you speak German, your parents were German Jews."

"My parents. I rarely speak of my parents. But when you told me the other day, Herr Wolf, I mean Max, that you lived in Chemnitz, I decided I wanted to tell you the whole story."

"You mean you come from Chemnitz too?" asked my father, his brown oval face held attentively to one side. My mother looked speechless.

"My name may be Yael Yadin, but that is just the Hebrew version. I was born Hettie Springer."

My father sighed. "I knew a Springer once. He helped me get started in business. In Chemnitz. But he is dead now."

"Just so. That was my uncle."

"Your uncle," exclaimed my mother. "We heard that he and his wife and the children had all died."

"As have my parents and sisters. I am the only one," said Yael, now quickly turning her face away. I did not want to see her cry, so I turned away too. Why did it always come to this? Why did everything always turn to sadness? "In 1936, three years after Hitler came to power, my family had a chance to go to Palestine. Everybody said 'Don't go. It's too dangerous. The Arabs will kill you. Europe is still best for us. Especially Germany. Germany will not hurt its Jews, the way Poland has.' My father said so too, but he had modern, democratic leanings. We took a family vote. And the vote was four to one against leaving Germany."

Everyone was quiet now. I looked at her stern, thin-lipped face and beautiful upright posture. A few droplets of sweat clung to her light-brown middle. Finally my father said: "A vote? Four to one? Your sisters, what were their names?"

Yael did not answer. Instead she said, "They were good girls, good students, never in trouble. I always was."

"How old were you?" asked my mother, obviously trying hard to remember the girls.

"I was sixteen and a bad girl. I was probably the only Jewish child in Chemnitz who dropped out of school. My parents could do nothing with me, nothing. Once or twice I ran away from home too. I played in a cabaret. They thought I would become a prostitute. Well, they weren't so far off."

"So then you set off for Palestine."

"Yes," said Yael, "I was not much older than Manny is now."

But of course she was. "I'm thirteen," I said.

"Yes, but you are big for your age." And Yael gave me a wide-mouthed smile, which made her look younger than twenty-eight.

My heart gave a jump, but my father pursued the conversation: "So how is it in Israel? Is it really Jewish? Are the police Jewish?"

"We have Jewish everything. Jewish police. Criminals. Even car thieves."

"Incredible," said my father. "Jewish car thieves."

"Well," said Yael, "I have to go. Two other Israelis are taking me out for peanut chicken and *funchi*."

"What's that?" asked my mother.

"It's cornmeal," I explained proudly. "Curaçaoans eat it a lot."

"Cornmeal," said my father flatly but with a glimmer of recognition.

"Don't you people eat the local food?" Yael asked scornfully.

"No, we eat European food."

Yael shrugged and rapidly said good-bye. "The Soviets were ahead of us all," said my father abruptly. "They created a Jewish national homeland in Birobidjan."

"Isn't that in Siberia?" teased my mother.

"Yes, but a good part of Siberia, a wholesome part, in the Far East. There Jews can live together and speak Yiddish. They drained the swamps and cut down the forest. I read about it in my socialist paper."

"Well, we now have Israel," sighed my mother. "That's obviously better than Siberia. In Haifa," she continued, "there are lots of European Jews. They came there in the thirties and speak German at home."

"Real Germans," smiled my father. "I'll bet they'll never learn Hebrew."

"Still, it may be a place for us some day."

"Yes," answered my father pensively. "You never know, maybe we'll have to go there someday."

"If we went to Israel," I said, "we wouldn't need to look for any more countries." I had never seriously thought of going there before.

"How can we be sure?" asked my father.

"So Israel won, wonderful," said Mr. Gos. "I'm sure you followed every skirmish and battle."

"I did."

"How did they manage to defeat those armies?"

"It was speed," I answered. "Motorized speed, like a blitzkrieg."

"Yes, and bravery too."

"Sure."

"I suppose these people, these Jews, have nothing to lose. But tell me, Manny, is Israel your country now?"

"No," I replied, "Holland is." How could he think that I wanted to be anything other than a Dutch boy, eager to return to Holland some day?

"And how about your parents?"

"You mean, would they want to live there?"

"Yes."

"Maybe my mother would, but my father doesn't think any country is safe."

"He doesn't? How could that be? They're all pretty safe now. The war has been over for three years."

How could I explain to him that my father was still looking for a safe place, and that he had said there must be such a place if only we could find it — but that he had also said there was no really safe place, though we might as well keep looking. There was nothing wrong with being one step ahead of whatever danger was lurking where you were.

Chapter 13. The Two Witch Doctors

M y mother was not without vanity, and when people started saying that she resembled Eva Perón, she was pleased. For several years in the late forties, she continued combing her hair back severely on both sides, the way the distant Argentinean beauty did. Eva Perón's doings were widely reported on our Caribbean island, and my mother frequently mentioned her. In our household it was understood that while Juan Perón might be a fascist, his wife tried to soften his ways and do all she could to help the poor. My mother pinned her picture up in the little hall near the kitchen next to that of Marlene Dietrich, with whom she also identified. Once in a while she even sang a line from the song Marlene had immortalized in *The Blue Angel*, which my mother had seen in Germany in 1930. "From head to toe, I'm primed for love. Everything else means nothing."

My mother was both fun-loving and melancholy. Sometimes she sat for hours in the living room, listening again and again to her favorite record, Fritz Kreisler's "Viennese Caprice," the tremulous, pulsating violin seeming to bring a glow to her face and make her want to say something. "That music has the romance of Europe. Things happen there and only there." She listened in great silence to Edith Piaf and other Parisian singers. Then with relief, she shook herself loose and sighed, "I really have to drive into town and help your father." Occasionally she looked downright unhappy and complained that my father was inconsiderate or even selfish. They rarely quarreled, but when they did it was about his inconsiderateness.

In the aftermath of the war my mother always said the most important thing was that we saved ourselves — "Personal things can always wait." She repeated this many times. "For me, the personal is secondary. It was different when I was a young girl." Another time she said, "When I turned thirty in 1941 in Holland, we were in a state of panic, wondering what to do, what we could still do. Now that I'm thirty-eight, I'm calmer. But of course I will never be at peace."

Seeing friends always cheered her. My mother had a great talent for friendship. After we arrived in Curaçao in 1943, she and Louisa Arends were close. Louisa was a heavy, cheerful Dutch Jewish woman of twenty-eight, who managed a stationery store called "Liberty," and so my grandmother called her "The Liberta," a name that others in this nickname culture started using for her. Because Louisa was single, my father declared that she was a bit odd: "When a woman at a certain age doesn't have a man, she becomes strange." My mother did not contradict him. She also was good friends with Flora Kamelink, but Mrs. Kamelink was "really" Dutch — that is, not Jewish — and her husband was a high colonial official on the island, both restraining influences. Unlike my father, who was always remote, my mother had an intimate manner; she asked direct questions and looked people in the eye. And she seemed to hear what people said, which made them want to confide in her. Mr. Dimanche, a friend in our refugee circle, called often to speak to her, sometimes about his unhappy marriage. When we were on vacation, frequently without my father, who had to manage the business, my mother was sought out by men who were business connections or simply tourists. They liked her youthful animation and direct manner.

One of my mother's best friends was Madame Escoli, whose first name I never knew and whom my mother always addressed as Madame. "*Se tutoyer, c'est folie,*" said Madame, firmly signaling her preference for the polite forms of speech. Not that Madame Escoli was formal: on the contrary, she spoke in rapid-fire French interrupted by bursts of laughter, and sudden conspiratorial mumblings, especially when they were talking about Maurice, her husband, a bald, dour, brooding presence, much older than Madame. They were Sephardic Jews from Turkey, who had come to the island ten years before we did, in a quest to make their fortune, and now ran a luggage and handbag store in one of the more cramped streets of downtown Willemstad. Maurice was sixty, Madame not yet forty. "My husband," she said in her quick French, "he is from Ankara; I'm from Istanbul," as if that explained the huge temperamental difference between them. "In Ankara people are gloomy. But Istanbul, they enjoy life there and it is beautiful. Ah, Istanbul, Constantinople, Byzantium," she rhapsodized. "Where has the Ottoman Empire gone? Like everything else: disappeared with the wind." And then, switching from French to Spanish, she spoke the title of the movie she had just told my mother about, "*Lo Que El Viento Se Llevó,*" "Gone with the Wind."

"Why did she never learn Dutch?" grumbled my father.

"Well, Max, both she and Maurice actually mastered Papiamentu, which is more than we can say."

"OK, but we haven't been here a dozen years."

My father didn't mind Madame Escoli, but he felt that she was not "solid," one of his favorite terms. She spent too much time driving around in her two-door, cream-colored Chevrolet, visiting people, gossiping. But my mother and Madame got along just fine and rarely discussed the war or the war's end or anything of great weight. My mother was happy to laugh with Madame about the foibles of mankind and especially the odd ways of the island, which Madame knew well. Certainly my mother got enough heaviness from my father.

I always loved listening to the two of them talk, because I was infatuated with French. I had gone to school for a few months in Nice in 1942 when I was seven, and I had liked the warmth there, the hills, and the sounds of French. Even before that time, my mother taught me some words and phrases, like *"Joie de vivre,"* *"Plus ça change, plus c'est la même chose"* or *"C'est le ton qui fait la musique."* She had studied French in high school in Germany, had lived in Belgium, and wanted to be an interpreter. With some of her friends, she dreamed of Paris. "French was what I wanted to speak when I grew up," she said. "I longed to live in Paris. Who knows what would have happened to me if I had been able to go? I spoke French every chance I got."

In Paris she would have met artistic people, living a bohemian life. In 1930, when she was nineteen, everything seemed possible for a bright, pretty girl brought up in Germany. Some planned to study, some to marry "interesting" men, different from those of their own Jewish circle, who were mainly in business. "But that was long before the war. Then I married. I had a family. And then this ghastly war changed everything. But I shouldn't complain. So now I'm trying to set something right, make something good for someone."

My mother and I sometimes confided in each other, and I liked to be with her then. But when she was in this mood I was uneasy and tried to steer her away from what made her so unhappy. Today, she looked tearful. "Yesterday I thought I saw that little girl. But that's impossible; she must be ten or eleven by now."

'What little girl?"

"No, that can't be true; she is no age at all."

"What do you mean?" I asked, hoping she would not explain.

"When we got caught in Nice in late '42 and sat in that assembly hall, there was a family with a little girl. We were released: they were not. Certainly deported. I wanted to take that little girl, rescue her; but the parents did not want to let her go."

I wanted to get away from the subject of the war. "Really, were you going to be an interpreter?"

"Yes, no chance of that now. Certainly not here, in the far reaches of the world. Well, we're lucky to be here."

"With whom did you speak French?"

"Oh, my girlfriends, even my sister Anna. We spoke French and sometimes held flowers near our face because we thought it looked glamorous." She smiled at the thought.

"Did they also want to move to Paris?"

"Yes, we all did. It was the most romantic place on earth. But what is left from those days? Nothing. Who is left from those days? Very few. Maybe you will go to Paris some day."

Every time I heard "*J'attendrai*" sung by Tino Rossi I thought of love, often in the shape of a girl I gazed at in class, and how I would someday live in Paris and stroll arm in arm with her along the Seine to the strains of Tino Rossi or Edith Piaf. I was an artist and she a schoolteacher, and we were on our way to a little apartment on the Left Bank. I remembered all the place names from the time we lived in France in 1942, the names my brother and I sang out in Marseilles or Nice: Rue du Maréchal Joffre, Avenue des Invalides, Place de la Victoire. And I remembered walking along the Promenade des Anglais in Nice with the beautiful dark-haired girl of fifteen who took care of my brother and me, her hypnotic voice soft and soothing.

I understood that Madame Escoli's French was not Parisian, but it certainly was swift. I listened all I could.

"Let's find someone for Louisa," said my mother to Madame one day, holding her head mischievously to one side. "We must do something for her. Everyone needs some love."

"Ah. Madame, you mean your young friend who is so ... what is she called, Mademoiselle Liberté," and she pantomimed a large bosomy woman.

"Yes, that's the one," frowned my mother. She did not like having her friend described that way.

Madame Escoli was sunk in thought. "But of course. I have just the one — a young refugee, spent the war years in Santo Domingo, where he grew up in that Jewish colony on the North Coast."

"Oh, really?" asked my mother. "What colony?"

"I don't know exactly, but the important thing is, he has nothing. They did farming in that community, you know, so they're all poor and he left. But because he's poor, he'll want Mademoiselle Liberté. After all, beggars can't be choosers," she chortled.

I knew the loose-limbed young man with his sober manner from our Jewish Club. Arturo Braverman's kinky hair was wild but he appeared older than twenty-four when he explained in Spanish that on the northern coast of the Dominican Republic the dictator Trujillo had created a settlement of German Jewish refugees in the thirties. "Roosevelt had accused him of slaughtering thousands of black Haitians who had moved across the frontier, and so in order to prove his good will he allowed a few hundred Jewish refugees from Europe to settle in the Dominican Republic."

"When was that?" asked my brother, who liked to get the sequence of things straight. He peered through his glasses at Arturo and ran his fingers through his hair.

One of the club regulars, Bruno, a gangly kid of around sixteen, looked up at Arturo from his comic book. "All this stuff about the war. I'm sick of it... So you're a Dominican practically. Why don't you stay in Santo Domingo?" Bruno had been born and raised in Curaçao and felt that the Caribbean was the world's best place.

"It's all farming. I want to go into business and have a leather shop."

"Besides, you want to get away from dictators, yes?" asked one of the older girls who came frequently to the Jewish club. Not waiting for his answer, she swayed over to a stack of records and put on a scratchy Xavier Cugat number, *"Amor, Amor, Amor."*

That evening I told my mother that Arturo wanted to have a shop, and I could see my mother's eyes starting to sparkle. Soon Mme. Escoli arranged a date.

But it was my mother who got an earful from her friend Louisa. At Madame's next visit, I heard my mother say:

"It did not go well. He kissed her too hard, a French kiss."

'Ah, what a scandal!" shouted Mme Escoli stamping her foot. "He is a crude farmer. Maybe he should go to Palestine. They can use more farmers there." Madame still called it Palestine, though it had recently become Israel.

"Maybe."

"He treated her like a prostitute."

My mother laughed. "I didn't think men kissed prostitutes."

But Madame had other things on her mind. "I have troubles," she said, "*Je vous dis franchement*, I am at the end of my wits." She patted her curly black hair but it remained limp.

"Why?"

"Maurice has got it into his head to take an external wife, an outside wife."

"An outside wife? Maurice?"

"Yes, an outside wife, a Caribbean invention, a wife outside the house. In Europe we would say mistress." And Madame shook her head in disbelief.

"But how is it possible?" My mother looked as if she was trying to suppress something, then blurted out: "He's no Maurice Chevalier." And then perhaps thinking that she should not have made a joke, she quickly added, "Or really handsome, like Mr. Dimanche."

"No, he's not," said Madame glumly, "but this woman bewitched him.

"She did? How?"

"In the usual way."

"Who is she?"

"A wild woman, Encarna. Dark, of course. What does she want with my Maurice?"

"How did you find out?"

"Oh, Madame Wolf. I have my spies, my helpers. The island is full of eager eyes. Anyway, Curaçao is not a place for secrets. She is a wild, wild woman from the country. She'll be his outside wife, and I ... what is an inside wife to do?"

"What will you do?"

Madame spread her arms wide. "What can I do? But still, I have a plan, a devilish plan, *très diabolique.*"

"What is it?"

"I will have her bewitched."

My mother laughed hard, and despite her misery, Madame joined in.

"This is what I'll do. I'll hire a sorceress, a witch doctor, to put a spell on her, turn her away from him."

"Will that really happen?"

"Things happen on this island that no one can explain." And on that, Madame swept out of the room.

A few weeks later, my mother and I were walking in downtown Willemstad and bumped into Madame Escoli, who looked somber, her face tight and her olive skin sallow. "I fired the magician."

"Why? Didn't she succeed?" My mother looked at her attentively.

"She did some of her magic, but to what effect? It was all foolishness. We came home one day and found a cow in our bathroom.

"A cow?"

"Yes, she was trying to demonstrate to me that she could do the magic, but I lost confidence."

"Still, if she can do that, maybe she can do other things."

'Well, *chère* Madame Wolf, there was something else: she knew the outside wife, and they were both plotting against me. How could I know that she was a friend of that woman? When I dismissed her, she threatened me, but I said, 'What can you do to me? Put a crocodile in my bedroom? I already have one.'"

I'm sure my mother never told my father about any of this. I was glad I heard these stories; they made me feel that my mother and I had a shared interest. I heard her on the phone with Madame, doing what she so often did: asking questions, giving encouragement, drawing out the other person, making appropriate, encouraging sounds. It was difficult to know what was happening because I heard only one end of the telephone conversation. Nor did I always pay attention: I had my school work and my friends and was beginning to feel smitten with Melda, a girl at school. I looked forward to catching a glimpse of her on weekends at the Piscadera Swim Club, which was frequented by Dutch people and a sprinkling of Curaçaoans.

My parents, who worked in the store all week, never missed a Sunday at the beach, my mother vivacious with her many friends, my father nodding abstractedly and gazing about absent-mindedly, even when he swam.

Both my father and mother would lapse into German or Yiddish when they did not want to be overheard. Now my mother was looking at my physics teacher, a tall, middle-aged Dutchman, drying the back of a pretty woman in a modish black two-piece bathing suit, definitely not his wife.

"Where is Mrs. Overland?" asked my mother in German.

"Oh, she must be on vacation in the Netherlands," answered my father, not knowing why my mother asked the question.

'Well, Max, this is something to behold."

"What is?"

"Now he's not only drying that woman off but doing her up in the back."

"Who?" asked my father.

"Don't you see? Over there."

"Where?" My father looked confused.

"There."

"There. But who?"

"Mr. Overland."

"Mr. Overland," said my father, enunciating the name slowly as if he heard it for the first time.

"Yes, Max, the boys' physics teacher."

"Oh, yes, yes…" said my father, now finally looking at the pair, who were strolling toward the far side of the beach, their hands touching.

"I wonder what's going on there," said my mother.

"Not a good thing," said my father slowly. "No, not a good thing. Dutch people, they have to uphold a standard. And this, no … But I thought Mr. Overland had such a nice wife."

"Well," sighed my mother. "You never know what a marriage is like. Sometimes even husband and wife don't know about each other, what their needs may be."

"What?" asked my father in the way he sometimes did, saying it flatly, as if it was not really a question. "What!"

Suddenly, none other than Madame Escoli arrived. Behind her, somewhat sheepishly, walked Maurice, his large, bald head seeming to fall to one side. He wore a Hawaiian shirt of the kind President Truman was always photographed in at Key West, which the Dutch people called "a little horror shirt."

Though my mother beamed as if she had been rescued, my father looked annoyed. "Hello, Maurice, how's business?" he finally said. And the two men walked toward the water's edge.

I sat next to my mother and now heard all.

"Everything has come out roses. I hired a better witch doctor, from Martinique, a woman who comes here to buy leather goods, which she sells over there. She comes a few times a year and stays a few weeks."

My mother had a skeptical curl around her mouth. "So did she tell you what she did?"

"No, but two days later I heard that the wild woman had fallen ill, with dengue, or something."

"Does Maurice talk about it at all?"

"Ah, what does Maurice know? Men do not understand these things. Magic is woman's business." And Madame looked away dreamily.

My mother gazed across the sand to the blue sea. For a moment, she seemed disturbed by something. Then she waited for Madame to continue. It was one of her techniques for drawing people out. She looked directly at them and waited. I had seen her do it with friends and strangers, women and men. Once she and Mr. Dimanche had sat in silence for a long time.

"I felt good," confided Madame. "I started realizing, I was invulnerable, the wife, the real one. That woman, she is the *putain*."

My mother looked sideways at me, but I pretended to be reading my book. "OK," she said, now firmly trying to get Madame back on track, "So she got sick. Then what?"

"Well, then, for a few weeks, nothing, but I realized Maurice was very friendly to me, which he had not been for years."

"He was?"

"Yes, indeed, he was, very much so."

"That doesn't make sense. You'd think he'd be resentful being deprived of his new romance."

"Some things make little sense. The magician said that on her next trip, she would bring along from Martinique some special ingredients to turn that whore Encarna against love, love in any form. She who had been a mistress in the arts of love would now be clumsy and indifferent."

"And is this what happened?"

"Yes, but with a difference. Encarna chased another man, old doctor Petrucci. And she became indifferent to Maurice."

"Well, that's exactly what you wanted."

"Yes, except that I would have preferred if Maurice had become indifferent to her."

My mother looked sympathetic and was beginning to speak when suddenly Madame became agitated. "*Tiens*, there is that woman, that bitch, that *putain*." I looked up from my book and no more than a few yards away Encarna paraded by, swaying her hips, displayed to advantage in her white swimsuit, over which she wore a Guatemalan peasant blouse that left her shoulders bare.

"*Asanti*," muttered Madame, "*Asanti, upsule, engala.*" And she took a small bell out of her purse and made a tinkling sound.

My mother looked embarrassed, but Madame had regained her composure: "*Asanti*," she muttered. "*Asanti.* No dengue, that's for sure."

Not far from us, Encarna sank into a beach chair and adjusted a delicate ankle bracelet. She turned almost at once to a Dutch man who was sprawled in his beach chair facing the blue Caribbean. "Have you got a cigarette, friend?"

"You bet I do," answered the man, gave her a cigarette, and lit it. Soon they were talking animatedly, Encarna's accented Dutch audible over his. Madame had grown silent. My mother sighed. Maurice and my father swam silently in the water. I moved my chair, pretending to get into the shade but actually to look at Encarna and to hear what she was saying. She and the man were laughing. "All these white women have to remember is to be women. What is it we have? We are southern, Latin; we have fire, passion. That's all."

A few months later, Madame Escoli, smiling and heavily made up, walked into our house and started scattering pieces of hard white candy all over the living room. "*Ramassez, ramassez,*" she called to my brother and me, urging us to pick them up from the floor, as if we were toddlers instead of teenagers. My mother had bought a new carpet, and Madame explained that this was the way to celebrate it. The children were to gather up the candy, which would initiate the new rug. "Besides," she said, "I have a lot to celebrate."

"Tell me," smiled my mother, after my brother and I had picked up the candy and deposited it into an old shoe box. "Spare no detail." She motioned Madame on to our large, overstuffed sofa.

"Soon after I saw you last, the woman from Martinique started blackmailing me. It was *chantage*, I tell you. *Chantage.*"

"What could she blackmail you with?"

"Black magic is against the law. The Dutch think that they have done away with voodoo, with the Tamboo dance, with Caribbean sorcery. How wrong they are. But still, it's strictly forbidden."

"Would something really have happened to you if she denounced you?"

"Probably not. But we can't afford to alienate the Dutch authorities. I don't have to tell you. We need them for business permits."

"True."

"I was not too worried. But then she said if I did not give her what she wanted, she would take away the hex on that woman Encarna."

"And then Maurice would go after her again?"

"Yes, that's what worried me. She wanted me to get her a residence permit. To be able to live here, on this island of greater wealth." Madame Escoli laughed scornfully.

"There's no way you could obtain that for her."

"I tried to tell her so, but she thought because I was white I could persuade the Dutch authorities. Little does she know how stiff-necked those Dutch colonials are, and how there's no love lost between them and us."

"Of course."

"So I said I'd try, that she would have to go home and wait for word from me. She said I was trying to get rid of her."

"Well, you were," laughed my mother.

"Naturally."

"Then what?"

"Then? Oh, yes. Then I took the initiative. I said if she did not wait patiently I'd put a spell on her."

"You what?"

"I said I would hex her, voodoo her, bewitch her, with Turkish magic. She would lose her gift, if she did not leave me alone."

"Surely she didn't fall for that."

"She did. She was frightened. And in fact I can do it. I think I have the gift. I went back to the first witch doctor, that fraud, and said I wanted to study magic."

"And you did?"

"I did. There isn't that much to it. But I'm not allowed to tell you what goes into it." Madame smiled serenely and lifted a tiny seashell from her purse and listened to it.

"Secret, is it?"

"Yes, just like the Freemasons Maurice goes to, but anyway, instead of putting a spell on her, I put one on Maurice."

"On Maurice?"

"Yes, I first went to the beauty parlor and had myself made over. Then I applied my secret knowledge, and now he wants to spend all his time with me."

My mother looked surprised. "You mean he loves you as he did Encarna?"

'Something like that. I also confessed everything to him, told him about hiring the magician, her blackmail, etc."

"Everything?"

"Well, not everything. I did not tell him about my own instruction into the black arts."

"That was wise of you. And now he loves you as before?"

"Better. All I know is that he tells me I'm beautiful and asks me to wear my tiger pajamas and dance for him."

My mother said, "What a useful gift," then dissolved into a fit of giggles, and Madame suddenly joined in.

Right after my fourteenth birthday, my mother asked me, "How did that Dominican fellow, that Arturo Braverman, strike you?"

"Weird," I said, "Why do you want to bother with him?"

"Madame Escoli had the idea he might be good for Louisa."

"He is still a young man, too young for an older lady like Louisa."

"I wish I had some magic for poor Louisa."

I looked up, startled. My mother noticed.

"Have you been listening to my conversations with Madame Escoli?"

I said I had heard some of them, but she continued, unperturbed. "I have to do something for Louisa, but what?"

"Why is it so important?" I asked.

"Oh, she is lonely, and it's important to do something, to create something good for another person. I could certainly use some witchcraft now. No, not for myself, for Louisa. It's not too late for her."

My mother seemed unusually agitated. "At least I can try to do something for other people. It's good for them and it's good for me. It would take witchcraft to do something for myself. I always had to take care of other people. But what does it matter, here we are, we are alive. Best of all, you two are alive."

I felt uncomfortable and quickly asked, "So how could witchcraft be used for Louisa?"

"Maybe Madame Escoli could …I like Madame. She has real spirit. When I married your father, I was nineteen. My father told me, 'You must marry him. Do not throw away this chance.' I so wanted to wait, to go to France, to have friends there, to study. But I did what my father said. And then the Nazis came to power… We were beginning to be nervous, frightened."

"Nervous" and "nerves" were among the first words I could remember. Only my parents used them; nobody else I knew did.

"Your father and I were a team. He was not good at dealing with the German authorities. His German did not sound perfect, mine did. When it was still possible to talk to them, I was the one who did. And later of course in '42 — in Holland and in France — I spoke for all of us when we needed something. That was my strength: I could always talk to everybody."

She paused, almost seeming to speak to herself only now. "Your father got us the false papers, and I, I spoke to the French police, pretending we had just arrived in Lyon when we had been cowering in that awful hotel room for weeks, pretending we were just passing through Nice, when we stayed eight months. At any moment they could have arrested us, deported us. We had to stick together or we would have been lost."

Why was she telling me this? These were all things I knew. "But witchcraft?"

"Oh yes," she said, calmer now. "Witchcraft — if I could use it to set something right, to recover something, to bring it back. But never mind. We could have used some witchcraft in Europe. We had the ghosts but not the witchcraft."

My mother seemed to give up for a while trying to arrange anything for Louisa, but then a whole new opportunity presented itself. Mr. Dimanche suddenly became a widower.

Despite his French name, Mr. Dimanche was Central European, very much so. He spoke German with a rich, vibrant baritone, at once patrician and warm. Though he had been a radio announcer as a young man, Mr. Dimanche came from a cosmopolitan Viennese family. In tropical Curaçao, he talked about the glory days of Vienna in the last century or about Theodor Herzl, the founder of Zionism and a good friend of his father. My mother enjoyed this sort of cultured talk, which was more in her background than that of my father, who never wholly escaped the *shtetl* of his youth.

Tall, dark-haired, blue-eyed, with his handsome, faintly pitted face and elegant manners, Mr. Dimanche had a commanding presence, almost military, except for his courtly attentiveness. His wife was short, blonde, and squat. She had a shrill, pea-hen voice, and was frequently in a dither. Mr. Dimanche had married her, a Christian farmer's daughter, shortly before the war. Because of his Aryan wife, the Germans allowed him to work at forced labor in a munitions factory in Northern Germany. When it became clear in early 1944 that he too would be deported to Auschwitz, she arranged with a trustworthy farm relative to hide him till the end of the war.

Although they were not a happy couple, Mr. Dimanche never failed to mention that his wife had saved his life. He was sympathetic to her feelings of displacement, he told my mother, but tired of his wife's selfish outbursts. "There was no logic to her moods," my mother quoted him at dinner once. I liked Mr. Dimanche and was shocked when in late 1949 his wife died of a heart attack.

His telephone calls to our house increased, and my mother became high-spirited when he called, her voice animated and humorous. At first, Louisa's name was mentioned often, but then that stopped after a while. I could tell that my mother brought her up and that Mr. Dimanche was not interested. Once in a while, she and Mr. Dimanche spoke in French, and her replies always seemed terse and mysterious to me: *Ça dépend* and *hélas* and *on verra*. To my father she said: "Oh, it's just Dimanche." She seemed abstracted and uncommunicative when he asked, even a little angry. Mr. Dimanche came by the house once to lend her a recording of Mahler songs with a scarlet cover, and they spoke intently to each other for a few minutes. But much of the time I did not pay attention. I wanted to have more phone calls myself; friends of mine were beginning to spend hours on the phone talking to their girlfriends.

One evening after we heard Yehudi Menuhin performing Schubert in the sweltering Roxy Theater — a movie house that doubled as a concert hall — I told my mother how difficult it was getting Melda to return my love. I thought she would make the distinction I already knew from books and magazines, between what the Dutch call "calf love" and real, adult love, which is based on affection and respect and grows over the years, and so on, and so on. But she surprised me by saying, "People scorn infatuation, but what is life lived without it?" Her blue eyes were serious, urgent. "Do not hold yourself back. Do not throw yourself away on the wrong people. No reason at all you should, unless, of course, there is another war."

I have always thought of that unexpected little speech. My mother stayed interested in love, and a bit of far-away glamour always remained visible, even to her children. Her friends kept mentioning Eva Perón, and when the news came from Argentina that she was ill and that she might have cancer, my mother was sorrowful. She looked often at her picture in the hall off the kitchen. Eva Perón's death at the age of thirty-three in 1952 came only seven years before my mother's death from the same disease at forty-seven.

Chapter 14. Campo Alegre

When I was thirteen, I started to make serious efforts to get the girl across the street into my room. In 1948 that was not easy, and in Curaçao for a Dutch boy, especially a refugee to the island, it was particularly difficult. Curaçaoan boys and girls managed to meet each other, but the Dutch were more restrained. Els was one of those straight up-and-down Dutch girls who walked stiffly and never unbent in the Caribbean sun. My Curaçaoan friends used to say if a girl walked that way she was "frigid." Or sometimes they said she was "asking for it."

To my urgent requests to come look at my new 8mm film projector, Els replied, looking genuinely puzzled, a little blonde frown on her face, "Why?" Since we came home from school at the same time every day, I talked to her often in front of her house, but she answered with few words in a terse, Dutch-laconic tone, though not unfriendly. Still, I liked to look at her thin, lanky body and guess at the curves under her white dress.

After asking her for several weeks, she finally came. I had begged my parents for a film projector for months and then instantly lost interest, so I had very few films — one or two Andy Panda movies, highlights from World War II, and, unaccountably, a Dutch documentary about glass-blowing in Rotterdam. To this day, the projector stands unused in my closet, a source of shame when I spot it.

But when Els finally came over, I cursed my scarcity of options. She settled for Andy Panda and did not comment after it was done.

"Do you want to see anything else?" I asked.

"Yes," she replied to my surprise, looking straight ahead. "What do you want to see?"

Embarrassed, I had to claim that I wanted to see "Glass Blowing in the Netherlands." All I wanted was to get my hands on her. I had imagined the scene a hundred times. I would draw her to me and whisper words that made her melt. Now at last, I approached her face with mine and suddenly kissed her lips. Her face looked different from close up. She let me kiss her but not touch her breasts. With her angular features and soft skin, she looked pretty in a prim sort of way.

My Curaçaoan classmates in school were considerably more advanced. Not only did they talk very graphically about what they had done with a girl the evening before, but they stood around vocally admiring them as they passed.

"This one, this one, she is *gitarra-gitarra*," said a lanky fellow with rolled-up short sleeves, who sketched the curves of a guitar with his muscular right arm.

"*Esta dushi pia*," "What delicious legs," murmured another softly, with sucked-in breath, as a languid Curaçaoan beauty passed, her hips swiveling under her tight dress.

The others joined in admiringly, "What lovely thighs."

The excitement built and a chorus of voices swelled, admiring, whispering, buzzing, calling, "What a lovely, lovely ass."

Soon eight thirteen- and fourteen-year-old boys were all murmuring and humming, the girl turning around coyly, or striding off angrily, as her nature inclined. Even after she was gone, the drawing in of breath continued, a low lascivious slurping that sounded as if the boys were sucking on their own tongue.

My yearnings were less carnal, more emotional. It had something to do with talking and touching, the whispers of mutual confidences. Still, it felt good to be here, though I was embarrassed when a teacher approached. "Poyoyo," whispered one of the boys. All the Dutch teachers had Papiamentu nicknames, a sort of code the boys had worked out. Nobody knew what Poyoyo meant. The whistling and cooing stopped abruptly. He was a large man with a lurching gait, which we mimicked behind his back.

"Bunch of overgrown boys standing on the sidewalk. Is this what you do with your spare time? 'Early to ripen, early to rot,' I always say."

"Yes, Mr. Pover. Certainly Mr. Pover... We're just standing here warming ourselves," soothed Ricardo.

"*Mal basha*, badly poured," growled Hipolito, using the Curaçaoan expression for misshapen.

"In this blistering heat?" bawled Mr. Pover.

After Mr. Pover shambled off, Frank bent over to tie his shoelaces, his tidy round behind curving under tan slacks, which made Wilmoo instantly thrust his crotch at it, lightly touching Frank. "*Mi ta dal bu un frescu.* I'm giving you a squeeze," called Wilmoo.

Frank did not mind. "Next time you're down, my prick will be in your ass, dear brother-in-law."

Suddenly Mary, a fifteen-year-old dream vision in Guatemalan peasant blouse, floated by. Her bare shoulders gleamed in the sun. A melody of whispers and murmurs surged forward. Mary looked boldly at us and smiled a practiced smile. She aspired to become a model in Venezuela. Even the Dutch kids among us breathed a few words to her, though they did not usually participate in the chorusing. You needed to know Papiamentu as well as Papiamentu body-language. As for me, though I was regarded as Dutch, I had an uncertain refugee status.

I longed to be free and easy as the Curaçaoans were and envied them for being able to get a response out of those lovely creatures. Ever since we had a dazzling nanny in the middle of the war in Nice in 1942, whose hypnotically mild manner stirred me unaccountably, I had understood that my future happiness would be linked with girls and women. It was their presence that would make life complete. Now, at thirteen, I started noticing the marriages of the people my parents brought home, and I envied those couples that looked happy. What serenity and pleasure must be theirs, though I could not define that pleasure.

It would be a miracle if I could ever get a girl of my own, but if the miracle happened I would talk to her differently. These Curaçaoan kids were saying the wrong things to girls who wanted to be spoken to of love. Yet for some reason the girls talked to them and not to me. If I could become freer, more Curaçaoan, then I would talk to these girls in my way, explain to them how they stirred me, and have them realize I understood them and could make their own like-minded dreams come true. Surely they would prefer it to these shouts and hisses. So I redoubled my efforts with Els, until one day she said she had enough of Andy Panda movies.

When my friend Peter and I went to the Roxy Theater, next to my grandmother's house, I was astonished at how loudly the kids screamed. My own enjoyment was more furtive. On Saturday afternoons, the Roxy showed a grab-bag of different films. The big hit at this time was a National Geographic documentary called "Wild Beasts at Bay," which featured seven or eight naked, large-breasted women in Africa striding toward us. The matinee crowd consisted mainly of kids who screamed whenever these women appeared.

"You've got to see this," said Anton when it was over. He was a light-skinned, wild-haired roughneck, who wore a turquoise shirt. He spent a long time combing his curly black hair and slicking down his little mustache. He was the kind Dutch teachers, probably rightly, typed as delinquent.

"We just saw it," grinned Peter, his flaxen hair sweaty with excitement.

"It doesn't matter. You've got to see it again."

"What a shirt, Anton!" said Peter.

"I give it to you." Anton grimaced and rapidly unbuttoned his shirt. In a minute, he was down to his undershirt and flung the shirt toward Peter. But Anton was not to be distracted and came back to the movie.

So we went again, and waited for the lithe black women with their large, pendulous breasts. Anton screamed the loudest. From then on, Peter and I went every Saturday to hear Anton scream.

"Did you hear that noise?" I asked my grandmother when I came in the door.

"Noise, when is there no noise?" She was a small woman with a bun of gray, thick hair, who looked directly at you but sometimes did not see you.

"I mean from the movie theater."

"I don't have to listen to hear noise. I hear a lot of noise in my head." But then she softened and said, "Better Curaçao noise than Europe noise. The people here like to make noise. They mean no harm. I'm making dinner. Do you want to eat?"

My grandmother stood in the dining room next to her pride and joy, a large white refrigerator she always referred to as *"De Kelvinator."* "This makes it easier to keep kosher," she said, patting it. "We need to live a Jewish life."

She now told the story of a friend in Amsterdam just before the war whose wife had died and who needed a new suit.

"And you know, when a person is in mourning, he is forbidden to buy new clothes for a year.'"

"Is that in the Bible?" asked my brother helpfully.

"No, it's in the Talmud. But anyway, Opa bought it for him and wore it once."

"What was the point of that?"

"So he could turn it over to him. After all, he hadn't bought it."

"But wasn't it a new suit?"

"No, you see, he wore it once. So it was a used suit."

"But that isn't fair. It's just a trick."

She laughed heartily. "I suppose it was a trick, but it was a good trick."

"I don't think God likes to be tricked," I said argumentatively.

"Opa would say these are not things we should delve into."

Being Jewish always felt strange. Imagine explaining any of this to my new friends. Of course, some of them went to church and had similar things to put up with, but it could not be this strange. Besides, we also carried another load — the all-enveloping gloom of what had happened in Europe. I felt a great sadness but also a kind of shame about it, an aversion: even to talk about it was embarrassing. If I was to live my life, I would have to free myself from that sad weight. If I was to experience any sort of pleasure, I had to get away from being Jewish. Real life, ordinary life, the only life I wanted, was with Anton and Peter and school, and real happiness would come from a girl. When I was with them, I didn't have to think about anything else. With them, it was easier to think of the future than it was at home.

"Why don't you guys come to Campo Alegre?" shouted Anton as I stood talking to Peter in front of the school. "It'll teach you two virgins what men do." He combed his mustache with a curved little pocket comb.

"Anton, we know what men do. We don't need to go to Campo Alegre for that."

"Maybe you know, but you Dutch guys need to actually do it. Theory and practice, remember, just like the teacher said. You talk about it in that weird Dutch way, 'Yes, yes, uhm, um so, so, yes, that would be nice...' but we Curaçaoans do it because our blood is hotter than yours."

"That's not so," argued Peter. "Our blood is just as hot as yours."

"No. It isn't. That's why we always have to have several girlfriends. Or a wife and a girlfriend. Not like Dutch people.

They're ice-blooded." And he started mimicking a stiff-legged Dutch walk that instantly put me in mind of Els.

"What about Latin Americans then?" I asked, just to have something to say.

Now Anton grew thoughtful. "They're like us and they aren't. You know, those women in Campo Alegre are almost all Latin Americans. They must be hot to become whores."

"Yes, they must be."

"Anyway, we Curaçaoans do what we want. That's the difference between you and us. We don't worry about what's allowed." And he mimicked a Dutch voice saying, "*Dat kan niet, dat mag niet*," "That's not possible; that's not permitted. No, you must not do that."

"Oh, come on, Anton," said Peter to keep his country's honor high. "You're so dumb."

But we both knew Anton was right. Curaçaoans did what they wanted. And of course we did not go to Campo Alegre.

Campo Alegre was constructed when the prostitutes were cleared out of the hotels of downtown Willemstad. It was in all the papers. The boys at school knew about it, and one teacher grumbled, "Dirty things know no venue." After weeks of preparation, the well-publicized move came: fifty small bungalow-like cement houses with barren porches had been readied near the airport. I saw several pictures in the paper of local officials pointing at ugly box-like mounds. The whole cluster was quickly dubbed Campo Alegre, the happy field, the camp of joy, not by the island government, nor by the Dutch Ministry of Foreign Affairs in The Hague, which probably did not know about this big move in its far-flung West Indian colony, but by the patrons, the people. Anyway, that's how I heard it referred to.

The local government organized the whole affair, but there was also a certain Mr. Bakhuis, a white Curaçaoan, a rich businessman, who was rumored to be the real proprietor of the place, and people started calling the big yellow buses that bore the name CAB, Curaçao AutoBus, Campo Alegre Bakhuis, also

CAB. It was a form of Curaçaoan poetic play I enjoyed, just like the spontaneous song-making that accompanied any major event. Such songs doing the rounds would then find their way into the local language Papiamentu.

My friends talked about Campo Alegre but my parents seemed not to know or care. It had taken all their spirit to escape Europe, all their strength, and now they were spent and numb. Even before war's end, the suspicion of a holocaust, whose fires had somehow spared us, was palpable. Their new tropical home held little interest for them, though my mother did acquire friends among both Dutch and Jewish people, and did here what she had always done: speak to people and charm them, so that my father wouldn't have to: "Curaçao is an easy place, with easygoing people. They missed the war. I'm glad for them."

The island, vibrant and prosperous, had been far removed from any war zone. Even the war's passing was distinctly less important than new songs and plans for Campo Alegre. I liked that. It was easy to be distracted here. I was full of the future, and American movies gave me a picture of what that future might look like: the girls in shorts, the way kids talked to parents and other grown-ups, so free and almost impertinent; young high-schoolers dancing in formal dress, and one young man approaching a dancing couple, saying, "May I cut in?" But when I saw "The Bachelor and the Bobby-Soxer," I thought less about the young girl than her serious, romantic older sister.

When Campo Alegre had been around for a while, along with its new futbol (soccer) stadium and the shiny open-air movie house, it was no longer the source for jokes and anecdotes and music and legend, though there were, of course, stories that circulated, especially among adolescents like me. One was of the newly arrived Frenchwoman, so tall, so elegant in her Parisian dresses, that her little house in the compound was stormed by a mob of eager, too-long-in-line men. Twenty men had actually entered her house when the police arrived. I pictured the enthusiasm of the men, imagined myself one of them, the glamorous Frenchwoman recognizing the superiority of my words and speaking to me, saying that she had waited for someone to say these words to her, which showed so much understanding. Then she would undress for me. But the other boys also caught a certain lyricism in the story of the elegant Frenchwoman: my friend Simon, on hearing it, would be rapt and fall in a mock faint on the sandy beach of the dark-blue Caribbean Sea where we were all standing; he couldn't hear the story often enough. Sometimes he stood in the schoolyard and let himself fall to the pavement, knowing that he would be caught by one of us.

Another friend, Monty, the stocky son of a Lebanese merchant — a very old, small man I always remember as sitting on the porch of his large house or on a straight-backed chair in his prosperous, messy store — was once caught going into Campo Alegre. Monty was stopped by security guards at the gate, an underage minor. For some reason, his picture appeared on the front page of the daily newspaper. Monty was not acquainted with the sensation of embarrassment: he bought several copies of the paper and went down the Herenstraat, the narrow shopping street where most of the best stores were located. To the owners and clerks who had a habit of standing in front of their stores, many of them good friends of his parents, he said proudly, "*Mi ta den courant,*" "I'm in the paper," and he showed off his picture. Even at the time I realized vaguely that here was something to be learned, about brazenness and poise and style. Monty got into absolutely no trouble for this caper.

At about the same time that Campo Alegre stopped being a novelty, Curaçao had a new sensation. It happened at the Roxy, next to my grandmother's house, the theater with all the best films. A movie, oddly called "Mum and Dad," made in England as an educational film, was part of a long series of "important" pictures. "Hamlet" would play at the Roxy, as would Laurence Olivier's "Henry V," which so enraged dozens of moviegoers who had expected much *spada*, Papiamentu for sword fighting, that they jumped on stage and fought mock sword fights with each other. Letters to the editor abounded, but one stood out: my high school teacher saying in his elaborate, florid Dutch, that "given the excessively long character of Shakespeare's declamations, it was not altogether surprising that the good people in the audience had become restive."

So despite its repertory of good movies — or because of it — "Mum and Dad" was to be featured at the Roxy. The advertisements in the newspaper said with a sort of heavy-handed discreetness that the film would feature a "live birth" and that therefore men would have to see it separately from women. Every two days there was to be a rotation of the sexes. Something in this message proved inflammatory. From my grandmother's balcony, I could see a massive line forming, two full days before the opening of the movie: it was all male. Young men, old men, middle-aged men, black, white, brown, some in torn sport shirts, some in *guayabera*, the all-purpose tropical garment that can be worn casually or formally with a black bow tie, some in "Palm Beach" (any light-colored suit was called Palm Beach) — all waited in the furnace sun.

My grandmother's front balcony was a rickety wooden thing on stilts no more than ten feet above and fifteen feet away from the waiting crowd. Through the always-open windows of my grandparents' bedroom I heard in the heavy, humid air the droning British voice from the Roxy and later heard the crowd leave, laughing, jostling, yelling to others across the street. Meanwhile, a new line had already formed for the next performance twenty-four hours later. Every afternoon I watched the lines in the blazing day, and while no one ever fainted from the heat, many in the audience — always men — fainted when that "live birth" was finally shown. I learned to listen to it from my hideaway in my grandmother's bedroom; the sounds of the audience swelled, heaved, then broke into a kind of heavy, hoarse shouting, with an undertone of jeering and then the ambulance would come, always for the men's performance.

I longed to see this movie, as did Peter, but the age limit of eighteen was strictly enforced. Besides, neither of us could stay away from school to stand in line for days. My grandmother, who barely noticed the lines in front of her house, could answer none of my questions. At best she shook her head and said in Yiddish that this now was all she needed. But at last she noticed my extraordinary interest in these lines of waiting people and asked me, "What kind of film is that?"

Suddenly embarrassed, I answered, "Oh, it's an educational movie."

"When you get married I hope you and your wife will keep a kosher home."

"Yes, Oma."

"We were fleeing the Nazis, and Opa was in one prison in Spain and I in another, we thought we had troubles. But we were lucky compared to the others. But even there we kept kosher."

"Sure, I know that."

I did not want to hear this, I did not want to be sad, I did not want to be drawn into the past. As soon as I could, I ran outside. Anton was sure to be somewhere nearby. Maybe he would know why so many men had fainted. I wished it were Saturday afternoon so that we could look at the bouncing women again. I ran past the enormous crowd in front of the Roxy, my head full of images of smiling girls in some future landscape, maybe Dutch, maybe American, and, to my relief, found Peter, looking more oafish than usual, his starched white shirt in pristine contrast to his ever lurid thoughts. He told me that he heard one of the men say after seeing "Mum and Dad," "Man, this is worse than Campo Alegre."

Well, maybe that man was right. When I finally did go, at sixteen, I was surprised by how domestic and placid Campo Alegre was, the little bungalows leaning into the grid of narrow streets and open pathways. Around the bungalows, men and women stood, conversing, laughing quietly. The little streets looked like lanes in a peaceful, though shabby, village. I had come there with George Gabrielides, a Greek sailor I had met in the hospital, when my foot was operated on. He had fallen on his back, broken it, he said, but he expected to walk again — but all George talked about was Campo Alegre.

"You know what this island is," he asked rhetorically, his brown eyes glittering in his small face, as he sat up in his hospital bed. "I've been all over the world, but this is the best. It's the pearl of the Antilles — and all because of Campo Alegre. Do you have a girlfriend?" And he hummed a few bars of a popular song about gypsy violins.

Els was the closest thing to a girlfriend I ever had, but she had returned to the Netherlands. I was eager for a girl, an experience, a taste of life.

"Is this man you met in the hospital, this Gabrielides, this sailor, taking you to the city?" asked my father, mildly giving voice to the danger he sensed.

"No, we're just going for a drive," I answered. "He is now well enough to drive."

I strolled through Campo Alegre. Groups of men were standing in a little plaza, talking animatedly but not rowdily. One smiling, strapping fellow, his powerful hands on his hips, said earnestly to an older fellow with glasses and close-cropped gray hair, "She sucked my cock so hard — so hard she sucked my cock. It's unbelievable how hard she sucked." The two black men faced each other intently, in that aggressive but playful Curaçaoan manner, as if no subject of greater importance could be discussed.

'Yes, but did she suck it well?" asked the older man, as if he were trying to fathom a scientific puzzle. He looked unsmiling, attentive.

"Man, I'm telling you that," said the younger man, his index finger pointing downward. "That's exactly what I'm telling you. I'm telling you how well."

"Don't you know a cock can be sucked hard but not well?" said the man, now taking off his glasses and looking in the distance.

Other men were reclining on benches in front of the porches. Between two bungalows, men and women were sitting on packing crates drinking out of beer bottles. On paths between the bungalows a few men sauntered past.

I was ready. Though I would have preferred love to sex, especially paid sex, I settled for the latter. George left me quickly enough. Carelessly, without choosing anyone, I walked on to a porch with an open door. A brown, worn-looking woman, wearing only a skirt and a white bra, who looked almost elderly — she must have been in her thirties — seemed surprised that anyone chose her. Her room was bare, except for a bed and a tiny refrigerator. I gave her ten guilders and she lay down on her back, matter-of-factly but somewhat stiffly, and instantly took down her underpants. "*Venga*," she said, "do come." I noticed that she used the polite form as if I were an adult.

I hesitated, having expected some kind of touching first, kissed her bare brown shoulder ardently, and again she looked surprised and said, "*Qué?*"

"I haven't done this very often," I said because I wanted her to talk to me. Of course I had never done it.

"*Venga*," she said again, raising her head a little and guiding me in.

I came into her and kissed her shoulder again, feeling a sudden surge of gratitude and pleasure. She rocked back and forth without saying anything. I wished I knew what she was feeling.

When I came, she said, "*Gracias*."

And I said, "*Gracias a usted*," and meant it wholeheartedly. It wasn't my dream, but it brought me closer, just as kissing Els had brought me closer.

It was over so quickly. She hadn't talked to me. She hadn't listened to me. It was sex, not love. And I paid for it. But it was a taste of that pleasure I had thought so much about, of the future I so eagerly wanted. I was happy.

It was my first and last visit to Campo Alegre or any brothel anywhere, but I never regretted having gone.

Chapter 15. The Gentiles Have Patience

Some time in the late forties, when we were comfortably settled in Curaçao, my parents attempted to embrace the normality that had eluded them during the long war years by doing what other young couples were doing — entertaining friends. These guests were very Dutch and chosen in part because my parents, who had lived in Holland but were not born there, wanted to be considered Dutch, and because there were few other refugees with our background on the island. My parents also valued them because they were prominent, influential people.

Our visitors would often talk at length about their hobbies and travels. Afterwards, my father would sigh to my mother, "The Gentiles have such patience."

I can still see my mother on the veranda of our house nodding quietly to our Dutch friends, the Kamelings or the Zaalmans or the Stierendragers, who had shown us innumerable slides of their vacations in Haiti, Jamaica, Costa Rica and the Virgin Islands, all of them convenient vacation spots for high Dutch colonial officials at that time. My mother usually conveyed an impression of deep interest, while my father seemed almost stuporous. Mrs. Kameling might talk for a long time in animated tones about native costumery and leather craft, while Mr. Kameling concentrated ponderously on deep-sea fishing and alligator hunting. Did we know that Lake Managua in Nicaragua was the only body of fresh water in the world to "host" sharks? We did not. Occasionally he would comment on a slide and say to no one in particular that "a large iguana is bigger than a small alligator" and my father would shake himself out of a deep reverie and nod abstractedly, with the same remote half smile he often had for my brother and me.

These visitors were "important people"; my parents felt they might, who knows, do us a favor some day. That was certainly one of the attractions of these particular people. This was not always explicitly stated, but my parents had acquired that habit in Europe, before and during the war. There was not only the Dutch cop my father had befriended who tipped us off early in 1942 that we were about to be deported by the Nazi occupiers of Holland, but even before the war, when my parents lived in Germany, they had experienced the value of knowing important people.

In her high school in Chemnitz, Germany, my mother had befriended a young, shy girl who had few friends, was clumsy and not pretty. Ilse was small and longed for attention; my mother was outgoing and popular, and paid attention to her. That was in the twenties. Ilse's parents had been delighted with the friendship and invited my mother again and again to their house. Only because of my grandfather's objections that a Jewish girl should not stay over in a Christian home did my mother never spend the night.

They remained on good terms even during the early Hitler years, when Ilse's father had become an officer in the SS. But suddenly in 1937, my mother received a call from her friend. "I cannot speak long. You must leave Germany. Forever."

We left Germany for Holland the next year, in 1938. Now ten years later, and eight thousand miles away, they courted Mr. Kameling, a florid, rotund man, whose job as head of the department of Social Security could in no way do anything for my parents, who were quietly running a modest import-export business. "But you never know," they said.

"Well, why do we have to come along?" my brother asked, giving his serious, bespectacled face a little shake.

"Because," said my mother kindly enough, "we need your help. Your Dutch is perfect, and you can ask them questions that we just wouldn't know to ask."

Essentially polite boys, my brother and I asked questions. I squirmed in my chair and yawned but I thought of things I could ask. My brother hated to take time off from his schoolwork, but he was an excellent question-asker. "Why do the natives of Haiti" — it was always the natives — "not get along with the Dominicans they share the island with?" he wanted to know.

"Because," said Mr. Kameling, "they are black, and the Dominicans aren't. Also, the Haitians try to look for work in the Dominican Republic, and the Dominicans resent that."

And why was Columbus's name for the island, Hispaniola, never used anymore?

Mr. Kameling was less sure about that.

Both of my parents looked pleased. But Mr. Kameling really would have preferred questions about his activities, the more technical the better. He had fished in the deepest waters, sought out the most far-fetched folklore. In that regard we were inadequate and couldn't think of anything to ask; in our family the word "hobby" had a bad name, it was thought of as frivolous, even though my brother and I got endless pleasure from our stamp collections. Besides, Mr. Kameling was actually more a naturalist than a hobbyist.

In the Kamelings' darkened house overlooking the harbor, we watched home movies and slides. A beam of light cast by the whirring projector revealed hundreds of gleaming specks of dust. Sitting on their large, white sofa, I felt sleepy and stifled a yawn. We were now in the jungles near Limón, on the Caribbean coast of Costa Rica. "The people here are English-speaking," discoursed Mr. Kameling. "They're descended from Jamaicans, who... Dear, did they come to work on the Panama Canal?"

"I think so," answered Mrs. Kameling.

"But then, how did they end up in Costa Rica?" And Mr. Kameling lumbered over to the Winkler Prins Encyclopedia, which we had in our house too.

This was more interesting than what came next, because the Kamelings were avid bird-watchers, a hobby my parents detested. "How can anyone spend his time this way?" my father asked. "So you see a bird. You look at it. You photograph it... so?"

"And why a bird?" chimed in my mother. "Why not a curtain or a chair?"

They saw no point in two grown people looking at birds; it made no sense to them. My father once told me that the only flower with its own name in Yiddish was a rose. I did not think there were many words for "bird" either. And yet my parents seemed ambivalent, envious as well as dismissive. On the one hand, they felt that bird-watching, woodworking, deep-sea diving, underwater photography, and matchbook and insignia collecting were alien pastimes, childish, tiresome and trivial; on the other hand, that they were wonderful activities, which gave pleasure and added richness to life, and that we refugees had been robbed of the patience required to pursue them. In some other life, maybe we would have had the peace of mind to do such things.

We had all seen hundreds of slides of different birds, most of them, though not all, in flight. Lovingly, the Kamelings called out names of exotic birds: "Vermilion Fly-catcher!" "Plain Xenops!" "Belted Kingfisher!" "Stripe-breasted Spine-tail!" "Red-faced Spine-tail!"

"So many of these birds are red," observed my mother irrelevantly.

"Waxwing!" called Mrs. Kameling.

"No, that's not a waxwing, dear. Look at those rough feathers."

"How can you tell the feathers are rough?"

"Can't you see how rough they look? That fellow is a palm-chat."

"But notice his rump. It's brown."

"That just means, dear, he's a young palm-chat."

"Oh... is that a booby?"

"No, that was last year. We saw a booby last year."

"Last year?"

"Yes, don't you remember, last year on the island of Margarita?"

"You mean two years ago on St. Lucia."

"No, dear, it was the year you stepped on that driftwood, don't you remember?"

"That was not Margarita, dear. How can you think so?"

"Birds are wondrous creatures," intoned Mr. Kameling. "Their glands give off an oil; they rub their heads in that oil and spread it over themselves." A slide of a nondescript-looking bird preening glowed on the screen, interminably.

"When do they molt?" asked my brother helpfully.

"Look, Bertha," yelled Mrs. Kameling in her high-pitched squeal, "there are the people I told you about, with the parrot." I could tell that my mother was frantically trying to recall a story about parrots, and I could guess what she would say to my father afterwards. "How in the world can these people care about a parrot? Well, I suppose if we had lived as they did, we would care too."

The slide, for once, was sharp and clear. Around a wretched hovel in a clearing stood Mr. Kameling like a fat giant surrounded by small black figures in ragged shorts. One of them held two sad-looking cages.

My mother finally said, "Yes, yes, the parrots."

"It's an Amazon, and it actually spoke Dutch. The people didn't even know what a treasure they had; gorgeous green plumage and a handsome yellow head."

My father came out with, "Oh, what happened to that bird?"

"No, Max," said Mr. Kameling with some exasperation, "we did not take it home: we just looked at it when the natives told us they had some. Costa Rica has more species of birds than any other country in the world."

After we got home, my father seemed uncharacteristically zany. I had never seen him like that. "Is a chicken a bird?" he asked my mother.

"No idea, Max," my mother said, looking at him, worried.

We thought of the Kamelings as great travelers, but they were considered mere tourists by our other guests, the Zaalmans. Husband and wife had a reputation for being strange; they were young and energetic and traveled to outlandish places and scoffed at the usual vacation retreats of other high Dutch colonial officials. Dr. Zaalman was deputy inspector of public health for the islands of Curaçao, Aruba, and Bonaire. He and his wife had climbed Machu Picchu twice, long before it was all the rage. "Dr. Zaalman is a real Cossack," said my father.

"They're both Cossacks," affirmed my mother.

They were a sturdy pair, he short and wiry, she tall, lanky and red-faced. On the slides, both wore mountain-climbing shorts and hobnailed boots. Traveling and photography were not pastimes but passions for them. They spoke of their trips with an almost proselytizing eagerness. Most of their colleagues, said Dr. Zaalman, had no idea what travel was. Real travel was adventure, testing your stamina in unfamiliar surroundings. You got to know people, unfortunate people, invisible people, and you photographed them to give them life. Dr. Zaalman explained that every picture must tell several stories. He liked to say that one vignette was not good enough.

One slide made me giggle hard: a whole row of somber bowler-hatted Indians appearing to lead the Zaalman couple to an ancient sacrifice on the shores of Lake Titicaca, a name my brother and I enjoyed for days afterwards. Dr. Zaalman said that it all showed a primitive culture being able to absorb a technologically advanced culture. For him photography was a kind of twentieth-century genre painting. On another slide, Mrs. Zaalman was unaccountably alone in a small boat on the gun-metal water. Her toothy smile and bright sweater looked oddly out of character with the stark surroundings.

Like many Dutch officials, they had spent the war years on the island and had grown to love their rank and privilege in this new world. They regarded the Netherlands with chagrin and the hopeless anger of those who have seen a beloved place utterly changed. Out of touch with the mother country, they were appalled at the new freedoms that were beginning to flourish there, of which they spoke with indignation. "Yes," Dr. Zaalman said, "people did not have enough to eat during the war, but is that an excuse for carrying on like that now? As if suddenly everything were allowed?" Dr. Zaalman spoke with that exaggerated enunciation that many well-educated Dutch people have. "You just can't imagine what goes on there now. The country is ruined. You should see it… My God: people are having children who have no business having children. It's chaos."

My mother looked interested but it was hard to tell if she was. My father may have thought that Dr. Zaalman was not enlightened politically; surely a socialist government would have cured these post-war ills.

To illustrate his point, Dr. Zaalman told us the following tale. A friend of his, whom he had visited last summer in The Hague, had brought Coca Cola into his house, and his five-year old daughter had become addicted to it. The Dutch word is *verslaafd*, enslaved, and Dr. Zaalman paused with relish before he continued. "The father tried to discourage his little girl from this habit, but she carried on so that he finally made an agreement with her." Again, a heavy pause. "What was the agreement, Max?" My father looked startled for a moment in the comfortable wicker chair in which he sat slumped, as if he thought Dr. Zaalman wanted him to provide the answer. "The agreement was," continued the doctor expansively, "that she could have all the Coca Cola she wanted, but he would spank her every time she did.

"So there we were, Max" — for some reason he addressed only my father, though my mother was clearly the better listener — "and the girl had a Co-Ca and then came over to her father and took off her little *directoire* and climbed over his knee and said, 'But please, not too hard, Daddy.'"

Dr. Zaalman's little glasses glistened in the tropical night air. He used the word *directoire* for 'panties,' a word that still suggested the naughty ladies of the French Revolution and probably had not been used much in the Netherlands since the turn of the century. There was a humid silence on the porch, which Dr. Zaalman gave every indication of enjoying.

I looked at my father, but he did not look more uncomfortable than usual. He was always ill at ease in social situations and escaped into blankness and absent-mindedness.

Just then, the maid came in and asked people what they wanted to drink and my father said to her, before my mother could speak, "Don't ask the guests — just give... assorted."

Dr. Zaalman — my parents never used his first name —was actually among my parents' favorite guests; my brother and I liked him too. He joked around with us and said we should become sailors; that was the only way to see the world. The worst thing was to become the kind of man who sat on his ass all day. Mrs. Zaalman gently chided her husband: what language for the children! "But it's true, isn't it?" said he and playfully raised a finger at his wife. "You wouldn't like such a man, would you, treasure?"

My parents' other friends, the Stierendragers, were a somewhat older couple in their mid-forties. Joop Stierendrager was exceptionally quiet when his wife was with him and rather loose-lipped when she was not. He had the reputation of being a first-rate civil servant in the Curaçaoan Department of Water, a difficult assignment in that drought-plagued island which had once imported water from far-away Ireland. Since we almost always saw the Stierendragers together, we had mainly the benefit of her voice. And that voice was insistent and confined largely to one subject: horses.

It was Mrs. Stierendrager's ardent wish to buy a horse and bring it to Curaçao. For that purpose, she and Joopje — she called her husband by the diminutive — had already made several trips to Venezuela and Costa Rica. "Dressage, that's what it's about... A good show horse," she explained to my parents, "holds its head down." And she tilted her head downward, looking rather contented in a horse-like way. "But not this far down," she suddenly burst out, her chin pressing against her throat.

My father looked alarmed. His idea of a good horse was one that was far away. My brother and I had once been on a horse but much preferred the donkeys at the burro-polo corral of the Curaçao Beach Club, where dozens of small boys on sweating donkeys swatted at a large soccer ball with brooms. Mrs. Stierendrager, whom my mother bravely called Ria, suddenly crossed her bony legs.

"The head is down, so that the back can swing more freely and the hind legs carry more weight. In fact, the hind legs go under further than in an ordinary horse; the hoof prints of the hind legs actually go in front of the print of the front legs. The hind legs take more of the weight and the front legs move more freely, so that the horse can stride. I want a horse that can stride."

"Wasn't there such a horse to be found in all of Venezuela?" asked my mother, a little less tactfully than she usually did.

"I can't say that," said Mrs. Stierendrager, suddenly very precise and pedantic. "All I can really say is that I didn't find him."

Mr. Stierendrager sipped at his whisky soda. One reason he was a comfortable presence was that he sometimes seemed even more abstracted than my father. But in a Gentile way: rumor had it that he had a local girlfriend. Mrs. Stierendrager again swung her legs over each other with such force that her skirt made a cracking sound. She gave the impression of unbridled, frustrated, furious energy.

My brother and I were ready for what was coming now: "Oh, I want, I want above all to breed horses!" The Dutch word for breeding is *fokken*, and we were both intensely familiar with the English word "fucking," which American GIs had brought to the island during the war, and which the local language, Papiamentu, promptly, eagerly, gratefully, assimilated. The wonder was that Mrs. Stierendrager did not know that, but a great many Dutch people didn't: they saw the "natives" but didn't hear them. A few learned to speak Papiamentu, but most of them did not, feeling that they would not be in Curaçao forever and that, after all, the locals spoke Dutch well enough.

After a few years, my annoyance with these visits gave way to a feeling of embarrassment. People like the Kamelings must have noticed my father's inattentiveness and his often not seeming to know what was being said to him. I could do better in their company, I thought, if I were alone, or just with my mother. Without my father present, I could speak to those Dutch people without worrying about what he would say or how he would appear to them. I knew what to say to them and how to say it. You had to show interest and understand that they loved many small things, that it wasn't just foolish of them to be caught up by their activities but revealed a love for what they saw.

Sometimes I even envied them. They might be dull, but they enjoyed themselves in a way my parents never did. My mother, too, started saying that she learned from them, and she made some visits on her own, without the rest of us. At times she seemed almost desperate to absorb their ways. "Why should they be the only ones who take pleasure in things?" she said. "OK, they're Gentiles, we will never understand them and they will never understand us, but isn't it healthier to be with such people than to stay at home? I want to try at least to live a normal life."

I liked her saying that. It made me feel good. Of course, she was more gregarious than my father, more talkative, more animated. She also had a talent for drawing new people to her, whatever her motives were in doing so. "Max," she would say, "have you met that new couple from the Netherlands?"

"New couple? What new couple?"

"She's the glamorous one. He looks older."

"Oh, yes, he's going to do something new here."

"Advertising, advertising." My mother smiled at the mention of this glamorous activity.

"How can anyone do advertising here? What's there to advertise?" asked my father.

"I don't know, but I'd like to meet them. Wouldn't you?"

"Yes, yes," lied my father.

"Good, maybe we'll be invited." And soon they were off to see Mr. and Mrs. Heider, who, my mother declared, acted like people just released from prison; they so loved the island.

My mother continued her visits. She always dressed up for these occasions. "Dutch people are formal," she said. "It makes small things important. Sometimes these things are silly, of course; but the Gentiles have the patience and peace of mind to take them seriously, and we should also try to. For us it's important that we see that side of life too."

My father looked at her blankly. "What side of life?" he asked.

"These people don't even give in to the heat," my mother continued. "Look at the way they dress. The women in girdles and stockings. Maybe life improves if we dress up for it."

However hot it might be in those pre-air-conditioning days, our guests arrived in coat and tie and skirts and dresses. The informality that had started washing over the Netherlands in the late forties had certainly not reached this distant Dutch colonial shore. Both at work and on social occasions, the men wore their coats and ties. My friends and I addressed our parents with the honorific "*U,*" rather than the informal "*Je.*" Dr. Zaalman might speak informally and even crudely, but that was because he was unconventional and an adult. It would never have been tolerated from a youngster. But of course, among ourselves we did what adolescents have always done: we were foul-mouthed, liberally mixing Dutch, Papiamentu and Spanish swear-words.

I always thought of the Dutch colonial officials as an indestructible species. Long after I left Curaçao to study at an American university, I bumped into Mr. Kameling in The Hague. I was thirty-three and teaching at San Francisco State University, and he must have been close to sixty. We recognized each other at once. He had grown shorter and fatter but looked remarkably the same. Mrs. Kameling had died five years before of breast cancer, and he had never remarried.

Now he was on his way to an Adult Education Center, where he was studying Italian to prepare for his next trip to Italy. He had taken up butterfly hunting and had found a valley in the Italian Alps where some as yet unclassified specimen of butterfly was to be found. "Even Nabokov," he said, "doesn't know a thing about these species. You know, the novelist and butterfly expert?" He said NA-bo-koffff, sounding happy, and for a moment I was startled at the intersection of my American college teacher existence and my Curaçaoan childhood. Not surprisingly, he was doing better than my father, also a widower, but still living in Curaçao, still working in his business, and ever more consumed with grief over my mother's death and his shattering losses during the war.

Two years after that meeting in Holland, in 1970, my father retired from his business in Curaçao to San Francisco, a lonely, obsessive man. Without work, without any hobbies, he filled his days wandering the streets. He made up schemes, plotted escape routes in the event of another outbreak of war. While Mr. Kameling was hunting butterflies, my father haunted hotel lobbies, trying to find people with experiences similar to his own, to engage them in conversation about such subjects as the Holocaust and the war. He had once cultivated important friends and was now alone. All the people about whom he said that "you never knew what they can do for you" were not able to do anything for him. He was alone with his memories.

I no longer scorned that formula, as I had during childhood and adolescence. Ever since leaving Curaçao I had begun to understand how crucial that way of doing things had been for us, how it had saved our lives. It was easy for me, here, now, not to court important people, as my parents had to. Without all the important people they befriended along the way of our escape route, courted, bribed, fooled, we would never have escaped. There would have been no escape route. And what I used to see as an irritating Jewish habit of maneuvering and sliding, I now began to realize was a crucial adaptation to ever-changing, ever-worsening dangers.

Throughout my childhood I heard my parents speak of important people who could conceivably help you in a crisis; the word for such a person was '*puritz.*' A *puritz* was to be befriended, flattered, bribed, manipulated, or courted. It was a word I disliked when my father used it. My mother was more ironical about it and said things like, "That *puritz* over there, selling tickets." There it meant that someone insignificant had achieved a momentary position of power.

I had changed my thinking too about the interests, the hobbies, the pastimes of the people who had them, which looked trivial to those bent on survival, but no longer did to me. It was precisely these things that gave pleasure to life; this importance we attach to things gives meaning to them. While I still do not like to hear unrelenting narratives about such activities as weaving or putting on plays for children or ceramics or the care of ancient carpets, I recognize the value of living immersed in these pursuits. I understand the pleasures of distractibility. I crave some of the Gentiles' patience for myself. Fat old Mr. Kameling was soaring on his mountaintop, pursuing transcendent butterflies, while here below, my father, leaden, earthbound, grew ever more despondent with the burden he carried.

My mother, even in her grief and unhappiness, grasped the value of the Gentile pastimes she had often disparaged. "I like them, and also I try to like them," she said. She does not, I thought then. How can you try to like someone? But she struggled to make these undertakings hers, as I do now to make them mine. I wished I could tell my mother that I saw things her way. She had died in 1959, and there were so many things I now saw her way.

"You know what made the difference?" said my father one day in the mid-seventies when we were both sitting in the lobby of San Francisco's Hyatt Regency Hotel.

"About what?" I asked, irritated at his way of beginning many a conversation *in medias res*.

"Well, when we couldn't get out of unoccupied France, at the end of '42, and I kept trying to get documents from the Spanish consul in Pau — get them quickly before the Nazis took over that part of France as well. I went to see him several times. I tried to do what your mother could do so well — get to know him. But you know what made the difference?"

"No," I repeated, looking at the waves of dancers in the lobby, swirling around us, two solitary Dutch-speaking figures marooned in Eden.

"It wasn't the money I kept trying to give him. He was afraid of taking money, though he took it. I heard about him and his many hobbies from a Jew who also was trying to save himself. The consul was a gardener, he collected wines, he owned stamps. Even during the war he traveled to see other stamp collectors." My father shook his head in disbelief. "He was one of those patient Gentiles. No, not the money — it was your and your brother's stamp-album, which I gave him. He was so ardent a collector of stamps that when he saw the album he wanted it. So then he gave me the visa to Spain. Only then did he give me the visa. The Nazis took that part of France only a few days later. We would have been lost." And now my father stared unseeing at the dancers.

Something welled up in me, deep and nameless, as if an unknown, unsuspected body of water were suddenly rising to ground level. I felt tears in my eyes and no longer saw the dancers at the Hyatt Regency. Had my father, against his nature, taken the time to study this Consul's habits, to learn about his ways? Had my parents prepared this present for him long in advance? If so, they were in their own way patient beyond belief, with a patience the Gentiles could not have mustered — or needed.

I had forgotten about that stamp album, which we had dragged across many a frontier. It was a large, beautiful book with a pale-blue cover and many illustrations my brother and I had been eager to cover with stamps. Each town we came to, whether it was Lyon, Nice, or Perpignan, my brother and I talked earnestly about the advantages of splitting up our collections, into his and mine. But then the question became how we would do this and whether the separate collections would not look meager, compared to what we once had.

One time, we actually divided our collection and laboriously took out all the stamps, but there turned out to be no way to buy another album. Besides, said my brother, with so much going on, so many serious things happening, to think about stamp collecting was silly. "Trifling," is the word he used.

I agreed with him, but after the loss of the album decided that I would not collect stamps again. What was the point? We could never hope to retrieve all the stamps we lost. But I did anyway, and now the only album I really remembered in detail was the one we started up again in Curaçao, long after the stamp-collecting consul in Pau had been bribed.

Manny, 17, and roommate Marvin at Brandeis
in 1951

With friends at Brandeis, in 1951

Part III: Forward

Chapter 16. The Tree of Memory: From Curaçao to Brandeis

N
ow on the KLM plane, almost seventeen years old, I was finally on my way to Brandeis University in Waltham, Massachusetts. I was wearing a jacket and tie and sat up straight, but people around me were relaxing; some had taken off their shoes. They must be Americans returning from a Caribbean holiday. My Dutch passport was a reassuring hard place in my right, inside jacket pocket. I kept tapping to feel if it was still there. Once I drummed my fingers on my right inside pocket and felt an alarming softness, the comforting passport ridges missing. Instantly my heart started to hammer until I realized that the passport was on the other, the left side. I checked there again, and the hard little square quieted me down.

America loomed beckoningly before me. Could it restore the happiness I had felt long ago, eleven years ago, in Holland, as a child before the war, when everything felt so perfect and the cool air around was filled with keen anticipation? After the years in Curaçao, I wanted to live in a country which resembled the country of my childhood more than Curaçao could. I did not want America to be yet another country to escape to but the one to replace Holland, making all the other escape countries unnecessary.

American movies, with their pictures of carefree boys and girls flirting with each other, carrying each others' books, quickened my desire to go to the U.S. These movies once or twice mentioned the word "Jewish," as if it were an ordinary word and even the words 'war' and 'Jews' and 'Hitler' as if they were ordinary words. I learned English in school and from the comic books I devoured. Bugs Bunny and Porky Pig became as real to me as the boys in Dutch children's books. There was something zany about these comic books, as if the American adults who created them were enough like children themselves to know what children were like.

> "Porky's my name and I stutter.
> When I see my girl,
> My head's in a whirl,
> And my heart begins to melt like butter."

I could practically hear Americans saying things like that, and they often did in the movies.

Even in Holland, when I was a small child, people talked about America. It was not as "normal" as Europe but more so than Curaçao. "In America," my father said, "people don't wash dishes. When they're done eating they throw the dishes out and then put their feet on the table." The first Americans I saw, tourists to Curaçao, looked as if they could put their feet on the table. Large and self-confident in their brand-new tropical clothes, they spoke loudly and brashly, as if English were the only language in the world. "Everything in America is always so exaggerated," my Dutch teacher said. My mother thought that Americans boasted a lot, but my father declared that "the Jews there are almost like Gentiles." I liked that idea.

At last the plane landed in Miami, and trembling with nervous anticipation, I waited in line at Immigration as a thermometer was clapped into my mouth by a pale, uniformed woman. If it registered a fever, I would be ordered to get a new certificate of health. I carefully looked through my papers: the health certificate lay neatly next to a document attesting to my Good Conduct, alongside a detailed financial statement outlining how my first American year would be paid. I patted my stiff passport side. Across from me sat two Dutch KLM pilots with thermometers hanging drolly from the corners of their mouths. The American officials chuckled at them and smiled at us.

"Hey, Joe," I heard one official say in imitation of the movies, "what'd you do last night?"

"You wouldn't believe it if I told you," answered Joe with a wide grin, loosening the collar of his white uniform shirt and deftly tucking his dark-blue tie, G.I. style, between two shirt buttons. Several of Joe's colleagues laughed and kept right on talking while smoking and glancing casually at travelers' documents. The slow, drawling banter contrasted with the rigid, anxious line the passengers formed. Every once in a while, a thumping sound made on paper allowed someone in line to pass on to the next station. They never asked my religion, though I did notice someone scribbling down "Caucasian," a word I did not understand.

I left on a scalding summer day in 1951. Standing at the Curaçao airport, holding the "bakobas," the fried bananas my friend Mundi had brought, I listened to him apologize. I had never heard him apologize before. "You must think I'm cheap, to bring these," he grinned, his brown face handsome and a little distant, looking away from me and my Dutch friend Peter. No Curaçaoan I knew had ever been stingy. On the contrary, we Dutch — real Dutch as well as refugee Dutch — always regarded Curaçaoans as extravagant, living beyond their means. Peter — real Dutch — ran a hand through his flaxen hair and smiled stolidly, his fleshy lips in a pleasant but puzzled grin: "Next year I'll be at the University of Amsterdam. Why aren't you going there? We could've been there together."

Only six weeks before I left for America, we had one last high-school outing to the Hato caves, the gloomy limestone caverns near Curaçao's airport. In the half darkness of an underground cavern, my classmates started one of their usual, zany routines: a low hum, growing ever louder; it was a way of talking to each other and excluding the teacher. But for once, the mood quickly darkened. Mundi stood still and whispered, "This is where my ancestors hid, the slaves who escaped. Some died here in these caves." A Dutch teacher overheard him and said in his "missionary Papiamentu," as the Curaçaoans called the way Dutch people spoke the native language, "Not to worry your head about that now, Mundi."

And I did not worry about it either: I was eager for my new life in America, away from Curaçao and away from my parents. I was eager to leave behind their gloom and our history. I wanted to be away from the daily reminders of our flight and the war concluded six years ago, the whispers about the horrors we escaped and the relatives who perished in Europe. And I wanted to get away from some of my own memories: the barking dogs during the night walk across the Demarcation line from occupied to unoccupied France, the hideous anxiety of my parents after our escape from captivity in Monte Carlo, the horror of uncertainty about whether we could proceed to Spain when the Nazis threatened unoccupied France in late 1942.

Even the aftermath in Suriname and Curaçao was not easy, though our life in Curaçao from 1944 on was relatively normal. Despite our safety in Curaçao, and despite the occasional zaniness of life in Curaçao, I felt nostalgic for life in Holland before the war and eager for the future in America after Curaçao. I would miss my friends in Curaçao and regretted not being able to go to Holland — which my parents felt would soon be in the grip of World War Three — but I longed to be in America. With my grandfather's death in 1950, another link was broken with the past. Now America would do the rest.

Mundi was frowning. "Why are you leaving? You could stay here in sweet Curaçao."

"You know there's no university here, Mundi."

"I know, but that's not why you're going."

"Mundi, I'm going to miss you," I said.

"Yeah, you're going to miss the dance tomorrow." He started dancing by himself, his arm encircling an imaginary girl.

I wanted to tell him that I did not belong in Curaçao, that I felt I was going to a place more congenial to me, but he suddenly said, "You colonials. You just leave here when you're done with us. Take a plane and get out. Without appreciating what's here. But America" — and here Mundi's rubbery face took on that Curaçaoan conspiratorial look — "In America the girls are hot, hot, hot." And he quickly sketched out a full female outline with his hands. I looked over at my parents, who, for the moment, stood apart. They looked strained, my mother trying to smile and my father with his unseeing, inward look. They were talking to each other in that sad, sorrowful way I knew well. I felt bad at how badly I wanted to leave. My brother had preceded me to America. My parents would remain alone in Curaçao.

I applied to the newly established Brandeis University, at once Jewish and obviously secular, because I thought the students would be Jewish like me and yet eager to live in a Gentile world. I thought they might be able to understand me and the different experience I brought with me. Our harrowing escape from Europe was not something I wanted to talk about but expected somehow to be known. Being Jewish themselves, they would care about it.

From my first days in America I retain the sense of having arrived on a movie set. Bright colors everywhere, hand-waving motions, loud, unabashed shouts. When school started, the fields of Brandeis glowed in the autumn sun. Students, some already holding hands, strolled on woody lanes between brightly painted wooden buildings, which housed classrooms and faculty offices. Laughter resounded in the administration building at orientation, in the cafeteria, and in the dormitories. My future classmates' voices rang out, accompanied by broad gestures and easy embraces. My parents had taught me not to "speak with my hands"; it would typify me as Jewish. Here students used almost theatrical body language, just like in the movies. My puzzlement, during those early American days, was less with language than with unaccustomed ways of behaving. How could they be so uninhibited?

My first class at Brandeis was in an auditorium — a sea of color, red shirts, green and blue and white scarves, yellow rain slickers. Boys and girls were sitting in all sorts of attitudes and postures — slumped, slouched, upright, leaning over each other, smiling, talking, calling. One fellow stood up and waved his arms as if he had just claimed a new continent. The students had a kind of larger-than-life, cartoon look about them. Their boldness was enviable, but, to my Dutch eyes, a trifle overdone. "You have to be crazy to wear a red shirt," my father used to say.

I felt comfortable here but not fully at home. This easygoing warmth I met everywhere was preferable to the sternness of manner of the Dutch, the frowns that were unabashedly disapproving. The good cheer all around me was comforting, though also puzzling. Why was everyone so happy? It was as if they did not know any other way. I tried to smile as much as my classmates did but often forgot to do so. Once, my face cracked painfully and a fellow student asked me, with a smile, if something was wrong. I also tried to speak with greater animation but found that difficult. For a while, I practiced speaking loudly, the way as a child I practiced saying dirty words and making rude gestures.

My roommate Marvin greeted me with a warm embrace. He had a finely chiseled face and a crew cut and always wore a tweed jacket and white shoes of a kind I had never seen before called "white bucks." "The two of us, we'll paint the town red," he exclaimed, while greeting a girl with a kiss on the lips. "You're so fast you make my head spin, Marv," she grinned. "Yeah, any more of this and I'll be spinning out of control," he bubbled. Marvin always flashed a phrase at someone and possessed the sort of joking verbal wit I seemed incapable of. His was an American ease, and I envied it. But Marvin was too quicksilvery to listen well. Throughout my acquaintance with him, he occasionally introduced me as "Manny from Caracas" or "Manfred who's from the tropics."

Marvin knew lots of girls, and he encouraged me to "date" them. I looked forward to this American activity of dating but did not realize that it centered around having fun. What I wanted to talk about with my dates was my hopes for a life of love and contentment. I tried to turn every conversation into a serious one. Despite this handicap, I soon had a girlfriend, Carol, dark-haired, Jewish, but as American as the blonde girls in the movies. She had a ready smile and a frequently impatient manner. I was excited by having a girlfriend and listened to her stories of parents and former boyfriends. Once, though, she accused me of never talking to her.

"How is that?" I asked, genuinely puzzled.

"You are a listener, and you listen to me, which is unusual for a boy. But I don't see that you're telling me about your own feelings."

"That's silly," I answered.

Carol drew herself up, her beautiful gray eyes hardening. "Sometimes I feel you're angry but refuse to tell me about what. You dismiss me, dismiss all Americans, because we haven't gone through what you have."

"That's not true. I don't even like to talk about that subject."

"Well, maybe you should," glowered Carol. "What do you really want? You want something, but what is it?"

"I want to be understood."

"Then you'll have to explain yourself."

"It would be nice to be understood without always having to explain myself," I said, now angry. "Maybe some people should use their imagination."

"You expect too much."

That night I dreamed a recurrent hallucinatory dream, which has lived in me ever since I realized what it meant to have survived the war, when the news from Europe came to Curaçao in 1945 — only six years ago — and is with me still: my brother and I are on a school bus, on a field trip with all our friends crowding all the seats in that shiny silver bus. Some of the children carry little satchels; others have unwieldy paper bags for the outing. The smaller ones have only toys and stuffed bears or rabbits. But something happens. When we return, only my brother and I are in that cavernous bus. All the seats are empty, and we two are the only ones left over from what promised to be a golden picnic.

I was content at Brandeis, in the company of boys and girls who liked to read and talk. Our conversations revolved around teachers, ideas, sex, and politics. Though surrounded by Jewish kids, I rarely got any questions about my past. In my classes, too, the war was the subject of analysis, rarely the occasion for feeling. I was now in a place where the past counted for little, and attention was lavished on the present and the future. Though I sometimes yearned to talk, I had found in America a place where I could live free from the darkening past, without history and without memory.

There were several survivors of the European catastrophe at Brandeis, but I remember only one: a young Polish woman whom we all shunned, her haunted, pallid face forbidding all interchange. Her name was Luba, and I never talked to her or even said hello. She spoke in a gray monotone when she spoke at all. I felt embarrassed in her presence, pained, as if remembering something hurtful that kept me from breathing. To look at her was to see the past and risk being devoured.

Carol may have wanted me to talk about the past, but she was fixed on the future — and the present. She taught me many American things, even a whole set of terms I did not know and a whole complement of attitudes. Americans had an astonishing vocabulary to indicate the variety of their wants: eggs "sunny side up," "open-faced sandwiches," lobster "thermidor," steak "rare, medium, or well-done." These were terms I did not know and concepts I did not understand. What difference did it make how you ate your sandwiches? It took me years to master such words and the preferences they signified. I did not feel easy enough to want so many things and lacked the comfort of thinking that so much was my inalienable due.

My father once said to me, "These American Jews are like goyim. They eat slowly; some of them even drink liquor. In America, it's not only the Gentiles who are calm." That was the calm I craved too, though I feared I would never own it. I had never heard the word *fun* underlined so meaningfully, except, of course, in the American movies I had seen in Curaçao.

My teachers at Brandeis differed from the Curaçaoan and Dutch teachers I had in the last few years. They were generous in a way many Americans seemed to be and curious in a way most were not. Even the older ones displayed a youthful, friendly manner. Spirited lecturers for the most part, they lacked the stiffness of the Dutch, the rigidity. Gone was the love of crisp, caustic expressions of the Dutch, the sardonic put-downs. Gently they nudged me out of my own Dutch reliance on formulas. One day in early October, during a class discussion of tolerance, I quoted one of my Dutch teachers' favorite French expressions, "*Tout comprendre, c'est tout pardonner.*"

"Not necessarily," replied Dr. Finkelpearl, smoothing down his tweed jacket and puffing at an imaginary pipe. His handsome, thoughtful face looked away for a moment; he blinked into the afternoon sunlight and gazed out the classroom window. "You can understand how someone became a murderer and still not forgive."

He was right, of course. Other things he said took longer to digest. And he asked me questions, not about my background but my opinions. No teacher in Curaçao had ever done that.

Brandeis was America, but for me it was also Europe. The cool days, the lush vegetation, the pleasure my fellow students took in the future, all were much more Dutch than Curaçaoan. It was as if the far distant past was being restored to me. That long-ago time suddenly seemed sharper than the intervening years of war and living in Curaçao, and sometimes I felt as if I were a child back in Holland, looking at the promising green park with its ponds and ducks and children and bicycles across the street from our house in Bilthoven. So it was easy to get used to Brandeis: I felt an affinity for what I had missed in Curaçao, that temperate way of life, that avoidance of tropical excess. For all the difference between Dutch people and Americans, the life at Brandeis was instantly recognizable.

And I recognized, too, a certain resemblance to the atmosphere in my father's stories about Europe before Hitler. "Germany was a pleasant country, an orderly country; people were so much quieter than in Poland." My father would smile ruefully, nostalgically. "Yes, there were economic troubles in the twenties, but if you worked hard you could have everything." In 1935 when I was born, those happy, prosperous years were already over. But now in 1951, when I heard lectures from refugee professors like Rudolf Kayser, the friend of Max Brod, himself an intimate of Kafka, or heard Aaron Gurwitsch with his thick accent, or Ludwig Lewisohn, it was as if the war had not happened, and a European Jewish culture still flourished undisturbed by Hitler.

One October day, Professor Lewisohn roused me from a reverie. The late-afternoon light slanted into the stuffy classroom. Lewisohn had drifted away from American literature to stories of how unfettered love had been in Europe, especially Central Europe, and then suddenly pronounced that after the terrible death of six million Jews it behooved us, the "remnant," to return to Judaism and lead a Jewish life.

Small, wizened, dapper, the sixty-nine year old professor stared straight ahead of him.

"No," I said standing up, tremulous but firm. "No."

Lewisohn's cool, blue, heavy-lidded eyes now appraised me. He waited for me to continue.

"Just because we have been persecuted is no reason for us to embrace religion," I said hoarsely. "We cannot let the enemy define us. What's more, the only real response to what happened is revenge."

"Revenge, Manfred?" asked Lewisohn coolly.

"Revenge," I said now coming into my own. "Neither silence nor acceptance. Revenge."

"Revenge is always a bad idea. It leads to more revenge," countered Lewisohn, tugging at his natty suit jacket.

"We cannot let things pass," I said, barely knowing why I was so insistent. "I myself don't like to dwell on it — but I cannot understand how we can blithely go on," I said, barely knowing what I meant. The memory of sitting in that huge hall in Nice at the end of 1942, with all those doomed people on narrow benches, flooded through me. From there they were shipped to Auschwitz. We were unaccountably saved, but who would speak for those pale, forgotten people now?

After we filed out, a classmate slapped me on the back. "You sure stopped the old man in his tracks," he said.

I told Carol what I had said to Lewisohn in class. Her head tilting to one side, she looked puzzled, then happy, smiling. "Well, at least you talked. But what did you mean?"

"I'll tell you what I mean. Ever hear of the Palestine Brigade? Young guys from Israel, fighters, before it was even Israel. A few years ago, they went to Germany and started killing Nazis. There has to be some justice."

"Justice?" Her gray eyes narrowed against the fierce afternoon sunlight. "You can't just go there and kill Germans. They're likely to kill the wrong ones. Forget it, Manny. There'll never be justice for what happened."

I felt tears welling up and yet felt foolish: compared to the others, nothing terrible happened to us. I said as much to Carol.

"You cry for what you feel," she said. "But sometimes I don't know what you feel."

"Sometimes I don't know either."

"You want something. But what?"

"Brandeis is a Jewish place. Why would explanations be needed here?"

Carol paused and ran her fingers through her dark hair. "Maybe they shouldn't be, but you still have to provide them."

"I know I do. But I don't know how. I thought I would be so happy to leave all that behind. But now I sometimes feel like my father — always brooding about what happened."

I who had spent all my time trying to forget was now trying to get others to remember.

Shortly after the first snowfall in that autumn of 1951, the foreign students at Brandeis were parceled out to different nearby families to celebrate Thanksgiving. I looked forward to this evening, both out of curiosity and a desire to impress the other guests with my foreign background.

My host was active in the Newton, Massachusetts, synagogue to which the university president also belonged. A surgeon in Boston, Dr. Stanley Wyman had a gleaming bald head, which he kept perfectly straight, and sat up with the sort of posture I had noticed in American movies. He told us about his years at Harvard, which he pronounced "Haaahvahd," and beamed and smiled, exuding peacefulness. It was hard for me to picture him in a synagogue or reading a Hebrew prayer, wearing a skull-cap.

The Wyman house was opulent, stuffed with seemingly new furniture, some of it a rich cream color. The Thanksgiving table was laden with food. To my astonishment, the ritual was as distinct as that of my grandfather's Sabbath dinners. When the turkey was brought in, we sat at attention, a low gasp emanating from the other guests. The huge bird was brown, glistening on the brightly polished altar of a silver tray.

Some of the foods were explained to me, but the way certain words were spoken — sweet potatoes, rice stuffing, yams, corn bread, cranberries — was evidently part of the ceremony. I saw a blur of orange and yellow and brown on large platters. Dr. Wyman sat at the head of the table, while his wife, a small woman in her forties, busied herself with innumerable chores, observations, chuckles, and explanations for me. She clearly felt sorry for anyone who had never participated in a Thanksgiving dinner.

At last it came, a clarion call, like the blowing of the shofar at the High Holidays:

"Stanley, Stanley, will you caahve the tuhkey?"

"I certainly will, Ceil."

"Stanley," she called again, "Stanley." I was surprised that neither she nor anyone else felt like outsiders in this tradition and comfortably behaved as if they were descended from those Yankees who fought, befriended, and ultimately betrayed the Indians. "Stanley, will you please carve the turkey?"

"Indeed, I will." Stanley moved with stately deliberateness.

"Now Stanley is carving the turkey," Ceil explained to me, leaning over me, her friendly green eyes fixed on some point in the distance. "My father, may he rest in peace, always, but always, carved the turkey. He was a small boy when he came to this country from Russia. Manfred, will you take white meat or dark?" The distinction meant nothing to me. Chicken was chicken, neither white nor dark. Turkey was unknown. I knew two or three vegetables, which arrived in Curaçao in expensive cans. Why the fuss?

Out of habit I patted my jacket pocket and felt the familiar outline of the passport. An unselfconscious chatter resounded.

Another guest, Walter, an attorney, and his wife Sandra had brought their two sons — Frederic, a quiet, amiable man of twenty-seven, a war veteran, and a boyish college freshman named Robert. Their mother explained that Robert had trouble getting into college because of being Jewish, so she could well understand the "discrimination" we suffered in Europe.

Frederic swallowed hard. "Not the same thing at all," he sighed. "No, not the same at all." His kindly, blushing face looked thoughtful. I waited for him to say more. He had fought in France and Germany, he told me later, and now attended law school on the G.I. Bill.

His father, Walter, turned to me, pleasantly enough but pursing his thin lips with a touch of censoriousness. "Why didn't you just leave Europe earlier and come to the U.S.?"

I laughed before I could catch myself. "The U.S. wouldn't admit us. We had no visa, no papers." I patted the inside pocket of my jacket again.

"But still," interjected Stanley, "still, Roosevelt was a great president."

"Yes," I said, and remembered listening to Roosevelt on the radio in Curaçao. I was beginning to feel disappointed in this evening.

The other guests had fallen silent. Walter carefully readjusted the collar of his blue Oxford shirt. "Papers? Oh, papers. You mean documents?"

Frederic's expression looked pained. Then he blushed, as if he had to say something urgent, but he seemed to think better of it. Finally, he asked if I knew that Curaçaoan Jews had built the Touro synagogue in Rhode Island, the first in the U.S.

After dinner, Stanley picked up an apple and gazed at it reverently, saying in his infinitely calm way, "There is nothing... like a good New England apple... on a cold day in November ..." Stanley's wife beamed at him. He looked like a character in a comic book. I decided to brighten up. Why should I be somber?

After dessert, another guest, Libby, a blonde woman of about fifty who worked for Hadassah, asked about my war experiences. She posed questions intently, but did not always seem to hear the answer. Lighting a cigarette in a long green holder, she said expansively, "You know, I have friends who escaped Europe. I forget now if they left before or after the war."

"That makes rather a lot of difference," I answered laconically.

"Oh, really?" she sighed. "These friends lost everything. They owned gorgeous furniture, clothes, jewelry, everything; they lost everything."

"But they got out; they survived," I said.

"Well, yes." She looked at me quizzically. I fought a surging tide of discontent. I wished this subject had not come up, but since it had, I wanted to make myself understood.

Frederic tried to speak, but he could only get a few words out. He was obviously embarrassed and smiled at me conspiratorially.

Clattering sounded in the kitchen. Ceil shouted, "Gentlemen, let's not talk about the past. Let's talk about your future, Manny. What are you going to study?"

"Psychology," I half-shouted back.

"Psychology? How nice. I wish Stanley had studied psychology. Stanley, I wish you had studied psychology."

"No, Ceil, psychology isn't for me. I like something a little more exact."

"Oh, Stanley. Exactness, always exactness. That's not how the world turns."

Libby returned to the subject of the war, though, now wearing a reflective face. She stuck another cigarette in her holder. "World War Two was no picnic here either. We had shortages. Sometimes we couldn't get soap or sugar or butter or even underwear, at least with elastic. For some reason we couldn't get elastic. You know, a lot of material was put in parachutes. Silk or nylon."

"I think nylon was invented right after the war, Libby," said Stanley suavely.

"No, you're wrong there, Stanley. Nylon was invented during the war, or even before... Ceil, Ceil — did we have nylon stockings during the war?" shrieked Libby.

I never heard the answer because I was enveloped in a thickening mist, conscious of a leaden feeling, which lessened my gladness about attending an American university, studying important ideas, and meeting friendly, book-loving girls. I thought of Carol and of Jenny, with whom I had recently walked to the library. The room with all those smiling strangers felt stiflingly hot. I half rose from my chair, swallowing painfully, almost choking, but no one noticed, and I sat down again, my forehead sweaty and cold. I feared that if I spoke I might sob. For a flickering moment I remembered that little gypsy boy in his locked compartment in The Hague in 1941, whom we rescued at the last moment when almost all the air in his wagon was used up. I could still hear his muffled cries. Where did he flee to and what subsequent disaster came his way?

Suddenly there was a crash. Frederic had knocked over a glass of water and a great fuss ensued about mopping up the water and drying the table cloth, everybody assuring Frederic that it did not matter. Astonishingly, Frederic did not look embarrassed. It was what I liked so much here, that American ease. If you knocked over a glass at a Dutch dinner party, you would not look so calm, nor would others go out of their way to make you comfortable. But, of course, you would not have knocked over anything at a Dutch dinner party in the first place; you would have been too careful.

I liked Frederic, and gratefully accepted his offer to drive me back to the dorm. He was more talkative in the car. "You know, you can't expect people who have no experience with war to understand it. They're really kind people."

"I know that," I said vehemently, "but they're not thinking; they don't understand."

He went on. "Take Libby. She may sound superficial, but do you realize that during the war she worked ten, twelve hours a day for the JOINT Distribution Service?"

The JOINT had been spoken of with reverence in our household in Curaçao. The organization had aided Jewish refugees during the war, while afterwards it had busied itself with the Displaced Persons — homeless refugees in special camps or wandering all over Europe. I had been too hard on Libby, as I had been on all these people. They understood to the best of their experience. And if I did not want to think about the war, why should they? I looked at Frederic's kindly face. His light-blue eyes and cleft chin appeared childlike, yet he was obviously a mature man. We drove over the wet, darkened roads, the car performing flawlessly, as everything seemed to in this country; the war had been worlds away and now was fading quickly into the past.

I talked to my French teacher, Claude Vigée — who had left Europe at the same time we had, in late 1942 — and told him about my evening. "These American Jews are so well assimilated, they're so American," he said, "that it's hard for them to imagine what went on in Europe." Perhaps ten years older than I, Vigée looked serene in his intellectualism and his devotion to poetry. A slender man with a fine beak of a nose, he had a coterie because of his poetic gifts and his aestheticism. We were walking on a winding road, almost a footpath, through the rolling hills of the campus. To my pleasure, he spoke of what we shared. "I yearn for my childhood. I'm in exile from it and from my own country. But I will not dwell on the immediate past."

"How do you avoid it?" I asked.

"Easier for me than for you. I'm older."

I puzzled over this and thought perversely that I could argue that same point another way. Suddenly he wheeled around and pointed skyward. "Look around you, Manfred. We are in paradise here. To live fully is to be in heaven."

It was precisely what I knew he excelled at — and could not do myself. I wanted to live "fully" but seemed incapable of doing so.

Vigée continued. "From the tree of memory, birds fly up."

I was a little embarrassed by this dramatic utterance, and confused too. Did he want those birds to fly up? I looked up at the trees and hoped no birds of memory would fly up for me.

*   *   *

On a suddenly warm winter day, I strolled to a bank in Waltham. "Could I please rent a safety deposit box?" I asked a distracted-looking teller. After repeating my question several times to several other bank officials, an earnest, middle-aged manager in a prim black dress took me to a back room and led me to a small chamber with safety deposit boxes. I inserted my Dutch passport into the narrow, gun-metal drawer, surprisingly like a little coffin. A passport was not needed in this country, and I did not want to have it near me. I wanted it buried forever.

As I left the bank, the middle-aged lady gave me a sudden, radiant smile. She did not know what I was doing, and did not care why I was doing it, but she obviously wished me well in her country.

My mood soared. Clearly, I had come to the right place. Back on campus, a very pregnant student and her fiancé strolled hand in hand. They looked happy and did not seem to mind "having to get married." In the distance, Carol waved at me. She wore a white scarf over her open coat. I felt a sudden rush of wanting her. "Let's go somewhere," she smiled, "I've already signed out." My heart did a turn.

We spent a day in Boston, seeing the sights, the Old South Meeting House and the Paul Revere House, with Carol explaining their significance for the American Revolution. The next day we toured Concord, and I listened again to Carol, who seemed to feel that she was preparing me for American citizenship. For once, I felt that all my yearnings had been fulfilled. We stopped sightseeing when in the late afternoon we saw a busload of tourists coming at us, on a green field near a historical site, and I thought one of them looked alarmingly like my Polish classmate Luba.

Back on campus that evening, winter had returned. We braced against a suddenly polar wind, warming our hands on each other. After twenty-four hours of contentment, an unease came over me. Something pulled at me, called out to me, distressed me. I felt a weight in the pit of my stomach.

I said to Carol, "After so looking forward to being in America, I sometimes find it hard to enjoy."

"Why is that?" asked Carol.

"To be here in America, to have survived — isn't that a betrayal of the dead?"

So many times I had given thanks for having lived, for not being one of the numberless dead. So many times that gratitude had struck me as an insult to those who did not live.

"Would it really have been better for Hitler to have one more victim?" countered Carol.

"I know, but I just can't think that we were more deserving than anyone else."

Carol shook her head. "This sounds like guilt, Manny. Why on earth should you feel guilty?"

No reason. And yet there was more to it than guilt: should I compound the insult of thanksgiving for my survival by deliberate forgetfulness, which is what I craved?

Looking back was fatal; the past would rise up and devour me, as it always tried to do. But facing the future, though essential, required being oblivious, courting coldness and denial. What was the answer?

I did not want to spoil the evening, so I changed the subject. But I continued to feel ill at ease, as if I were untrue to myself or betraying a friend and somehow complicit in stifling a barely audible cry for help.

The icy wind blew harder, and we almost ran to the cafeteria. At my dormitory building, a small group of students stood in the courtyard looking up. Curious, we stopped, but Carol saw something before I did. "Let's just go," she said. "It's that boy from your dorm. You don't want to see this."

"No, let's see," I insisted. I knew which boy she meant. He lived down the hall from me. Like so many Brandeis students he was from New York and Jewish, but, uniquely, he claimed he went frequently to Germany to visit his fiancée, an opera singer. Tall, curly-haired, often silent, he had no friends. He hinted that

269

his bride-to-be was an aristocrat with a mysterious past in former Nazi circles. During the Christmas holiday, he went to Germany "to get married." When he returned, he told his roommate that his fiancée had killed herself.

The crowd grew by the moment. It was so cold that we huddled together. I felt the ice seeping into my shoes. At a second-floor window stood a tall, pale young man in the grayish green uniform of a Nazi officer, his curls distinctly visible under his military cap. He stood stiffly, distantly, as if not present in his body, and he did not gesture or speak. We watched for some time, none of us speaking, until he disappeared behind the curtains. The next day he was driven to New York, to recover from his "nervous breakdown."

As if we had taken a vow of silence, my classmates and I never mentioned this scene to each other, and, incredibly, neither did Carol and I at dinner that evening.

This ghostlike apparition haunted me. It spoke of pain not confronted and history not faced.

Why the Nazi uniform, I pondered. Did a victim need to identify with his oppressor if he wants to go on living?

Or maybe it was simply that victims can be tyrants too. The Israeli woman Yael who had come to Curaçao a few years ago intimated as much. But if there was less of a difference between victims and oppressors, then the world of victims was less separate, less distinct, and the special status of Jews as victims lessened. That thought brought some relief. I did not want to be in the company of victims.

And, pondering further, maybe I was not as alone as I felt. Someone else, however deranged, turned out to be as preoccupied with the past as I was. Here was someone who brooded enough about it to don a Nazi uniform. Maybe this grotesque fantasy showed that Jewish Americans were not as oblivious as they had seemed that Thanksgiving night. Some little lump had risen to the surface; some bit of undigested experience had come, however weirdly, to the fore. Like me, they found it hard to talk; we each chose our own form of silence, and each broke it in our own way.

I think now that my biggest relief that night came from understanding that the ghost of what I could not talk about had finally appeared. Something was embodied, even for me, in this bizarre phantasm that struggled to be born.

Dimly, distantly, I apprehended that the past could not be ignored or wished away, though the future had to be recognized — and while I was not yet capable of doing either, any more than this boy was, I now started to recognize that both had to be done.

I looked around, before me, expectantly, hopefully, at a life that suddenly asked to be lived.